HEINE: *Selected Verse*

Heinrich Heine (1797–1856) was born of Jewish parents in Düsseldorf. In 1816 he went to Hamburg to learn the rudiments of commerce from his uncle Salomon, a rich and successful merchant and banker. The young man was set up in a business of his own, but was bankrupt within a year. His uncle then agreed to finance a university course for him. He entered Bonn University in 1819 to study law – though literature claimed more of his time. In October 1820 Heine transferred to Göttingen University, where he graduated as a doctor of law in July 1825. Two of the intervening years were spent pleasantly in Berlin, where his first two books were published; he also began to write political and cultural journalism and to travel widely. *Buch der Lieder*, his most famous collection of lyric verse, was published in autumn 1827. Though Heine continued to write poetry, his publications in the following years were mainly prose: the satirical *Reisebilder* (travel sketches; 1826–31) are only the best-known of a series of polemical writings. In 1831, disillusioned with Germany and inspired by the July Revolution in France, Heine moved to Paris. For many years his principal source of income was the series of articles he wrote for German and French newspapers. Heine's first major poetic publication for seventeen years was *Neue Gedichte* of 1844, an uneven collection which included early poems as well as brilliant political satires. His finest achievements of the decade are the mock-epics *Atta Troll. Ein Sommernachtstraum* (1847) and *Deutschland. Ein Wintermärchen* (1844). By 1848 failing health left him totally bedridden and in increasing pain, but he sublimated his sufferings in what he called his 'mattress-grave' in the beautiful collection of lyrics and narrative poems, *Romanzero* (1851), and in two later books, *Gedichte. 1853 und 1854* (1854) and the posthumous *Letzte Gedichte* (1869).

*

Peter Branscombe was born in Kent in 1929. He was educated at Dulwich College and, after National Service in Austria, Worcester College, Oxford, where he read modern languages and was President of the University Opera Club. He taught at Lancing College for three years before taking a Ph.D. in German at Bedford College, London. In 1959 he joined the German Department at the University of St Andrews, where he has been Professor of Austrian Studies since 1979. He has broadcast frequently on BBC radio and is the author or editor of various literary and musical studies. He is married and has three children and a ginger cat. His principal hobbies are bird-watching, walking, and reviewing gramophone records.

SELECTED VERSE

HEINE

INTRODUCED, EDITED AND TRANSLATED BY
PETER BRANSCOMBE

PENGUIN BOOKS

PENGUIN BOOKS

Published by the Penguin Group
Penguin Books Ltd, 27 Wrights Lane, London W8 5TZ, England
Penguin Books USA Inc., 375 Hudson Street, New York, New York 10014, USA
Penguin Books Australia Ltd, Ringwood, Victoria, Australia
Penguin Books Canada Ltd, 10 Alcorn Avenue, Toronto, Ontario, Canada M4V 3B2
Penguin Books (NZ) Ltd, 182–190 Wairau Road, Auckland 10, New Zealand

Penguin Books Ltd, Registered Offices: Harmondsworth, Middlesex, England

First published 1968
Reissued in Penguin Classics 1986
5 7 9 10 8 6 4

Copyright © Peter Branscombe, 1968
All rights reserved

Printed in England by Clays Ltd, St Ives plc
Typeset in Monotype Fournier

FOREWORD

THE purpose of these Penguin books of verse in the chief European languages is to make a fair selection of the world's finest poetry available to readers who could not, but for the translation at the foot of each page, approach it without dictionaries and a slow plodding from line to line. They offer even to those with fair linguistic knowledge the readiest introduction to each country's lyrical inheritance, and a sound base from which to make further explorations.

The selections in each book have been made by the anthologist alone. But all alike reflect contemporary trends in taste, and include only poetry that can be read for pleasure. No specimens have been included for their historical interest, or to represent some particular school or phase or literary history.

CONTENTS

CONTENTS

CONTENTS

CONTENTS

CONTENTS

CONTENTS

CONTENTS

INTRODUCTION

'ONE of the first men of this century ...' That is what Heinrich Heine affected to call himself when he claimed to have been born in the early hours of 1800. Here, as in most of his autobiographical writings, we must temper the poetic worth of what he is saying with scepticism as to its factual validity. For Heine was primarily a poet— a poet whose popularity has been restricted in his native land by his sharply critical tongue, and is abroad based chiefly on the early lyrics made immortal by the settings of Schubert and Schumann. Yet it is precisely these poems which are least typical of the mature Heine: semi-precious gems of great brilliance though many of them are, and saved from cloying sentimentality by the sharpness of their contours, they mark only a stage through which Heine had to pass in his search for a mature and personal poetic language: it is to the late poems that we must turn to find the authentic blending of imagination and discipline, gaiety and squalor, pain and indomitable courage that makes Heine unique even in a nation of great lyric poets.

Heine was born at Düsseldorf in the Rhineland on 13 December, and probably in 1797, the son of a colourful but not particularly efficient or successful Jewish tradesman, and a courageous, stable mother who came from a respected and comfortably placed medical family in Düsseldorf; she was likewise Jewish. Heine in his autobiographical writings paints vivid pictures of his parents – especially of his father, with his love of dogs and horses and military display. And it was following the whim of his father, whose great joy in business was the importation of English cloth, that young Heine, the eldest of four children, was called Harry: the name of the Liverpool merchant who supplied Samson Heine's business with much of its material.

Düsseldorf was a pleasant little backwater in Heine's time, a town of some 15,000 inhabitants; it had a distinguished artistic past, and it was to flourish again in the future. The French occupation of the Rhineland brought civic rights for the Jews, who numbered no more than 300 in Düsseldorf, and did not live in a ghetto; the population was mainly Roman Catholic, though there were some 2,000 Protestants. Heine's parents were not strict Jews; Harry was sent to a dame's school, then to a small Jewish school, and at the age of seven to a lycée run mainly by Jesuits. The rector made a considerable impression on Heine: here was a man who perhaps introduced the boy to the conflict between the intellect and religion. For Rector Schallmeyer taught doctrines inspired by the latest French rationalist philosophy – and also officiated at divine service. From this we in part trace Heine's scepticism: in his own home, too, he saw both spiritual indifference and an observance of Jewish rites.

There was little to disturb the smooth flow of Heine's upbringing. The most memorable event was Napoleon's entry into Düsseldorf in November 1811; Heine leaves a glowing description in the prose work entitled *Ideen. Das Buch Le Grand* – Le Grand being the drummer from the Grande Armée who was (at least in Heine's imagination) billeted on the family. The portrait of the Emperor riding easily along on his great white horse deserves to be set alongside 'Die Grenadiere' as one of the finest literary tributes to the magnetic appeal of Napoleon.

Heine's mother had practical plans for her son. She thought first that he should become a great soldier, or an administrator of occupied territories; then when Napoleon's fortunes began to wane her mind turned to a business career. It was certainly not from her that Heine inherited his love of legend and fairy story. From an early age he showed a remarkable imagination and a natural ability to clothe his dreams and fantasies in vivid and immediately recognizable forms. Yet for all that he also showed an awareness of reality and a healthy scepticism towards people and things: in the light of his later development it is interesting to note that his earliest surviving poem is a satire directed against a school-fellow.

Heine probably first felt his Jewishness in the autumn of 1815 when he and his father went to Frankfurt for the trade fair. Here the Jews still lived in the dark, damp ghetto which he describes so powerfully in the *Rabbi von Bacharach* fragment. Heine stayed two months in Frankfurt, working at a banker's and then at a grocer's, but without success or pleasure. In the summer of 1816 he went to Hamburg, where his uncle Salomon was one of the most respected merchants of the city. Heine naturally found it difficult to show, and perhaps even to feel, gratitude. For the rest of his life he was to be more or less dependent on the generosity of his uncle (and after his death, on that of his son Karl), yet his attitude towards these Hamburg relations was one of the least attractive sides of his character. They welcomed him kindly, though as the poor relation from the country he scarcely felt at ease – a feeling exaggerated by a rebuff when he found himself in love with his pretty young cousin Amalie. It is in 'Affrontenburg' (p. 219) of three decades later that we find the strongest expression of his bitter feelings for this family. For two years Heine learnt the rudiments of banking from his uncle, who then set him up with a business of his own – though 'Harry Heine & Compagnie' was bankrupt within a year. Uncle Salomon now agreed that Heine should study law at his expense. He returned to his parents in May 1819, and in the autumn entered Bonn University – on qualifications which would surely be considered insufficient nowadays. During his year in Bonn he went to more lectures on literature than on law, and he was by now busy writing poetry – such famous ballads as 'Die Grenadiere' and 'Belsatzar' date from the Bonn period. In the autumn of 1820 he moved on to Göttingen University (of which his *Harzreise* gives an entertaining satirical picture); he was sent down in January 1821 for wanting to fight a duel with pistols, and he went on to Berlin.

The two years in Berlin were a period of leisure and progress – he had the entrée to some of the leading salons, and from these years date his first two publications in book form. In the summer of 1823 Heine stayed some weeks with his parents, now at Lüneburg; he got to know the sea for the first time during a holiday at Cuxhaven; and he also revisited his uncle's family at Hamburg – it was during this visit, if at all, that he fell in love, equally in vain, with Amalie's younger sister Therese.

In January 1824 Heine took up his studies again, once more at Göttingen, and despite the Harz journey which he undertook that summer, and the writing of the book that bears that name in the autumn, he made sufficient progress to be able to graduate doctor of law in July 1825, a month after he had entered the Protestant church (taking the opportunity to change his name from Harry to Heinrich). Prudence rather than conviction lay behind the conversion – medicine alone of the higher professions was at that time open to non-baptized Jews.

Heine was now twenty-eight, and he was no clearer about the choice of a career than he was on questions of religion, patriotism or poetry. In the coming months he considered a number of different careers – lecturer in Berlin, advocate in Hamburg, and later a chair at Munich and the post of syndic in Hamburg. In the end he accepted a job as a political journalist in Munich, but he only kept it for six months. He was, in fact, becoming ever more surely the poet and free-lance journalist which he was to remain for the rest of his life. He was by now well embarked on the four volumes of his *Reisebilder* (Travel Pictures), and it was during his holidays on the islands and mainland coast of north-west Germany that he gathered the impressions which bore fruit in the *Nordsee* poems.

Heine's first volume of verse had been published in Berlin in 1822. It and the other books of poems which followed were carefully sifted and rearranged by Heine soon after his return from a visit to England in the summer of 1827. The resulting *Buch der Lieder*, published in October, is the volume on which Heine's fame as a lyric poet is founded, and it is still by far his most popular book.

The first section of the *Buch der Lieder*, *Junge Leiden*, comprises the eerie 'Traumbilder', followed by 'Lieder', 'Romanzen' and 'Sonette'. This last is a form in which Heine does not often shine, but the three earlier categories recur almost throughout his poetic career.

The *Lyrisches Intermezzo* contains for many readers the quintessential Heine. This is the book of short lyrics in which a poet's love and the sorrows it almost inevitably brings are expressed with a spontaneity and also a degree of gentle irony which has endeared Heine to poets, composers and general readers alike – and when people have the chance to recite a few lines of once-learnt German verse, they are quite likely to come from the *Lyrisches Inter-*

mezzo. It is easy with Heine to make the mistake of interpreting too biographically the loves and sadness which he sings. We hardly doubt that in 'Ich grolle nicht' (p. 27), for example, the poet is reaching down into the depths of a genuine grief, but far more often he treats his sorrow ironically, holds it at arm's length and smiles at it even as he suffers ('Es liegt der heiße Sommer', p. 32; 'Sie saßen und tranken am Teetisch', p. 33; 'Die alten, bösen Lieder', p. 36). Frequently Heine achieves the desired effect of distance between himself and his sorrows by another device for which he is famous: conventional flower and bird images are given a highly personal twist when Heine makes them into symbols of the impossibility of full harmony in love. 'Am leuchtenden Sommermorgen' (p. 32) invites us to believe in a liaison between a man and a flower; 'Die Lotosblume ängstigt' (p. 25) and 'Ein Fichtenbaum steht einsam' (p. 29) express in the terms of a romantic conceit the physical impossibility of union. It is, of course, less the subject-matter than the artistry of the poems themselves that holds the admiration of the reader.

In *Die Heimkehr* there is an increase both in frequency and in intensity of the wit and irony found in the early sections of the *Buch der Lieder*. There is sometimes a gentle melancholy and nostalgia too, ostensibly depersonalized in 'Die Lorelei' (p. 40) – but shining through is Heine's fascination with the Venus or Circe figure – and overtly personal in 'Mein Kind, wir waren Kinder' (p. 48). And there are poems like 'Das ist ein schlechtes Wetter' (p. 46) in which a mood is created without our feeling the colouring touch of the poet at all. There is a wealth of genuine feeling in the famous 'Doppelgänger' poem (p. 44) which makes it as hauntingly memorable as Tonio Kröger's description, in Thomas Mann's story, of his return to his northern home-town when he stands at night below the house in which his first love had dwelt. Then there are the poems in which socially conventional attitudes are expected to take the place of real feeling ('Als ich, auf der Reise', p. 41; 'Die Jahre kommen und gehen', p. 45; 'Doch die Kastraten klagten', p. 54). In these poems, too, the recurring, but for commentators exaggeratedly important, image of love trans-

ferred to the little sister may perhaps admit of a biographical inter-
pretation ('Als ich, auf der Reise' and 'An Jenny', p. 113, widen
the concept of little sister). New, however, and warmly welcome
for their vitality and fresh self-criticism, are the poems in which
Heine mocks himself, forcing himself to laugh at emotions which
are none the less real. The two 'Teurer Freund' poems (pp. 50 and
52) are outstanding examples, though the last two lines of 'Sag,
wo ist dein schönes Liebchen' (p. 56) are gleefully taken up by
those who wish to see the whole book as a reflection of Heine's
unhappy love for his cousin.

The last two *Heimkehr* poems are in many ways more closely
linked with *Die Nordsee*, from which they are separated by the
small but genial section from the *Harzreise* – poems which, like
almost everything Heine wrote, would in the best of possible
worlds only be read within the context which he, careful arranger
that he was, intended. 'Götterdämmerung', the only one of the
longer poems from the end of *Die Heimkehr* included in this antho-
logy, is a strange, involved and disturbing piece. While outside
everyone gaily greets the advent of spring, the poet bolts his door
against the intruder (Tonio Kröger again, and his writer friend!)
and inveighs against the falsity and sickness of the world. The poem
ends with a vision of cosmic destruction, with God a fugitive and
his angels routed.

If it is seen as a fault that *Die Nordsee* (like the *Harzreise* poems
originally published within the vivid and episodic prose *Reisebilder*)
fails for long to avoid the wordly concerns of the salon poetry of
the earlier sections of the *Buch der Lieder*, these sea-poems must be
accounted splendid failures. Their free rhythms and invigorating
sturdiness make them at their best the outstanding sea-poems in the
German language; and even when (as in 'Seegespenst', p. 71, and
'Untergang der Sonne', p. 75) the poet is caught in the toils of
hopeless love, or indulges in the ridiculous conceit of an unhappy
mariage de convenance between sun and sea-god, his wit and sheer
poetic craft see him through.

In many ways the most interesting of the *Nordsee* cycle, and one
which forms a bridge with 'Götterdämmerung', is 'Die Götter

Griechenlands'. I am aware that this book does not adequately cover Heine's religious doubts, questionings and blasphemies. Here as elsewhere there is so much contradictory evidence. Heine could refer to his baptism into the Protestant church as an 'entry ticket to European culture', yet a poignant description in *Die Stadt Lucca* of Christ suffering but militant reveals that he at times deeply admired the son of the God of his new religion. 'Götterdämmerung', and particularly 'Die Götter Griechenlands', show another aspect of the picture. In the latter Heine is the champion of the underdogs, the unloved but defeated gods of Greece – he sides with them not because he respects them, but because the new gods who have displaced them are even less sympathetic to him: 'malicious ones in the sheep's skin of humility', he calls them.

Seventeen years passed between the publication of *Buch der Lieder* and Heine's next collection of verse, the *Neue Gedichte* of 1844. The intervening years had been momentous for Heine as well as for the Europe in which he lived – years in which his hopes of a career in Germany finally vanished, and in which almost all his published writings were critical and polemical rather than poetic. His journalistic career in Munich did not last long, and by the summer of 1828 he was convinced that his future should lie in the academic world: one of the ministers of the King of Bavaria (the Ludwig whom Heine was later to revile in the 'Lobgesänge', p. 144) promised him a chair at Munich, and in expectation of it Heine set off on a hedonistic and restorative journey to Italy. However, the autumn brought the end of his hopes of Munich University, and on his journey homewards he learnt of the death of his father. 1829 was spent mainly in Hamburg and Berlin, working away at the *Reisebilder*, and included another interlude on the north-west coast in the late summer. And it was on Heligoland in the following summer that Heine learnt of the July Revolution in France – an event which fired him with enthusiasm, but did not yet draw him to that country. The move to Paris, when it did come in 1831, was not planned as a permanent farewell to Germany; and it was brought about as much by Heine's quarrels and disillusionment in Germany as by enthusiasm for things French. Heine had done himself lasting harm by his public revenge against the aristocrat Platen, a man whose poetry Heine was at liberty to detest, but whose personal perversions would have been better left unmentioned. He had enemies among adherents of his old faith and his new one, and still no job which might have caught and held his interest came his way. So at the end of April 1831 he set out via Frankfurt, Heidelberg and Strasbourg for Paris, where he arrived in May.

The last poems he wrote before his emigration are contained in *Neuer Frühling*. Many of them are simply reworkings of familiar themes, in others there is a maudlin sentimentality which at its least attractive is not even alleviated by wit or cynicism. But this book does also contain strikingly original poems: the double pathetic fallacy of 'Unterm weißen Baume sitzend' (p. 88) where the seasons change as quickly as in a fairy story or a dream; the sparrow's skilfully disguised catechism in 'Im Anfang war die Nachtigall' (p. 91). There are also many poems in which human characteristics (especially feminine fallibility) are given a new slant by their transposition into the world of trees, birds and flowers. This book also contains that perfect little ballad, 'Es war ein alter König' (p. 96), which in its ellipsis and also its musicality rivals the later 'Der Asra' (p. 182); and the mysterious 'Durch den Wald, im Mondenscheine' (p. 98) where the poet is more than a mere observer of the elfin hunt. A healthy purging after so much of spring and love is provided by the last poems of the cycle, though here too the metaphors remain mannered.

Verschiedene, the following section of *Neue Gedichte*, apostrophizes various women with whom the poet in fact or fancy enjoyed relationships during his early years in Paris. Heine's hedonism and the pantheistic creed of Saint-Simon are combined in 'Auf diesem Felsen' (p. 102). The frank sensuality of these urban poems shocked readers when they first appeared in a Berlin journal early in 1833, and I suppose some of them may still disturb people today – though less by their titillation of the senses than by their easy assumption that love is a casual affair, an accepted part of the everyday business of life in a big city. Occasionally (e.g. 'Fürchte nichts', p. 107) Heine returns to the playful artifice of earlier cycles, but on the whole the theme is the attraction of physical love, and the only thing to fear is an attempt by the woman of the moment to invest it with permanency. The trio from 'Kitty' (pp. 111–13) – a light glance back to Heine's English visit, perhaps – has been inserted here, as also have 'An Jenny' (p. 113), a touching expression of the recurrent frustrations of love, and 'In der Frühe' (p. 115), a greeting to the plump, good-natured but thoughtless French girl whom he finally married in 1841, and to whom a less complimentary tribute is 'Der Tannhäuser' – its length could alas allow it no place in this book.

The *Romanzen* in this anthology range from the cynical directness of 'Ein Weib' (p. 117) through the brief tribute to Byron of 'Childe Harold' (p. 118) and the nostalgia for Germany which, voiced in 'Anno 1839' (p. 118), had taken the place of Heine's early enthusiasm for life in Paris, to delightful ballads of love. Some of these are witty and urbane in the vein of *Verschiedene*. The best of them, 'Begegnung' (p. 124), a delicate and haunting tale of the meeting at a village dance of two handsome visitors from the spirit world, shows how attached Heine still was to the poetic traditions of his native land. The 'Altes Kaminstück' (p. 128) of the *Zur Ollea* section (*olla podrida*, a Spanish soup) is again more German than French in its evocation of a winter's evening.

The *Zeitgedichte* are quite the most important and revolutionary – in two senses – of the *Neue Gedichte*. These poems dealing with contemporary events and attitudes (the term 'Zeitgedicht' defies translation) are a logical growth of Heine's twin preoccupations of recent years, politics and poetry. 'Adam der Erste' (p. 131) is a Promethean outburst against the vetoes of authority; 'Entartung' (p. 133) debunks the conventional romantic nature-symbolism which Heine had himself so often employed, and it also underlines the degeneration of man; the brilliantly effective, halting conclusion of 'Die Tendenz' (p. 134) shows a mock respect for the censor. In 'Der Kaiser von China' (p. 135) and 'Zur Beruhigung' (p. 137) Heine turns his attentions to Frederick William IV, whom he depicts as a bibulous, self-satisfied and weak Emperor of China: the 'Middle Kingdom' is hopefully equated with Prussia; Schelling, the transcendentalist Romantic philosopher, is seen as the counsellor Confucius (Heine calls him Confuse-ius, playing with the 'clear' of the following line); Cologne Cathedral – in actual fact not completed until 1880 – is the great pagoda. The attack on cosy complacency is even more obvious in 'Zur Beruhigung'–sharply etched in the third and fourth lines of the second stanza by the bathos so often and effectively achieved when Heine couples elevated concepts with unexpected food metaphors. Even sharper, though, is the play on father figure and nursery. In 'Nachtgedanken' (p. 140) we find perhaps the most touching expression of Heine's nostalgia, the poem which he originally intended to preface *Deutschland. Ein Wintermärchen*. Many of the *Zeitgedichte*, and especially of those not published until later, are attacks on individuals and cannot be appreciated without lengthy critical comment (would that 'Die Audienz' were anywhere near self-explanatory!). 'An Georg Herwegh' (p. 144), however, sums up in two concise stanzas the aspirations of the well-intentioned but impractical German liberals of the early 1840s. Two of the evil, acute songs in praise of Ludwig I are included (p. 144) as evidence of Heine's ability to hate deeply; and 'Die schlesischen Weber' (p. 148) with its sombre refrain of the exploited weavers shows Heine's deep but seldom so unequivocally stated human sympathies. The last two poems in this section of the anthology are not really *Zeitgedichte* at all, but they deserve their inclusion for the light they throw on the gentler side of Heine's satire.

Atta Troll. Ein Sommernachtstraum is Heine's most inimitable creation. If outwardly its loose series of events and reflections seems to link it with the prose *Reisebilder* of the late twenties, it is truer to consider it as marking the beginning of Heine's later and predominantly lyrical creative period. *Atta Troll* has a poetic logic and beauty of its own such as can only be hinted at in an excerpt. The canto, or 'Caput', chosen comes roughly midway through the twenty-seven which constitute the whole; it describes an episode during the hunter's travels down to the Pyrenees where he hopes to shoot the great dancing-bear Atta Troll, who has escaped from captivity and returned to his wife and children in his native mountain forests. Here he criticizes the ways of men with a bourgeois half-logic in which his human enemies read a danger only to be removed by his death. As is probably already clear, Heine's tale functions on two levels; the symbolical meaning is more important than the simple tale. *Atta Troll* is so rich a cornucopia that the reader who fails to surrender to the charm and irony of Caput XIV (p. 161), the hunter's meeting with the children in their mountain aerie, may well find something more to his taste in the caricatures of various exponents of German letters and liberalism, the nature pictures, the bear's-eye view of heaven. The reader who wants to explore Heine's dreams of fair women should tackle Capita XVIII–XX, the Wild Hunt – though there is little traditional Romantic spookiness in these cantos, depicting as they do Heine's warring ideals of beauty: Diana, the Classical; Abunde, the Celtic; and the one to whom Heine awards the palm, Herodias/Salome, the Jewish. For all the satire there is enough simple nature poetry and romantic yearning for Heine to be able to claim in the closing canto that he had written 'perhaps the last free forest song of Romanticism'.

Although work on *Atta Troll* began when Heine was recuperating at a Pyrenean spa (1841) it is a journey of the imagination rather than of fact. *Deutschland. Ein Wintermärchen* is the account – distorted in the glass which the poet held up to the contemporary world – of Heine's visit to Germany in the autumn of 1843. He composed the poem in the spring of 1844, after his return home, and in July he went back to Germany to see through the press his *Neue Gedichte*, in which *Deutschland* originally appeared. The pleasure to be derived from the cantos included in this anthology (pp. 161 ff.) is one of accumulation and contrast: quite apart from the transformation of a nurse's tale to poetic reality in Barbarossa's underground kingdom, there is the interplay between the Romantic picture of Germany's legendary saviour at her hour of need, and the oppressive yet fundamentally weak Barbarossa of cantos XV–XVII, the fusty antiquarian (and antique) in whom the perceptive reader may recognize Frederick William IV. We see in this benign tyrant unable to control the power he is calling into being a link with the German militarism of the future (cf. 'Deutschland',

p. 142). His worst offence in Heine's eyes, however, is his complete lack of style and stature. Heine felt drawn to mock the old feudal ideals of his modern Barbarossa, though at the end of Caput XVIII he has to admit that genuine medievalism is preferable to the parody of it which Frederick William IV represents. The whole poem is rich in satire of things Prussian, but Heine also has a look at the Swabian poets and at many of his contemporaries – thereby conferring on them an immortality which his satire was at pains to deny them. Witty and unexpected rhymes, subtle use of enjambement, a sophisticated counterpoint of popular speech rhythms and urbanities – these are some of the qualities which make *Deutschland. Ein Wintermärchen* such an entertaining poem. It is, however, full of disillusionment, there is little here of the delicacy and lightness of *Atta Troll* – Heine is sounding a summons to German common sense and integrity, but he is at his happiest when attacking the church, the monarchy and German nationalism, and at his least impressive when he is trying to be constructive.

Even before the journeys to Germany in 1843 and 1844 Heine's health had occasionally given him cause for complaint – indeed, in childhood days he had frequently suffered from severe headaches. Now his health began to break, and the death of his uncle Salomon and the realization that his cousin Karl was prepared to continue the generous avuncular allowance of 4,800 francs per year (Heine received a similar sum from the French government until after the revolution of 1848) only if Heine refrained from publishing anything defamatory to the family, led him to anger and despair. By 1846 he was ailing visibly, and by the summer of 1848 he was bedridden, prey to the paralysis which gradually drained his life away in the course of more than seven years. In the postscript to the *Romanzero* (1851) Heine paints a moving picture of himself, confined like the magician Merlin to a 'melodious grave' – though Heine's living grave knew no flowers and trees (he envied the dog he saw cocking its leg against the only tree-trunk visible from his Paris attic); and the only melodies he heard were those he himself created in the miseries of his sleepless nights (see 'Wie langsam kriechet', p. 223). Yet however much he suffered, he continued to fight back, he never abandoned the search for beauty and pleasure, though for him the pleasures of the senses were of the past, and the poems he felt compelled to write were so often poems of cruelty and degradation.

The book which Heine's publisher christened *Romanzero* appeared at the end of 1851. The first of its three sections, *Historien*, is an attempt to find in history a parallel to and a refuge from the torments of the present. Past and present are hilariously, almost hysterically, linked in 'Rhampsenit' (p. 177); in the moral (you get a security-conscious king if you appoint a thief) there is a touch of the grim irony which recurs irregularly but frequently in the poetry of Heine's later years – even where the mood is ostensibly gay there lurks a gruesome quality which finds a modern echo in some of the songs of Mr Tom Lehrer. Very different are the sustained elegiac tone of 'Der Mohrenkönig' (p. 183) and the whispered, wistful evocation of a passion long dead and only to be fulfilled in the world of ghosts which we meet in 'Geoffroy Rudèl' (p. 186.) But the impossibility of human happiness in love is most poignantly summed up in the four stanzas of 'Der Asra' (p. 182).

The second book of the *Romanzero*, *Lamentationen*, contains bitterness and savagery, but also sustained dignity and pathos, along with flashes of the old wit. This book contains the series of twenty poems entitled 'Lazarus', to which the 'Zum Lazarus' (p. 222) section of the poems of 1853–4 form an adjunct. The Lazarus figure from St Luke's gospel, chapter 16, verse xix ff., formed a natural model for the ailing and impecunious Heine; these poems, with their variations on the theme of the inevitability of death, are the more poignant in that the sick poet dreams of past happiness, thinks tenderly of the wife he must leave behind so ill-equipped for the struggle of existence, and at times manages to summon up a touch of defiant pride that, though beaten in body, his spirit is unconquered ('Enfant perdu', p. 197).

The third book, *Hebräische Melodien*, takes its title but little else from Byron's *Hebrew Melodies*. It consists of only three poems, the one contained in this anthology being the first. 'Prinzessin Sabbath' (p. 199) is perhaps the most beautiful of Heine's poetic tributes to the religion of his fathers which was for him the source of such ambivalent feelings. Gentle irony touches the cantor, even the Princess herself; parody of Schiller's 'Ode to Joy' finds a place without seeming an intrusion – and the Jew is shown for the rest of the week as the dog which for so many non-Jews he always is. Yet the tone of the poem is predominantly one of nostalgia, of a quiet exultation which makes life for all its sufferings worth living.

The last poems which Heine published in book form appeared in the autumn of 1854 in the first of three volumes of *Vermischte Schriften* (Various Writings); in their context the *Gedichte. 1853 und 1854*, as he called them, separate the autobiographical *Geständnisse* (Confessions) from *Die Götter in Exil* (The Gods in Exile). These thirty-three poems contain works as fine as any he had ever written. To a friend who commented on their startling novelty Heine replied, 'Yes, I know it well, they are beautiful, frighteningly beautiful. They are like a lament from the grave, a cry in the night from one who has been buried alive, or from a corpse, or even from the grave itself. Yes, German lyric poetry has never heard such notes as these before – and has never been able to hear them, because no poet has ever been in such a plight.' The poems he is thinking of here are the eleven which are linked together as 'Zum Lazarus'. The others include a delightful fantasy, 'Rote Pantoffeln' (p. 209), which is a cautionary tale for pretty young mice, and the harshly brilliant subliminal plea for the underprivileged which is called 'Das Sklavenschiff' (p. 211). The still centre, however, is the group which shows the poet bounded by the four walls of his sick-room, questioning the goodness and justness of God's decrees, recording the anguish of his present lot, certain that the only change will be from attic to grave – unless he is, as he sometimes imagines, already dead and suffering the torments of the damned in hell. Despite his frequent longing for the ease of death his conclusion in the last of these poems is that any sort of life is preferable to even the most heroic of deaths. In the 'Epilog' (p. 230), as in 'Der Scheidende' (p. 254), Heine remembers Achilles's words to Odysseus: 'I would rather be a serf in the house of some landless man . . . than king of all these dead men that have done with life.' And indeed there is much besides in 'Zum Lazarus' which recalls the torments of the dead in that same eleventh book of *The Odyssey*, and not a little perhaps of Odysseus's unconscious fear of being lost in the realms of the dead.

Of the last poems which Heine did not live to prepare for the press a few continue the mingled tones of irony and respect for God which so memorably characterize many of his previous works; it would, though, be misleading to claim any marked difference in content, mood or poetic quality until we reach the poems of the final months of Heine's life when the visits of Elise Krinitz, whom he called 'Die Mouche' after the fly on her seal, brought him the last happiness he was to know. Until their kinship of souls, which Heine would dearly have liked to be a kinship of bodies too, he had continued in the vein of melancholy, resignation and anguish familiar from the Lazarus cycle. Intensification rather than novelty is the keynote of such poems as 'Mir lodert und wogt' (p. 236), the apotheosis of his 'Doppelgänger' works, and one of the most remarkable of all his poems. In it the poet's scornful *alter ego* takes over (as we realize only in the final stanza) from the slowly dying man in his Paris sickroom who had seemingly from the beginning been represented by the thirsty young poet in the tavern at Godesberg. To study this poem carefully is to be made aware of the consummate skill in the evocation of mood, character and tension of which Heine was master, and also of the saving power of irony and self-parody.

The love Heine felt for his wife Mathilde is explicit in such poems as 'Gedächtnisfeier' (p. 194), 'An die Engel' (p. 195) and 'Mich locken nicht' (p. 226), and it is especially tender in 'Ich war, o Lamm' (p. 244). True union of the minds, however, was something Heine could never enjoy with his child-like wife; it was the 'Mouche' who gave him that. His unrealizable passion for her is shown in 'Worte! Worte!' (p. 245); the deeper, spiritualized love which bound the young German girl to the dying poet is most perfectly expressed in the long dream-poem, 'Es träumte mir' (p. 246), in which the almost lifelong fight between the Nazarene side of Heine's nature (here simplified to Barbarian) and the Hellene, finds its last precipitate. But this poem is much more than a procession of the figures on the dead poet's sarcophagus (familiars from Heine's highly personal mythology); it is a silent colloquy between the dead man and the passion flower (= the 'Mouche'), doomed to be shattered by the discordant braying of Balaam's ass. Everything that is great and beautiful must perish – that is the message of 'Ganz entsetzlich ungesund' too (p. 239).

Heine's last request, painfully mimed since he had by then almost entirely lost the power of speech, was for paper and a pencil. Even opium, the drug to which he owed what alleviation he had during his last years, and to which he paid a beautiful tribute in the poem 'Morphine' (p. 243 – it was originally intended for the *Romanzero*) – even opium could no longer help. What he would have written on that early morning of 17 February 1856 if death had not at last carried him off, we cannot know. But since a question mark forms an unsatisfactory conclusion, it may be thought appropriate to end this anthology with 'Der Scheidende', a poem of parting. There is no false emotion, no self-pity as Heine pictures the audience leaving the theatre (that recurrent image!) to return to its several philistine homes. Suffering is now too overpowering for Heine to risk again the personal identification which ended 'Sie erlischt!' (p. 196); a gentle, mocking anachronism on the Odysseus theme is what we have (cf. 'Epilog', p. 230); and gentle too is the irony with which Heine countered the visitor who, near the end, asked him how he stood with the Almighty: '*Dieu me pardonnera, c'est son métier.*'

EDITOR'S NOTE

NO one is more conscious than the present writer of the sad but inevitable gaps in this collection. Every period and style of poem is represented, but no poem has been included simply because it is famous. The Schumann lover, for instance, may look in vain for the text of this or that favourite song; my hope is that though he may be disappointed in some respects, he will come across poems which illuminate some unexpected aspect of Heine's personality, and even that he will be encouraged to move on and sample more of the longer poems which considerations of space precluded: 'Waldeinsamkeit', perhaps, that lovely picture of a poet's first innocence amid the world of nature; and above all, 'Bimini', a glowing, fantastic allegory, at once witty and infinitely sad, of an old man's search for the waters of life which gush forth on the mythical island which is Heine's Avalon.

The ordering of the various published collections, and also of poems within collections, is as far as possible Heine's own. His numbering of individual poems, however, has only been taken over where sections of a longer work have been included. The poems which were not published until after Heine's death have been inserted as far as possible immediately after the published groups with which they seem to belong.* This procedure has the merit that the poems from beginning to end appear more or less in the order in which they were written. The editor offers no apology for maintaining in his English versions Heine's tense sequences. However difficult it may sometimes be to decide why Heine has in the middle of a poem switched from past tense to present and back again, it seems preferable to leave the reader to ponder over the resulting jolt for himself, rather than to iron out a difficulty which, however strange it may seem, was clearly not due to any superficial convenience or poetic licence. Take the well-known 'Belsatzar' (p. 9). The predominating preterite tense is broken six times – by both verbs in stanza two, by a sequence of five in stanzas seven and eight (after the indecision in stanza six where a present is followed by a return to the past); by a further four verbs in stanzas twelve and thirteen. The other two interruptions by the present tense are highly dramatic confrontations: in stanza nine the return to the preterite ('rief') is at once countermanded by two presents in the next line; and in stanza sixteen the repeated imperative ('Und sieh! und sieh!') is the last touch of immediacy in a narrative which, however long ago its events took place, nevertheless touches its readers to the quick with its unexpected present-tense highlights which then seem to grow more and more remote from us as the

* These are grouped in each case under the heading Nachlese.

vivid details of the blasphemy give way to the archaic dignity and stiffness of the Old Testament story.

Among the many people to whom I am grateful for help in the preparation of this book I must single out in particular Professor S. S. Prawer and Professor E. Purdie for their encouragement and advice, and Dr J. M. Lindsay for his assistance in reading the proofs. I should also like to thank the colleagues and students in St Andrews with whom I have discussed Heine's verse and from whose ideas and reactions I have derived so much benefit and pleasure.

*

This reissue provides me with the opportunity to make a number of minor corrections and improvements, and to bring the select bibliography up to date.

March 1985   PJB

TEXTUAL AND BIBLIOGRAPHICAL NOTE

THE German texts are based on the following editions:

Heinrich Heines Sämtliche Werke, edited by E. Elster, Bibliographisches Institut, Leipzig and Vienna, 1890.

Heinrich Heines Sämtliche Werke, edited by O. Walzel and others, Insel, Leipzig, 1911–20.

Heine's orthography has been modernized, except where he used anachronisms deliberately. Apostrophes have been preserved only where they differentiate between past and present tense of a weak verb.

The following books in English on Heine may be recommended:

ATKINS, H. G. *Heine*. Routledge, 1929.

BUTLER, E. M. *Heinrich Heine, a Biography*. Hogarth Press, 1956.

FAIRLEY, B. *Heinrich Heine. An Interpretation*. Oxford University Press, 1954.

HOFRICHTER, L. *Heinrich Heine*. Translated from the German by B. Fairley, Oxford University Press, 1963.

MARCUSE, L. *Heinrich Heine. A Life between Past and Future.* Translated from the German by L. Marie Sieveking and Ian F. D. Morrow. Sidgwick & Jackson, 1934.

LIPTZIN, S. *The English Legend of Heinrich Heine*. New York: Bloch Publishing Company, 1954.

PRAWER, S. S. *Heine: 'Buch der Lieder'*. E. Arnold, 1960.
Heine. The Tragic Satirist. Cambridge University Press, 1961.
Heine's Jewish Comedy. Oxford University Press, 1983.

REEVES, N. *Heinrich Heine. Poetry and Politics*. Oxford University Press, 1974.

ROSE, W. *Heinrich Heine. Two Studies of his Thought and Feeling.* Oxford University Press, 1956.
The Early Love Poetry of Heinrich Heine. Oxford University Press, 1962.

SAMMONS, J. L. *Heinrich Heine, The Elusive Poet*. Yale University Press, 1969.
Heinrich Heine. A Modern Biography. Princeton University Press, 1979.

BUCH DER LIEDER

BOOK OF SONGS

JUNGE LEIDEN

from TRAUMBILDER

Im nächtgen Traum hab ich mich selbst geschaut,
In schwarzem Galafrack und seidner Weste,
Manschetten an der Hand, als gings zum Feste,
Und vor mir stand mein Liebchen, süß und traut.
Ich beugte mich und sagte: «Sind Sie Braut?
Ei! ei! so gratulier ich, meine Beste!»
Doch fast die Kehle mir zusammenpreßte
Der langgezogne, vornehm kalte Laut.
Und bittre Tränen plötzlich sich ergossen
Aus Liebchens Augen, und in Tränenwogen
Ist mir das holde Bildnis fast zerflossen.
O süße Augen, fromme Liebessterne,
Obschon ihr mir im Wachen oft gelogen,
Und auch im Traum, glaub ich euch dennoch gerne!

YOUNG SORROWS

from DREAM PICTURES

I saw myself in a dream one night in black tail-coat and silk waistcoat, shirt-cuffs showing, as if going to a ball, and before me stood my darling, sweet and well-loved. I bowed my head and said, 'Are you engaged? Ah ha! I congratulate you, my dear!' But the long-drawn-out, politely cold phrase almost choked me. And bitter tears suddenly poured from my darling's eyes, and in floods of tears this lovely picture almost dissolved before my eyes. O sweet eyes, innocent stars of love, although you often lied to me while I was awake, and in my dreams too, I still like to believe you!

HEINE

from LIEDER

Schöne Wiege meiner Leiden,
Schönes Grabmal meiner Ruh,
Schöne Stadt, wir müssen scheiden, –
Lebe wohl! ruf ich dir zu.

Lebe wohl, du heilge Schwelle,
Wo da wandelt Liebchen traut;
Lebe wohl, du heilge Stelle,
Wo ich sie zuerst geschaut.

Hätt ich dich doch nie gesehen,
Schöne Herzenskönigin!
Nimmer wär es dann geschehen,
Daß ich jetzt so elend bin.

Nie wollt ich dein Herze rühren,
Liebe hab ich nie erfleht;
Nur ein stilles Leben führen
Wollt ich, wo dein Odem weht.

Doch du drängst mich selbst von hinnen,
Bittre Worte spricht dein Mund;
Wahnsinn wühlt in meinen Sinnen,
Und mein Herz ist krank und wund.

from SONGS

Fair cradle of my sorrows, fair tomb of my peace, fair city, we must part –
farewell! I call to you.

Farewell, sacred threshold, where my dear darling walks; farewell, sacred
spot where I first saw her.

Would that I had never seen you, fair queen of my heart! Then it would
never have come to pass that I am now so wretched.

I never wanted to touch your heart, I never begged for love; I only wanted
to lead a quiet life where you breathe and move.

But you yourself drive me away from here, your mouth speaks bitter words;
madness rages in my mind, and my heart is sick and wounded.

4

Und die Glieder matt und träge
Schlepp ich fort am Wanderstab,
Bis mein müdes Haupt ich lege
Ferne in ein kühles Grab.

WARTE, warte, wilder Schiffsmann,
Gleich folg ich zum Hafen dir;
Von zwei Jungfraun nehm ich Abschied,
Von Europa und von ihr.

Blutquell, rinn aus meinen Augen,
Blutquell, brich aus meinem Leib,
Daß ich mit dem heißen Blute
Meine Schmerzen niederschreib.

Ei, mein Lieb, warum just heute
Schauderst du, mein Blut zu sehn?
Sahst mich bleich und herzeblutend
Lange Jahre vor dir stehn!

Kennst du noch das alte Liedchen
Von der Schlang im Paradies,
Die durch schlimme Apfelgabe
Unsern Ahn ins Elend stieß?

And my limbs, weary and feeble, I drag away, my staff in my hand, until I lay my tired head in a cool, far-off grave.

WAIT, wait, wild seaman, I'll follow you to the harbour at once; I'm taking leave of two maidens: Europe, and her.

Stream of blood, run from my eyes, stream of blood, break forth from my body, so that I may write down my pains with my hot blood.

Ha, my dear, why is it precisely today that you shudder to see my blood? For long years you have seen me standing before you, pale and bleeding at the heart.

Do you remember the old story of the serpent in Paradise which through the evil gift of the apple plunged our ancestor into wretchedness?

Alles Unheil brachten Äpfel!
Eva bracht damit den Tod,
Eris brachte Trojas Flammen,
Du brachtst beides, Flamm und Tod.

from ROMANZEN

DIE GRENADIERE

Nach Frankreich zogen zwei Grenadier,
Die waren in Rußland gefangen.
Und als sie kamen ins deutsche Quartier,
Sie ließen die Köpfe hangen.

Da hörten sie beide die traurige Mär:
Daß Frankreich verloren gegangen,
Besiegt und zerschlagen das große Heer –
Und der Kaiser, der Kaiser gefangen.

Da weinten zusammen die Grenadier
Wohl ob der kläglichen Kunde.
Der eine sprach: Wie weh wird mir,
Wie brennt meine alte Wunde!

Apples have brought every disaster! Eve brought death with them, Eris brought flames to Troy, and you brought both flames and death.

from ROMANCES

The Grenadiers

Two grenadiers were making their way towards France; they had been prisoners in Russia. And when they came to German quarters, they hung their heads.

They both heard there the sad news that France was lost, the Grand Army beaten and broken – and the Emperor, the Emperor a prisoner.

The grenadiers wept together at the sad news. One said: What pain I'm in, how my old wound burns!

Der andre sprach: Das Lied ist aus,
Auch ich möcht mit dir sterben,
Doch hab ich Weib und Kind zu Haus,
Die ohne mich verderben.

Was schert mich Weib, was schert mich Kind,
Ich trage weit beßres Verlangen;
Laß sie betteln gehn, wenn sie hungrig sind –
Mein Kaiser, mein Kaiser gefangen!

Gewähr mir, Bruder, eine Bitt:
Wenn ich jetzt sterben werde,
So nimm meine Leiche nach Frankreich mit,
Begrab mich in Frankreichs Erde.

Das Ehrenkreuz am roten Band
Sollst du aufs Herz mir legen;
Die Flinte gib mir in die Hand,
Und gürt mir um den Degen.

So will ich liegen und horchen still,
Wie eine Schildwach, im Grabe,
Bis einst ich höre Kanonengebrüll
Und wiehernder Rosse Getrabe.

The other said: The game is over, I too should like to die with you, but I have a wife and child at home who will perish without me.

What do I care about wife and child, I have a far better desire; let them go begging if they are hungry – my Emperor, my Emperor a prisoner!

Grant me a request, brother: if I should die now, take my body with you to France, bury me in the earth of France.

You must lay my cross of honour with its red ribbon on my heart; put my musket in my hand, and gird my sword round me.

Thus will I lie and listen quietly, like a sentry, in the grave, until I hear again the roar of cannon and the trotting of neighing horses.

Dann reitet mein Kaiser wohl über mein Grab,
Viel Schwerter klirren und blitzen;
Dann steig ich gewaffnet hervor aus dem Grab –
Den Kaiser, den Kaiser zu schützen.

DIE BOTSCHAFT

MEIN Knecht! steh auf und sattle schnell,
Und wirf dich auf dein Roß,
Und jage rasch durch Wald und Feld
Nach König Dunkans Schloß.

Dort schleiche in den Stall, und wart,
Bis dich der Stallbub schaut.
Den forsch mir aus: Sprich, welche ist
Von Dunkans Töchtern Braut?

Und spricht der Bub: «Die Braune ists»,
So bring mir schnell die Mär.
Doch spricht der Bub: «Die Blonde ists»,
So eilt das nicht so sehr.

Dann geh zum Meister Seiler hin,
Und kauf mir einen Strick,
Und reite langsam, sprich kein Wort,
Und bring mir den zurück.

Then my Emperor may ride over my grave, many swords will clash and glitter; then I shall arise armed from the grave – to protect the Emperor, the Emperor.

The Errand

MY squire! To your feet, saddle up quickly and throw yourself on your horse and gallop fast through forest and field to King Duncan's castle.

Creep into the stable there, and wait till the stable-boy sees you. Question him: Say, which of Duncan's daughters is to be married?

And if the boy says 'It's the dark one', bring me the news quickly. But if the boy says 'It's the fair one', there's not so much need to hurry.

In that case go to the master rope-maker and buy me a cord, and ride slowly, speak no word, and bring it to me.

BELSATZAR

DIE Mitternacht zog näher schon;
In stiller Ruh lag Babylon.

Nur oben in des Königs Schloß,
Da flackerts, da lärmt des Königs Troß.

Dort oben in dem Königssaal
Belsatzar hielt sein Königsmahl.

Die Knechte saßen in schimmernden Reihn,
Und leerten die Becher mit funkelndem Wein.

Es klirrten die Becher, es jauchzten die Knecht;
So klang es dem störrigen Könige recht.

Des Königs Wangen leuchten Glut;
Im Wein erwuchs ihm kecker Mut.

Und blindlings reißt der Mut ihn fort;
Und er lästert die Gottheit mit sündigem Wort.

Belshazzar

MIDNIGHT was already drawing near; Babylon lay quiet and at peace.

Only up there in the royal castle do torches flicker, and the king's followers make a din.

Up there in the royal hall Belshazzar was holding his royal feast.

The vassals sat in shimmering rows and emptied the goblets of sparkling wine.

The goblets clinked, the vassals made merry; the headstrong king liked the noise.

The king's cheeks glow; from the wine an arrogant defiance grew within him.

And blindly this defiance carries him away; and he blasphemes the divinity with sinful word.

Und er brüstet sich frech, und lästert wild;
Die Knechtenschar ihm Beifall brüllt.

Der König rief mit stolzem Blick;
Der Diener eilt und kehrt zurück.

Er trug viel gülden Gerät auf dem Haupt;
Das war aus dem Tempel Jehovahs geraubt.

Und der König ergriff mit frevler Hand
Einen heiligen Becher, gefüllt bis am Rand.

Und er leert ihn hastig bis auf den Grund,
Und rufet laut mit schäumendem Mund:

Jehovah! dir künd ich auf ewig Hohn –
Ich bin der König von Babylon!

Doch kaum das grause Wort verklang,
Dem König wards heimlich im Busen bang.

Das gellende Lachen verstummte zumal;
Es wurde leichenstill im Saal.

And he boasts insolently and blasphemes wildly; the host of vassals roars him its approval.

The king called with haughty mien; the servant hurries and returns.

He bore many golden vessels on his head; they were stolen from Jehovah's temple.

And the king seized with impious hand a sacred cup filled up to the brim.

And he empties it hastily to the bottom, and shouts aloud with foaming mouth:

Jehovah! I proclaim my eternal scorn for thee – I am the King of Babylon!

But scarcely had the terrible words rung out, when the king grew secretly afraid in his heart.

The shrill laughter died away suddenly; it became deathly still in the hall.

Und sieh! und sieh! an weißer Wand
Da kams hervor wie Menschenhand;

Und schrieb, und schrieb an weißer Wand
Buchstaben von Feuer, und schrieb und schwand.

Der König stieren Blicks da saß,
Mit schlotternden Knien und totenblaß.

Die Knechtenschar saß kalt durchgraut,
Und saß gar still, gab keinen Laut.

Die Magier kamen, doch keiner verstand
Zu deuten die Flammenschrift an der Wand.

Belsatzar ward aber in selbiger Nacht
Von seinen Knechten umgebracht.

And look, look! On the white wall something came forth, like a human hand;
   and wrote, and wrote on the white wall letters of fire, and wrote, and vanished.
   The king sat there with staring gaze, with knocking knees and deathly pale.
   The host of vassals sat filled with cold terror, and sat very still, made no sound.
   The soothsayers came, but none knew how to interpret the flaming writing on the wall.
   But Belshazzar in that same night was slain by his vassals.

DIE FENSTERSCHAU

Der bleiche Heinrich ging vorbei,
Schön Hedwig lag am Fenster.
Sie sprach halblaut: Gott steh mir bei,
Der unten schaut bleich wie Gespenster!

Der unten erhub sein Aug in die Höh,
Hinschmachtend nach Hedewigs Fenster.
Schön Hedwig ergriff es wie Liebesweh,
Auch sie ward bleich wie Gespenster.

Schön Hedwig stand nun mit Liebesharm
Tagtäglich lauernd am Fenster.
Bald aber lag sie in Heinrichs Arm,
Allnächtlich zur Zeit der Gespenster.

DER WUNDE RITTER

Ich weiß eine alte Kunde,
Die hallet dumpf und trüb:
Ein Ritter liegt liebeswunde,
Doch treulos ist sein Lieb.

Seen at the Window

Pale Heinrich went past, fair Hedwig lay at the window. She said half aloud: God help me, that man down there looks as pale as a ghost!

That man down there raised his eyes, gazed full of yearning towards Hedwig's window. Fair Hedwig was seized as if by the torments of love, she too became as pale as a ghost.

Fair Hedwig then stood, filled with love's affliction, day in, day out watching at the window. But soon she lay in Heinrich's arms every night at the hour for ghosts.

The Sick Knight

I know an old story which rings heavy and sad: a knight lies love-sick, but his beloved is faithless.

Als treulos muß er verachten
Die eigne Herzliebste sein,
Als schimpflich muß er betrachten
Die eigne Liebespein.

Er möcht in die Schranken reiten
Und rufen die Ritter zum Streit:
Der mag sich zum Kampfe bereiten,
Wer mein Lieb eines Makels zeiht!

Da würden wohl alle schweigen,
Nur nicht sein eigener Schmerz;
Da müßt er die Lanze neigen
Widers eigne klagende Herz.

WAHRHAFTIG

WENN der Frühling kommt mit dem Sonnenschein,
Dann knospen und blühen die Blümlein auf;
Wenn der Mond beginnt seinen Strahlenlauf,
Dann schwimmen die Sternlein hintendrein;
Wenn der Sänger zwei süße Äuglein sieht,
Dann quellen ihm Lieder aus tiefem Gemüt; –

He must despise his own dearest love as faithless, he must consider his own
love-anguish as dishonourable.

He would like to ride into the lists and challenge the knights to combat:
Let him prepare for battle who accuses my love of a fault!

All would probably be silent, but for his own pain; he would have to level
his lance against his own sorrowing heart.

In Truth

WHEN spring comes with sunshine the little flowers bud and bloom; when the
moon begins its shining course the little stars swim behind; when the minstrel
sees two sweet little eyes, songs spring from the depths of his being; – but

Doch Lieder und Sterne und Blümelein,
Und Äuglein und Mondglanz und Sonnenschein,
Wie sehr das Zeug auch gefällt,
So machts doch noch lang keine Welt.

from SONETTE

AN MEINE MUTTER B. HEINE,
GEBORNE VAN GELDERN

Ich bins gewohnt, den Kopf recht hoch zu tragen,
Mein Sinn ist auch ein bißchen starr und zähe;
Wenn selbst der König mir ins Antlitz sähe,
Ich würde nicht die Augen niederschlagen.
Doch, liebe Mutter, offen will ichs sagen:
Wie mächtig auch mein stolzer Mut sich blähe,
In deiner selig süßen, trauten Nähe
Ergreift mich oft ein demutvolles Zagen.
Ist es dein Geist, der heimlich mich bezwinget,
Dein hoher Geist, der alles kühn durchdringet,
Und blitzend sich zum Himmelslichte schwinget?

songs and stars and little flowers, and little eyes and moonlight and sunshine,
however much this stuff pleases, it is nowhere near being the whole world.

from SONNETS

To My Mother B. Heine, née van Geldern

I AM accustomed to hold my head high, my mind is also a bit rigid and stubborn; if the king himself were to gaze into my face I would not cast down my eyes. But, dear mother, I will say it openly: however strongly my proud mind puffs itself up, in your blessedly sweet, familiar presence a humble timidity often seizes me. Is it your spirit which secretly subdues me, your exalted spirit which boldly penetrates everything, and flashing soars towards the light of

Quält mich Erinnerung, daß ich verübet
So manche Tat, die dir das Herz betrübet?
Das schöne Herz, das mich so sehr geliebet?

FRESKO-SONETTE AN CHRISTIAN S.,* VI

"Als ich vor einem Jahr dich wiederblickte,
Küßtest du mich nicht in der Willkommstund.»
So sprach ich, und der Liebsten roter Mund
Den schönsten Kuß auf meine Lippen drückte.
Und lächelnd süß ein Myrtenreis sie pflückte
Vom Myrtenstrauche, der am Fenster stund:
«Nimm hin, und pflanz dies Reis in frischen Grund,
Und stell ein Glas darauf», sprach sie und nickte. –
Schon lang ists her. Es starb das Reis im Topf.
Sie selbst hab ich seit Jahren nicht gesehn;
Doch brennt der Kuß mir immer noch im Kopf.
Und aus der Ferne triebs mich jüngst zum Ort,
Wo Liebchen wohnt. Vorm Hause blieb ich stehn
Die ganze Nacht, ging erst am Morgen fort.

heaven? Does the recollection torment me that I have committed so many
deeds which saddened your heart? That beautiful heart that has loved me so
much?

Fresco Sonnets for Christian S.,* No. VI

'When I saw you again a year ago you didn't kiss me when you greeted me.'
So I said, and my dearest's red mouth pressed the most beautiful kiss upon my
lips. And sweetly smiling she plucked a myrtle-twig from the myrtle-bush
which stood at the window: 'Take and plant this twig in cool earth, and put a
glass cover over it,' she said, and nodded. – That was long ago. The twig died
in its pot. I haven't seen her for years; but the kiss still burns in my memory.
And recently I felt impelled to go from far away to the place where my darling
lives. I stood in front of the house the whole night and departed only when it
was morning.

* Christian Sethe, a close friend of Heine's.

15

Nachlese

MINNEKLAGE

EINSAM klag ich meine Leiden,
Im vertrauten Schoß der Nacht;
Frohe Menschen muß ich meiden,
Fliehen scheu, wo Freude lacht.

Einsam fließen meine Tränen,
Fließen immer, fließen still;
Doch des Herzens brennend Sehnen
Keine Träne löschen will.

Einst, ein lachend muntrer Knabe,
Spielt ich manches schöne Spiel,
Freute mich der Lebensgabe,
Wußte nie von Schmerzgefühl.

Denn die Welt war nur ein Garten,
Wo viel bunte Blumen blühn,
Wo mein Tagwerk Blumenwarten,
Rosen, Veilchen und Jasmin.

Supplementary Poems

Love-Lament

LONELY I lament my sorrows in the familiar bosom of the night; I must avoid cheerful people, flee shyly from places where joy laughs.

Lonely, my tears flow, flow constantly, flow silently; but no tear will extinguish my heart's burning desire.

Once, a laughing, cheerful boy, I played many a delightful game, enjoyed the gift of life, never knew the feel of pain.

For the world was only a garden in which many brightly-coloured flowers bloom, in which my daily task was tending the flowers: roses, violets and jasmine.

Träumend süß auf grüner Aue,
Sah ich Bächlein fließen mild;
Wenn ich jetzt in Bächlein schaue,
Zeigt sich mir ein bleiches Bild.

Bin ein bleicher Mann geworden,
Seit mein Auge sie gesehn;
Heimlich weh ist mir geworden,
Wundersam ist mir geschehn.

Tief im Herzen hegt ich lange
Englein stiller Friedensruh;
Diese flohen zitternd, bange,
Ihrer Sternenheimat zu.

Schwarze Nacht mein Aug umdüstert,
Schatten drohen feindlich grimm;
Und im Busen heimlich flüstert
Eine eigen fremde Stimm.

Fremde Schmerzen, fremde Leiden
Steigen auf mit wilder Wut,
Und in meinen Eingeweiden
Zehret eine fremde Glut.

Dreaming sweetly in a green meadow I saw little streams flowing gently; when I look into little streams now, a pale image shows itself to me.

I have become a pale man since my eye saw her; I have become secretly sad, something strange has happened to me.

Deep in my heart I had long cherished little angels of quiet, restful peace; they have flown shivering, anxious, away to their starry home.

Black night clouds my eye, shadows threaten, hostile and grim; and in my heart a voice – my own, yet strange – whispers secretly.

Strange pains, strange sorrows rise up in wild fury, and a strange glow gnaws at my vitals.

Aber daß in meinem Herzen
Flammen wühlen sonder Ruh,
Daß ich sterbe hin vor Schmerzen –
Minne, sieh! das tatest du!

IM DOME

Des Oberkirchners Töchterlein
Führt' mich in die heiligen Hallen;
Ihr Haar war blond, ihr Wuchs war klein,
Ihr Tuch vom Halse gefallen.

Ich sah für einiger Groschen Preis
Die Gräber und Kreuze und Lichte
Im alten Dom; da ward mir heiß –
Ich sah in Elsbeths Gesichte.

Und schaute wieder hie und da
Die heiligen Kirchenmonstranzen;
Im Unterrock, Halleluja!
Die Weiber am Fenster tanzen.

But that in my heart flames rage without respite, that I am dying of pain –
love, see, that was your doing!

In the Cathedral

The head sacristan's little daughter led me into the sacred halls; her hair was
blond, she was slight of build, her kerchief had fallen from her neck.

For the price of a few pence I saw the tombs and crosses and candles in the
old cathedral; I grew hot – I looked into Elsbeth's face.

And then again looked here and there at the sacred monstrances; the women
in the stained glass window are dancing, hallelujah, in their petticoats.

Des Oberkirchners Töchterlein
Blieb mit mir zusammen stehen;
Sie hat ein Augenpaar gar fein,
Drin habe ich alles gesehen.

Des Oberkirchners Töchterlein
Führt' mich aus den heiligen Hallen;
Ihr Hals war rot, ihr Mund war klein,
Ihr Tuch vom Busen gefallen.

ICH mache die kleinen Lieder
Der Herzallerliebsten mein,
Die heben ihr klingend Gefieder
Und fliegen zu dir hinein.

Es stammen die kleinen Jungen
Vom schnalzenden Herrn Gemahl,
Die kommen zu dir gesprungen
Über Wiese, Busch und Tal.

Die Leute so gerne weilen
Bei meiner Lieder Chor;
Doch bei der Jungen Heulen
Sie halten sich zu das Ohr.

The head sacristan's little daughter remained standing at my side; she has a lovely pair of eyes; I saw everything reflected in them.

The head sacristan's little daughter led me out of the sacred halls; her neck was red, her mouth was small, her kerchief had fallen from her bosom.

I PRODUCE my little songs for the darling of my heart, they raise their sounding wings and fly in to you.

Your young boys are the product of your tongue-clicking husband, they come leaping towards you over meadow, bush and valley.

People are so glad to linger at my chorus of songs; but at the yelling of your boys they block their ears.

Und der dies Lied gesungen,
Der liegt allein in der Nacht
Und hätte weit lieber die Jungen,
Ach, als die Lieder gemacht!

Die Liebe begann im Monat März,
Wo mir erkrankte Sinn und Herz.
Doch als der Mai, der grüne, kam:
Ein Ende all mein Trauern nahm.

Es war am Nachmittag um Drei
Wohl auf der Moosbank der Einsiedelei,
Die hinter der Linde liegt versteckt,
Da hab ich ihr mein Herz entdeckt.

Die Blumen dufteten. Im Baum
Die Nachtigall sang, doch hörten wir kaum
Ein einziges Wort von ihrem Gesinge,
Wir hatten zu reden viel wichtige Dinge.

Wir schwuren uns Treue bis in den Tod.
Die Stunden schwanden, das Abendrot
Erlosch. Doch saßen wir lange Zeit
Und weinten in der Dunkelheit.

And the man who sang this song lies alone at night and would have been much happier producing your boys, ah, than the songs!

Love began in the month of March, when my heart and mind fell ill. But when May, the green month, came, all my grieving came to an end.

It was at three o'clock in the afternoon, on the mossy bank at the hermitage, which lies hidden behind the lime-tree, that I opened my heart to her.

The flowers smelt sweet. In the tree the nightingale sang, but we heard scarcely a single word of its warbling, we had many important things to say.

We swore to be true to each other unto death. The hours fled, the evening glow died away. But we sat for a long time and wept in the darkness.

Die Wälder und Felder grünen,
Es trillert die Lerch in der Luft,
Der Frühling ist erschienen
Mit Lichtern und Farben und Duft.

Der Lerchengesang erweicht mir
Das winterlich starre Gemüt,
Und aus dem Herzen steigt mir
Ein trauriges Klagelied.

Die Lerche trillert gar feine:
«Was singst du so trüb und bang?»
Das ist ein Liedchen, o Kleine,
Das sing ich schon jahrelang!

Das sing ich im grünen Haine,
Das Herz von Gram beschwert;
Schon deine Großmutter, o Kleine,
Hat dieses Liedchen gehört!

Es faßt mich wieder der alte Mut,
Mir ist, als jagt ich zu Rosse,
Und jagte wieder mit liebender Glut
Nach meiner Liebsten Schlosse.

The woods and fields grow green, the lark trills in the air, spring has appeared
with lights and colours and scents.

The lark's song mellows my mind, stiffened by winter, and from my heart
there arises a sad song of lament.

The lark trills very prettily: 'What are you singing so sadly and anxiously?'
–'It is a little song, o little one, which I've been singing for years!

'I sing it in the green grove, my heart heavy with grief; your grandmother,
o little one, heard this little song!'

My old courage comes over me again, I feel as if I were charging on horseback,
charging once more with loving ardour towards my dearest's castle.

Es faßt mich wieder der alte Mut,
Mir ist, als jagt ich zu Rosse,
Und jagte zum Streite mit hassender Wut,
Schon harret der Kampfgenosse.

Ich jage geschwind wie der Wirbelwind,
Die Wälder und Felder fliegen!
Mein Kampfgenoß und mein schönes Kind,
Sie müssen beide erliegen.

My old courage comes over me again, I feel as if I were charging on horseback, charging into battle with hate-filled anger: my adversary is there waiting.

I charge as fast as the whirlwind, the forests and meadows fly! My adversary and my lovely child, they must both succumb.

LYRISCHES INTERMEZZO

Im wunderschönen Monat Mai,
Als alle Knospen sprangen,
Da ist in meinem Herzen
Die Liebe aufgegangen.

Im wunderschönen Monat Mai,
Als alle Vögel sangen,
Da hab ich ihr gestanden
Mein Sehnen und Verlangen.

Aus meinen Tränen sprießen
Viel blühende Blumen hervor,
Und meine Seufzer werden
Ein Nachtigallenchor.

Und wenn du mich lieb hast, Kindchen,
Schenk ich dir die Blumen all,
Und vor deinem Fenster soll klingen
Das Lied der Nachtigall.

LYRICAL INTERMEZZO

In the wonderfully beautiful month of May, when all the buds were bursting,
love unfolded in my heart.

In the wonderfully beautiful month of May, when all the birds were singing,
I confessed to her my longing and desire.

From my tears shoot up many blossoming flowers, and my sighs become a
choir of nightingales.

And if you love me, little one, I'll give you all the flowers, and before your
window the song of the nightingale shall ring out.

Auf Flügeln des Gesanges,
Herzliebchen, trag ich dich fort,
Fort nach den Fluren des Ganges,
Dort weiß ich den schönsten Ort.

Dort liegt ein rotblühender Garten
Im stillen Mondenschein;
Die Lotosblumen erwarten
Ihr trautes Schwesterlein.

Die Veilchen kichern und kosen,
Und schaun nach den Sternen empor;
Heimlich erzählen die Rosen
Sich duftende Märchen ins Ohr.

Es hüpfen herbei und lauschen
Die frommen, klugen Gazelln;
Und in der Ferne rauschen
Des heiligen Stromes Welln.

Dort wollen wir niedersinken
Unter dem Palmenbaum,
Und Liebe und Ruhe trinken
Und träumen seligen Traum.

ON wings of song, my sweetheart, I shall carry you away, away to the meadows by the Ganges – I know the loveliest place there.

A red-blooming garden lies there in the still moonlight; the lotus-flowers await their dear little sister.

The violets titter and flirt, and gaze up at the stars; secretly the roses whisper fragrant tales into each other's ears.

The innocent, clever gazelles come frisking up to listen; and in the distance the waves of the sacred river murmur.

There we will sink down beneath the palm-tree and drink in love and peace, and dream blessed dreams.

DIE Lotosblume ängstigt
Sich vor der Sonne Pracht,
Und mit gesenktem Haupte
Erwartet sie träumend die Nacht.

Der Mond, der ist ihr Buhle,
Er weckt sie mit seinem Licht,
Und ihm entschleiert sie freundlich
Ihr frommes Blumengesicht.

Sie blüht und glüht und leuchtet,
Und starret stumm in die Höh;
Sie duftet und weinet und zittert
Vor Liebe und Liebesweh.

IM Rhein, im heiligen Strome,
Da spiegelt sich in den Welln,
Mit seinem großen Dome,
Das große, heilige Köln.

Im Dom, da steht ein Bildnis
Auf goldenem Leder gemalt;
In meines Lebens Wildnis
Hats freundlich hineingestrahlt.

THE lotus-flower is afraid of the sun's splendour, and with bowed head she dreamily waits for night.

The moon is her lover, he awakens her with his light, and for him she unveils her innocent flower-face in a friendly way.

She blooms and glows and shines, and stares silently into the heavens; she smells fragrant and weeps and trembles for love and love's woe.

IN the Rhine, the holy river, there is in the waves the reflection of great, holy Cologne with its great cathedral.

In the cathedral there is a picture painted on golden leather; it has cast its friendly beams into the wilderness of my life.

Es schweben Blumen und Englein
Um unsre liebe Frau;
Die Augen, die Lippen, die Wänglein,
Die gleichen der Liebsten genau.

O schwöre nicht und küsse nur,
Ich glaube keinem Weiberschwur!
Dein Wort ist süß, doch süßer ist
Der Kuß, den ich dir abgeküßt!
Den hab ich, und dran glaub ich auch,
Das Wort ist eitel Dunst und Hauch.

*   *
*

O schwöre, Liebchen, immerfort,
Ich glaube dir aufs bloße Wort!
An deinen Busen sink ich hin,
Und glaube, daß ich selig bin;
Ich glaube, Liebchen, ewiglich,
Und noch viel länger, liebst du mich.

Flowers and little angels hover around Our Lady; her eyes, her lips, her little cheeks are exactly like my darling's.

Oh, don't swear, just kiss, I don't believe any woman's oath! Your words are sweet, but sweeter still is the kiss which I kissed from you! I have it, and I believe in it too – words are nothing but mist and breath.

Oh, swear on, darling, for ever, I believe you by your word alone! I sink on to your bosom and believe I'm happy; I believe, darling, that you will love me for ever and even longer.

Ich grolle nicht, und wenn das Herz auch bricht,
Ewig verlornes Lieb! ich grolle nicht.
Wie du auch strahlst in Diamantenpracht,
Es fällt kein Strahl in deines Herzens Nacht.

Das weiß ich längst. Ich sah dich ja im Traum,
Und sah die Nacht in deines Herzens Raum,
Und sah die Schlang, die dir am Herzen frißt, –
Ich sah, mein Lieb, wie sehr du elend bist.

Ja, du bist elend, und ich grolle nicht; –
Mein Lieb, wir sollen beide elend sein!
Bis uns der Tod das kranke Herze bricht,
Mein Lieb, wir sollen beide elend sein!

Wohl seh ich Spott, der deinen Mund umschwebt,
Und seh dein Auge blitzen trotziglich,
Und seh den Stolz, der deinen Busen hebt, –
Und elend bist du doch, elend wie ich.

I bear no grudge, even though my heart is breaking, o love for ever lost, I bear no grudge. Though you gleam in the splendour of diamonds, no ray falls into the night of your heart.

I've known that for a long time. For I saw you in a dream, and saw the night about your heart, and saw the snake that gnaws at your heart – I saw, my love, how very wretched you are.

Yes, you are wretched, and I bear no grudge; – my dear, we must both be wretched! Until death breaks our sick hearts, my dear, we must both be wretched!

Indeed I see mockery hovering about your mouth, and see your eye flash defiantly, and see the pride which makes your bosom swell – and yet you are wretched, wretched as I am.

Unsichtbar zuckt auch Schmerz um deinen Mund,
Verborgne Träne trübt des Auges Schein,
Der stolze Busen hegt geheime Wund –
Mein Lieb, wir sollen beide elend sein.

UND wüßtens die Blumen, die kleinen,
Wie tief verwundet mein Herz,
Sie würden mit mir weinen,
Zu heilen meinen Schmerz.

Und wüßtens die Nachtigallen,
Wie ich so traurig und krank,
Sie ließen fröhlich erschallen
Erquickenden Gesang.

Und wüßten sie mein Wehe,
Die goldnen Sternelein,
Sie kämen aus ihrer Höhe,
Und sprächen Trost mir ein.

Die alle könnens nicht wissen,
Nur Eine kennt meinen Schmerz:
Sie hat ja selbst zerrissen,
Zerrissen mir das Herz.

Pain too quivers unseen about your mouth, hidden tears dull the light of
your eyes, your proud bosom nurtures a secret wound – my love, we must
both be wretched.

AND if the little flowers knew how deeply my heart was wounded, they would
weep with me to heal my pain.

And if the nightingales knew how sad and sick I am, they would joyously
let their refreshing song ring out.

And if the little golden stars knew my woe, they would come down from
their heights and speak comfort to me.

None of them can know it, only one person knows my pain: she herself it
was who rent my heart.

Wir haben viel für einander gefühlt,
Und dennoch uns gar vortrefflich vertragen.
Wir haben oft «Mann und Frau» gespielt,
Und dennoch uns nicht gerauft und geschlagen.
Wir haben zusammen gejauchzt und gescherzt,
Und zärtlich uns geküßt und geherzt.
Wir haben am Ende, aus kindischer Lust,
«Verstecken» gespielt in Wäldern und Gründen,
Und haben uns so zu verstecken gewußt,
Daß wir uns nimmermehr wiederfinden.

Ein Fichtenbaum steht einsam
Im Norden auf kahler Höh.
Ihn schläfert; mit weißer Decke
Umhüllen ihn Eis und Schnee.

Er träumt von einer Palme,
Die, fern im Morgenland,
Einsam und schweigend trauert
Auf brennender Felsenwand.

We felt deeply for one another and yet got on with each other extremely well. We often played at husband and wife, and yet did not quarrel or come to blows. We rejoiced and joked together, and tenderly kissed and embraced each other. Finally in childish glee we played hide-and-seek in the woods and hollows, and we were so good at hiding that we shall never find each other again.

A fir-tree stands alone in the north on a bare height. He is sleepy; ice and snow envelop him with a white blanket.
He dreams of a palm-tree who, far away in the east, grieves alone and silent on a burning wall of rock.

Aus meinen großen Schmerzen
Mach ich die kleinen Lieder;
Die heben ihr klingend Gefieder
Und flattern nach ihrem Herzen.

Sie fanden den Weg zur Trauten,
Doch kommen sie wieder und klagen,
Und klagen, und wollen nicht sagen,
Was sie im Herzen schauten.

Ein Jüngling liebt ein Mädchen,
Die hat einen andern erwählt;
Der andre liebt eine andre,
Und hat sich mit dieser vermählt.

Das Mädchen heiratet aus Ärger
Den ersten besten Mann,
Der ihr in den Weg gelaufen;
Der Jüngling ist übel dran.

Es ist eine alte Geschichte,
Doch bleibt sie immer neu;
Und wem sie just passieret,
Dem bricht das Herz entzwei.

From my great sorrows I make my little songs; they raise their sounding wings and flutter to her heart.

They found their way to my dear one, but they come back and lament, and lament, and don't want to tell what they saw in her heart.

A young man loves a girl who has chosen another; this other one loves another girl and has married her.

The girl in vexation marries the very first man who comes her way; the young man is in a sad plight.

It is an old story, but it remains ever new; and when it happens to someone, his heart breaks.

Aus alten Märchen winkt es
Hervor mit weißer Hand,
Da singt es und da klingt es
Von einem Zauberland:

Wo große Blumen schmachten
Im goldnen Abendlicht,
Und zärtlich sich betrachten
Mit bräutlichem Gesicht; –

Wo alle Bäume sprechen
Und singen, wie ein Chor,
Und laute Quellen brechen
Wie Tanzmusik hervor; –

Und Liebesweisen tönen,
Wie du sie nie gehört,
Bis wundersüßes Sehnen
Dich wundersüß betört!

Ach, könnt ich dorthin kommen,
Und dort mein Herz erfreun,
Und aller Qual entnommen,
Und frei und selig sein!

A white hand beckons from old stories, there's a singing and a ringing of a magic land
    where great trees languish in the golden evening light and tenderly gaze at each other with bridal faces; –
    where all the trees speak and sing, like a choir, and loud springs burst forth like dance-music; –
    and love-songs such as you have never heard ring out, until a wonderfully sweet yearning deludes you wonderfully sweetly!
    Ah, if I could only find my way thither to gladden my heart, and relieved of all torment, be both free and blessed!

Ach! jenes Land der Wonne,
Das seh ich oft im Traum;
Doch kommt die Morgensonne,
Zerfließts wie eitel Schaum.

Am leuchtenden Sommermorgen
Geh ich im Garten herum.
Es flüstern und sprechen die Blumen,
Ich aber, ich wandle stumm.

Es flüstern und sprechen die Blumen,
Und schaun mitleidig mich an:
Sei unserer Schwester nicht böse,
Du trauriger, blasser Mann!

Es liegt der heiße Sommer
Auf deinen Wängelein;
Es liegt der Winter, der kalte,
In deinem Herzchen klein.

Ah! I often see that land of bliss in my dreams; but when the morning sun comes, it dissolves like mere foam.

On a bright summer morning I walk round the garden. The flowers whisper and speak, but I, I walk in silence.
The flowers whisper and speak and look at me sympathetically: don't be angry with our sister, you sad, pale man!

Hot summer lies upon your little cheeks; cold winter lies in your tiny little heart.

Das wird sich bei dir ändern,
Du Vielgeliebte mein!
Der Winter wird auf den Wangen,
Der Sommer im Herzen sein.

Sie saßen und tranken am Teetisch,
Und sprachen von Liebe viel.
Die Herren, die waren ästhetisch,
Die Damen von zartem Gefühl.

Die Liebe muß sein platonisch,
Der dürre Hofrat sprach.
Die Hofrätin lächelt ironisch,
Und dennoch seufzet sie: Ach!

Der Domherr öffnet den Mund weit:
Die Liebe sei nicht zu roh,
Sie schadet sonst der Gesundheit.
Das Fräulein lispelt: Wie so?

That will change, my dearly loved one! Winter will be upon your cheeks, summer in your heart.

They sat and drank at the tea-table and spoke much about love. The gentlemen were aesthetic, the ladies of tender feeling.

Love must be platonic, said the dry councillor. His wife smiles ironically, and yet she sighs: Ah!

The canon opens his mouth wide: Love should not be too rough, or it is damaging to the health. The young lady whispers, How?

Die Gräfin spricht wehmütig:
Die Liebe ist eine Passion!
Und präsentieret gütig
Die Tasse dem Herren Baron.

Am Tische war noch ein Plätzchen;
Mein Liebchen, da hast du gefehlt.
Du hättest so hübsch, mein Schätzchen,
Von deiner Liebe erzählt.

Iᴄʜ hab im Traum geweinet,
Mir träumte, du lägest im Grab.
Ich wachte auf, und die Träne
Floß noch von der Wange herab.

Ich hab im Traum geweinet,
Mir träumt', du verließest mich.
Ich wachte auf, und ich weinte
Noch lange bitterlich.

Ich hab im Traum geweinet,
Mir träumte, du bliebest mir gut.
Ich wachte auf, und noch immer
Strömt meine Tränenflut.

The countess speaks sadly: Love is a passion! And graciously presents a cup of tea to the baron.

There was another place at the table; my darling, you were the missing one. You would have told them so prettily, my treasure, of your love.

I ᴡᴇᴘᴛ in my dream, I dreamt that you lay in your grave. I awoke, and the tear was still flowing down my cheek.

I wept in my dream, I dreamt that you left me. I awoke, and I wept on, bitterly, for a long time.

I wept in my dream, I dreamt that you were still fond of me. I awoke, and my flood of tears is still streaming.

Der Herbstwind rüttelt die Bäume,
Die Nacht ist feucht und kalt;
Gehüllt im grauen Mantel,
Reite ich einsam im Wald.

Und wie ich reite, so reiten
Mir die Gedanken voraus;
Sie tragen mich leicht und luftig
Nach meiner Liebsten Haus.

Die Hunde bellen, die Diener
Erscheinen mit Kerzengeflirr;
Die Wendeltreppe stürm ich
Hinauf mit Sporengeklirr.

Im leuchtenden Teppichgemache,
Da ist es so duftig und warm,
Da harret meiner die Holde –
Ich fliege in ihren Arm.

Es säuselt der Wind in den Blättern,
Es spricht der Eichenbaum:
Was willst du, törichter Reiter,
Mit deinem törichten Traum?

The autumn wind shakes the trees, the night is damp and cold; wrapped in a grey cloak I ride alone in the forest.

And as I ride, my thoughts ride on before me; they carry me lightly and airily to my dearest's house.

The dogs bark, the servants appear with flickering candles; I race up the spiral staircase, my spurs jingling.

In the bright, tapestry-hung chamber it is so sweet-scented and warm, my darling is waiting for me – I fly to her arms.

The wind rustles in the leaves, the oak-tree says: What do you want, foolish horseman, with your foolish dream?

Es fällt ein Stern herunter
Aus seiner funkelnden Höh!
Das ist der Stern der Liebe,
Den ich dort fallen seh.

Es fallen vom Apfelbaume
Der Blüten und Blätter viel!
Es kommen die neckenden Lüfte,
Und treiben damit ihr Spiel.

Es singt der Schwan im Weiher,
Und rudert auf und ab,
Und immer leiser singend,
Taucht er ins Flutengrab.

Es ist so still und dunkel!
Verweht ist Blatt und Blüt,
Der Stern ist knisternd zerstoben,
Verklungen das Schwanenlied.

Die alten, bösen Lieder,
Die Träume schlimm und arg,
Die laßt uns jetzt begraben,
Holt einen großen Sarg.

A star falls from its sparkling heights! It is the star of love that I see falling there.

Many blossoms and leaves fall from the apple-tree! The teasing breezes come and play their games with them.

The swan sings on the pond, and swims back and forth, and singing ever more softly he dives into his watery grave.

It is so quiet and dark! Leaf and blossom are scattered, the star has vanished with a crackle, the swan's song has died away.

The old, bad songs, the evil, disturbing dreams — let us now bury them; fetch a big coffin.

Hinein leg ich gar Manches,
Doch sag ich noch nicht was;
Der Sarg muß sein noch größer
Wie's Heidelberger Faß.

Und holt eine Totenbahre,
Von Brettern fest und dick:
Auch muß sie sein noch länger
Als wie zu Mainz die Brück.

Und holt mir auch zwölf Riesen,
Die müssen noch stärker sein
Als wie der heilge Christoph
Im Dom zu Köln am Rhein.

Die sollen den Sarg forttragen
Und senken ins Meer hinab,
Denn solchem großen Sarge
Gebührt ein großes Grab.

Wißt ihr, warum der Sarg wohl
So groß und schwer mag sein?
Ich legt auch meine Liebe
Und meinen Schmerz hinein.

I shall put many things into it, but I shan't yet say what; the coffin must be even bigger than the Great Tun at Heidelberg.

And fetch a funeral bier of firm, thick boards: it must be even longer than the bridge at Mainz.

And fetch me twelve giants too, they must be even stronger than the St Christopher in the cathedral at Cologne on the Rhine.

They are to carry the coffin away and sink it in the sea, for a big grave is needed for such a big coffin.

Do you know why the coffin is so big and heavy? I put my love too, and my pain, into it.

Nachlese

Du sollst mich liebend umschließen,
Geliebtes, schönes Weib!
Umschling mich mit Armen und Füßen,
Und mit dem geschmeidigen Leib.

*   *
*

Gewaltig hat umfangen,
Umwunden, umschlungen schon
Die allerschönste der Schlangen
Den glücklichsten Laokoon.

Ich glaub nicht an den Himmel,
Wovon das Pfäfflein spricht;
Ich glaub nur an dein Auge,
Das ist mein Himmelslicht.

Ich glaub nicht an den Herrgott,
Wovon das Pfäfflein spricht;
Ich glaub nur an dein Herze,
'nen andern Gott hab ich nicht.

Supplementary Poems

You must embrace me lovingly, beloved, beautiful woman! Entwine me with your arms and legs and with your supple body.

The most beautiful of serpents has powerfully clasped, enfolded, entwined the happiest of Laocoöns.

I don't believe in Heaven, of which the little priest speaks; I only believe in your eyes, they are my heavenly light.

I don't believe in the Lord God, of whom the little priest speaks; I only believe in your heart, I have no other god.

Ich glaub nicht an den Bösen,
An Höll und Höllenschmerz;
Ich glaub nur an dein Auge,
Und an dein böses Herz.

Ich kann es nicht vergessen,
Geliebtes, holdes Weib,
Daß ich dich einst besessen,
Die Seele und den Leib.

Den Leib möcht ich noch haben,
Den Leib so zart und jung;
Die Seele könnt ihr begraben,
Hab selber Seele genung.

Ich will meine Seele zerschneiden,
Und hauchen die Hälfte dir ein,
Und will dich umschlingen, wir müssen
Ganz Leib und Seele sein.

I don't believe in the Evil One, in Hell and the torments of Hell; I only believe in your eyes, and in your evil heart.

I cannot forget, beloved, charming woman, that I once possessed you, body and soul.
  I should still like to have your body, your body, so tender and young; they can bury your soul, I've soul enough myself.
  I will cut up my soul and breathe half of it into you, and I will enfold you in my arms, we must be wholly one body and soul.

DIE HEIMKEHR

Ich weiß nicht, was soll es bedeuten,
Daß ich so traurig bin;
Ein Märchen aus alten Zeiten,
Das kommt mir nicht aus dem Sinn.

Die Luft ist kühl und es dunkelt,
Und ruhig fließt der Rhein;
Der Gipfel des Berges funkelt
Im Abendsonnenschein.

Die schönste Jungfrau sitzet
Dort oben wunderbar,
Ihr goldnes Geschmeide blitzet,
Sie kämmt ihr goldenes Haar.

Sie kämmt es mit goldenem Kamme,
Und singt ein Lied dabei;
Das hat eine wundersame,
Gewaltige Melodei.

THE HOMECOMING

I don't know why I am so sad; I can't get out of my mind a tale from olden times.

The air is cool and it is growing dark, and the Rhine flows peacefully; the peak of the mountain sparkles in the evening sunshine.

The fairest maiden sits up there, wonderful, her golden jewellery glitters, she combs her golden hair.

She combs it with a golden comb, and sings a song the while; it has a strange, powerful melody.

Den Schiffer im kleinen Schiffe
Ergreift es mit wildem Weh;
Er schaut nicht die Felsenriffe,
Er schaut nur hinauf in die Höh.

Ich glaube, die Wellen verschlingen
Am Ende Schiffer und Kahn;
Und das hat mit ihrem Singen
Die Lore-Lei getan.

ALS ich, auf der Reise, zufällig
Der Liebsten Familie fand,
Schwesterchen, Vater und Mutter,
Sie haben mich freudig erkannt.

Sie fragten nach meinem Befinden,
Und sagten selber sogleich:
Ich hätte mich gar nicht verändert,
Nur mein Gesicht sei bleich.

Ich fragte nach Muhmen und Basen,
Nach manchem langweilgen Geselln,
Und nach dem kleinen Hündchen
Mit seinem sanften Belln.

It seizes the boatman in his little boat with wild woe; he doesn't see the rocky reefs, he only looks up to the heights.

I believe the waves finally swallow the boatman and his boat; and the Lorelei has done that with her singing.

WHEN on my journey I by chance met my darling's family, her little sister, father and mother recognized me and greeted me cheerfully.

They asked how I was and at the same time said I hadn't changed a bit, only that I was pale in the face.

I asked after aunts and cousins, and many a boring person, and the little dog and its gentle bark.

Auch nach der vermählten Geliebten
Fragte ich nebenbei;
Und freundlich gab man zur Antwort:
Daß sie in den Wochen sei.

Und freundlich gratuliert ich,
Und lispelte liebevoll:
Daß man sie von mir recht herzlich
Viel tausendmal grüßen soll.

Schwesterchen rief dazwischen:
Das Hündchen, sanft und klein,
Ist groß und toll geworden,
Und ward ertränkt, im Rhein.

Die Kleine gleicht der Geliebten,
Besonders wenn sie lacht;
Sie hat dieselben Augen,
Die mich so elend gemacht.

WIR saßen am Fischerhause,
Und schauten nach der See;
Die Abendnebel kamen,
Und stiegen in die Höh.

I also asked incidentally about my darling, now married; and they kindly gave me the answer that she was in childbed.

And I politely offered my congratulations and murmured lovingly that they were to give her a thousand hearty greetings from me.

Her little sister interpolated: the little dog, gentle and small, had grown big and wild and been drowned in the Rhine.

The little girl is like my beloved, especially when she laughs; she has the very same eyes which made me so wretched.

WE sat by the fisherman's house and looked out to sea; the evening mists came and rose high in the sky.

Im Leuchtturm wurden die Lichter
Allmählich angesteckt,
Und in der weiten Ferne
Ward noch ein Schiff entdeckt.

Wir sprachen vom Sturm und Schiffbruch,
Vom Seemann, und wie er lebt
Und zwischen Himmel und Wasser,
Und Angst und Freude schwebt.

Wir sprachen von fernen Küsten,
Vom Süden und vom Nord,
Und von den seltsamen Völkern
Und seltsamen Sitten dort.

Am Ganges duftets und leuchtets,
Und Riesenbäume blühn,
Und schöne, stille Menschen
Vor Lotosblumen knien.

In Lappland sind schmutzige Leute,
Plattköpfig, breitmäulig und klein;
Sie kauern ums Feuer, und backen
Sich Fische, und quäken und schrein.

The lamps were gradually being lit in the lighthouse, and in the far distance another ship was spotted.

We spoke of storm and shipwreck, of the seaman and his life balanced between sky and sea, fear and joy.

We spoke of distant coasts, of the south and the north, and of the strange peoples and strange customs there.

By the Ganges there are sweet smells and bright lights, and giant trees blossom, and beautiful, quiet people kneel before lotus flowers.

In Lapland the people are dirty, flat-headed, broad-mouthed and small; they squat round the fire and bake fishes, and croak and shout.

Die Mädchen horchten ernsthaft,
Und endlich sprach niemand mehr;
Das Schiff war nicht mehr sichtbar,
Es dunkelte gar zu sehr.

STILL ist die Nacht, es ruhen die Gassen,
In diesem Hause wohnte mein Schatz;
Sie hat schon längst die Stadt verlassen,
Doch steht noch das Haus auf demselben Platz.

Da steht auch ein Mensch und starrt in die Höhe,
Und ringt die Hände, vor Schmerzensgewalt;
Mir graust es, wenn ich sein Antlitz sehe –
Der Mond zeigt mir meine eigne Gestalt.

Du Doppeltgänger! du bleicher Geselle!
Was äffst du nach mein Liebesleid,
Das mich gequält auf dieser Stelle,
So manche Nacht, in alter Zeit?

The girls listened gravely, and finally no one spoke; the ship was no longer visible, it was growing too dark.

THE night is still, the streets are at rest, my darling dwelt in this house; she left the town long ago, but the house still stands in the same place.

A man stands there too and stares up, and wrings his hands in the violence of his pain; I shudder when I see his face – the moon shows me my own form.

You ghostly double! pale fellow! Why do you imitate the pain of love which tormented me in this very place so many nights in times gone by?

DIE Jahre kommen und gehen,
Geschlechter steigen ins Grab,
Doch nimmer vergeht die Liebe,
Die ich im Herzen hab.

Nur einmal noch möcht ich dich sehen,
Und sinken vor dir aufs Knie,
Und sterbend zu dir sprechen:
Madame, ich liebe Sie!

WAS will die einsame Träne?
Sie trübt mir ja den Blick.
Sie blieb aus alten Zeiten
In meinem Auge zurück.

Sie hatte viel leuchtende Schwestern,
Die alle zerflossen sind,
Mit meinen Qualen und Freuden,
Zerflossen in Nacht und Wind.

Wie Nebel sind auch zerflossen
Die blauen Sternelein,
Die mir jene Freuden und Qualen
Gelächelt ins Herz hinein.

THE years come and go, generations go down to the grave, but the love which
I have in my heart shall never pass away.

I should like to see you just once more, and sink down before you on my
knees, and say to you with my dying breath: Madam, I love you!

WHAT does this lonely tear want? It blinds my eye. It remained in my eye
from former days.

It had many bright sisters who have all dissolved, dissolved with my tor-
ments and joys in night and wind.

Like mists those little blue stars have also dissolved which smiled those joys
and torments into my heart.

Ach, meine Liebe selber
Zerfloß wie eitel Hauch!
Du alte, einsame Träne,
Zerfließe jetzunder auch!

DAS ist ein schlechtes Wetter,
Es regnet und stürmt und schneit;
Ich sitze am Fenster und schaue
Hinaus in die Dunkelheit.

Da schimmert ein einsames Lichtchen,
Das wandelt langsam fort;
Ein Mütterchen mit dem Laternchen
Wankt über die Straße dort.

Ich glaube, Mehl und Eier
Und Butter kaufte sie ein;
Sie will einen Kuchen backen
Fürs große Töchterlein.

Die liegt zu Haus im Lehnstuhl,
Und blinzelt schläfrig ins Licht;
Die goldnen Locken wallen
Über das süße Gesicht.

Ah, my love itself dissolved like an empty breath! Old, lonely tear, you too must now dissolve!

WHAT terrible weather, there's rain and storm and snow; I sit by the window and look out into the darkness.
A solitary little light flickers as it moves slowly along; a little old woman with her little lantern is tottering across the street there.
I think she has bought flour and eggs and butter; she will bake a cake for her big little daughter.
She is lying at home in the arm-chair, blinking sleepily into the light; her golden locks fall in waves over her sweet face.

MAN glaubt, daß ich mich gräme
In bitterm Liebesleid,
Und endlich glaub ich es selber,
So gut wie andre Leut.

Du Kleine mit großen Augen,
Ich hab es dir immer gesagt,
Daß ich dich unsäglich liebe,
Daß Liebe mein Herz zernagt.

Doch nur in einsamer Kammer
Sprach ich auf solche Art,
Und ach! ich hab immer geschwiegen
In deiner Gegenwart.

Da gab es böse Engel,
Die hielten mir zu den Mund;
Und ach! durch böse Engel
Bin ich so elend jetzund.

SIE liebten sich beide, doch keiner
Wollt es dem andern gestehn;
Sie sahen sich an so feindlich,
Und wollten vor Liebe vergehn.

THEY think I grieve from love's bitter sorrow, and in the end I believe it myself just as other people do.

O little one with the big eyes, I've always told you that I love you more than I can say, that love is gnawing away my heart.

But only in my lonely room did I speak in this way, and alas! I have always kept silent in your presence.

There were bad angels who kept my mouth closed; and alas! because of bad angels I am now so wretched.

THEY were in love with each other, but neither wanted to admit it to the other; they looked at each other with such hostility and nearly passed away for love.

Sie trennten sich endlich und sahn sich
Nur noch zuweilen im Traum;
Sie waren längst gestorben,
Und wußten es selber kaum.

MEIN Kind, wir waren Kinder,
Zwei Kinder, klein und froh;
Wir krochen ins Hühnerhäuschen,
Versteckten uns unter das Stroh.

Wir krähten wie die Hähne,
Und kamen Leute vorbei –
«Kikereküh!» sie glaubten,
Es wäre Hahnengeschrei.

Die Kisten auf unserem Hofe
Die tapezierten wir aus,
Und wohnten drin beisammen,
Und machten ein vornehmes Haus.

Des Nachbars alte Katze
Kam öfters zum Besuch;
Wir machten ihr Bückling und Knickse
Und Komplimente genug.

They finally parted and saw each other only occasionally in their dreams;
they had died long before, and scarcely knew it themselves.

MY child, we were children, two small, merry children; we crept into the little
hen-house, hid in the straw.
    We crowed like cocks, and when people passed by – 'Cock-a-doodle-doo!'
they thought it was a cock crowing.
    We papered the boxes in our yard and lived there together and set up an
elegant household.
    The neighbour's old cat often came on a visit; we bowed and curtsied to her
and paid her our respects.

Wir haben nach ihrem Befinden
Besorglich und freundlich gefragt;
Wir haben seitdem dasselbe
Mancher alten Katze gesagt.

Wir saßen auch oft und sprachen
Vernünftig, wie alte Leut,
Und klagten, wie alles besser
Gewesen zu unserer Zeit;

Wie Lieb und Treu und Glauben
Verschwunden aus der Welt,
Und wie so teuer der Kaffee,
Und wie so rar das Geld! – – –

Vorbei sind die Kinderspiele,
Und alles rollt vorbei –
Das Geld und die Welt und die Zeiten,
Und Glauben und Lieb und Treu.

WIE der Mond sich leuchtend dränget
Durch den dunkeln Wolkenflor,
Also taucht aus dunkeln Zeiten
Mir ein lichtes Bild hervor.

We asked after her health with courtesy and concern; since then we've said the same thing to many an old cat.

We often sat and talked sensibly, like grown-ups, and complained how much better everything had been in our day:

how love and loyalty and faith have disappeared from the world, and how very expensive coffee is, and how very scarce money is! – – –

Children's games are past, and everything passes away – money and the world and the times, and faith and love and loyalty.

As the moon forces its shining way through the dark gauze of clouds, so a bright image rises to the surface of my mind from dark times.

Saßen all auf dem Verdecke,
Fuhren stolz hinab den Rhein,
Und die sommergrünen Ufer
Glühn im Abendsonnenschein.

Sinnend saß ich zu den Füßen
Einer Dame, schön und hold;
In ihr liebes, bleiches Antlitz
Spielt' das rote Sonnengold.

Lauten klangen, Buben sangen,
Wunderbare Fröhlichkeit!
Und der Himmel wurde blauer,
Und die Seele wurde weit.

Märchenhaft vorüberzogen
Berg und Burgen, Wald und Au; –
Und das alles sah ich glänzen
In dem Aug der schönen Frau.

«Teurer Freund! Was soll es nützen,
Stets das alte Lied zu leiern?
Willst du ewig brütend sitzen
Auf den alten Liebes-Eiern?

We were all sitting on the deck, sailing proudly down the Rhine, and the summer-green banks glow in the evening sunshine.

I sat pensively at the feet of a beautiful and charming lady; the red gold of the sun played on her dear, pale face.

Lutes sounded, boys sang, a wonderful cheerfulness! And the sky grew bluer, and our souls expanded.

As in a fairy-tale, mountains and castles, forest and meadow passed by; – and I saw all this reflected in the eyes of the beautiful woman.

'Dear friend, what is the use of constantly strumming that old song? Do you intend to sit brooding for ever on those old love-eggs?

«Ach! Das ist ein ewig Gattern,
Aus den Schalen kriechen Küchlein,
Und sie piepsen und sie flattern,
Und du sperrst sie in ein Büchlein.»

HERZ, mein Herz, sei nicht beklommen,
Und ertrage dein Geschick,
Neuer Frühling gibt zurück,
Was der Winter dir genommen.

Und wie viel ist dir geblieben!
Und wie schön ist noch die Welt!
Und, mein Herz, was dir gefällt,
Alles, alles darfst du lieben!

DU bist wie eine Blume,
So hold und schön und rein;
Ich schau dich an, und Wehmut
Schleicht mir ins Herz hinein.

'Ah, there's no end to this waiting, and then little chicks crawl out of the shells, and they chirp and they flutter, and you shut them up in a little book.'

HEART, my heart, be not oppressed, and put up with your fate. The new spring will give back what winter took from you.

And how much still remains to you! And how beautiful the world still is! And, my heart, you may love everything, everything that is pleasing to you.

YOU are like a flower, so good and beautiful and pure; I gaze at you, and melancholy creeps into my heart.

Mir ist, als ob ich die Hände
Aufs Haupt dir legen sollt,
Betend, daß Gott dich erhalte
So rein und schön und hold.

MAG da draußen Schnee sich türmen,
Mag es hageln, mag es stürmen,
Klirrend mir ans Fenster schlagen,
Nimmer will ich mich beklagen,
Denn ich trage in der Brust
Liebchens Bild und Frühlingslust.

TEURER Freund, du bist verliebt,
Und dich quälen neue Schmerzen;
Dunkler wird es dir im Kopf,
Heller wird es dir im Herzen.

Teurer Freund, du bist verliebt,
Und du willst es nicht bekennen,
Und ich seh des Herzens Glut
Schon durch deine Weste brennen.

I feel as if I should lay my hands upon your head, praying that God may keep you so pure and beautiful and good.

LET the snow pile up outside, let it hail, let the storm rage, banging noisily at my window, I will never complain, for in my heart I carry the picture of my darling and the joys of spring.

DEAR friend, you are in love, and new pains torment you; your head grows darker, your heart grows lighter.
   Dear friend, you are in love, and you won't admit it, and I can see the glow from your heart already burning through your waistcoat.

Ich hab mir lang den Kopf zerbrochen,
Mit Denken und Sinnen, Tag und Nacht,
Doch deine liebenswürdigen Augen,
Sie haben mich zum Entschluß gebracht.

Jetzt bleib ich, wo deine Augen leuchten,
In ihrer süßen, klugen Pracht –
Daß ich noch einmal würde lieben,
Ich hätt es nimmermehr gedacht.

Wir fuhren allein im dunkeln
Postwagen die ganze Nacht;
Wir ruhten einander am Herzen,
Wir haben gescherzt und gelacht.

Doch als es morgens tagte,
Mein Kind, wie staunten wir!
Denn zwischen uns saß Amor,
Der blinde Passagier.

I have long tormented my brain with thinking and pondering, day and night, but your kind eyes have brought me to a decision.

I shall remain now where your eyes shine, in their sweet, wise splendour – I should never have thought that I should love again.

We travelled alone in the dark mail-coach the whole night; we lay heart to heart, we joked and laughed.

But when the morrow dawned, my child, how amazed we were! For Amor sat between us, a stowaway.

Das weiß Gott, wo sich die tolle
Dirne einquartieret hat;
Fluchend, in dem Regenwetter,
Lauf ich durch die ganze Stadt.

Bin ich doch von einem Gasthof
Nach dem andern hingerannt,
Und an jeden groben Kellner
Hab ich mich umsonst gewandt.

Da erblick ich sie am Fenster,
Und sie winkt und kichert hell.
Konnt ich wissen, du bewohntest,
Mädchen, solches Prachthotel!

Doch die Kastraten klagten,
Als ich meine Stimm erhob;
Sie klagten und sie sagten:
Ich sänge viel zu grob.

Und lieblich erhoben sie alle
Die kleinen Stimmelein,
Die Trillerchen, wie Kristalle,
Sie klangen so fein und rein.

Heaven only knows where the silly girl has taken lodgings; cursing in this rainy weather I run through the entire town.

I've run from one inn to another, appealing in vain to each loutish waiter.

Then I catch sight of her at a window, and she waves and titters clearly. Was I to know, girl, that you were staying at such a smart hotel!

But the castrati complained when I began to sing; they complained and said I sang much too coarsely.

And they all sweetly raised their little voices in song, their little trills, crystal-like, rang out so delicately and purely.

Sie sangen von Liebessehnen,
Von Liebe und Liebeserguß;
Die Damen schwammen in Tränen
Bei solchem Kunstgenuß.

KAUM sahen wir uns, und an Augen und Stimme
Merkt ich, daß du mir gewogen bist;
Stand nicht dabei die Mutter, die schlimme,
Ich glaube, wir hätten uns gleich geküßt.

Und morgen verlasse ich wieder das Städtchen,
Und eile fort im alten Lauf;
Dann lauert am Fenster mein blondes Mädchen,
Und freundliche Grüße werf ich hinauf.

ÜBER die Berge steigt schon die Sonne,
Die Lämmerherde läutet fern;
Mein Liebchen, mein Lamm, meine Sonne und Wonne,
Noch einmal säh ich dich gar zu gern!

They sang of love's desires, of love and love's outpouring; the ladies were
bathed in tears at such an aesthetic treat.

SCARCELY had we seen each other, when from your eyes and voice I could see
that you were favourably disposed towards me; if your wretched mother had
not been there, I think we would have kissed straight away.
   And tomorrow I'm to leave the little town again and take up life's old rush;
my blonde girl will be waiting at her window, and I shall throw friendly
greetings up to her.

THE sun is already rising above the mountains, the flock of lambs tinkles in
the distance; my darling, my lamb, my sun and joy, how I should love to see
you again!

Ich schaue hinauf, mit spähender Miene –
Leb wohl, mein Kind, ich wandre von hier!
Vergebens! Es regt sich keine Gardine;
Sie liegt noch und schläft – und träumt von mir?

DER Tod, das ist die kühle Nacht,
Das Leben ist der schwüle Tag.
Es dunkelt schon, mich schläfert,
Der Tag hat mich müd gemacht.

Über mein Bett erhebt sich ein Baum,
Drin singt die junge Nachtigall;
Sie singt von lauter Liebe,
Ich hör es sogar im Traum.

"SAG, wo ist dein schönes Liebchen,
Das du einst so schön besungen,
Als die zaubermächtgen Flammen
Wunderbar dein Herz durchdrungen?»

I gaze up with an expectant look – farewell, my child, I'm off on my way!
In vain! the curtain does not stir; she is still in bed and sleeping – and dreaming
of me?

DEATH is the cool night, life is the sultry day. It grows dark, I am sleepy,
day has made me tired.
Over my bed there grows a tree in which the young nightingale sings; it
sings of nothing but love, I hear it even in my dreams.

'TELL me, where is your lovely darling whose praises you once sang so
beautifully when the magically powerful flames wonderfully filled your heart?'

Jene Flammen sind erloschen,
Und mein Herz ist kalt und trübe,
Und dies Büchlein ist die Urne
Mit der Asche meiner Liebe.

GÖTTERDÄMMERUNG

DER Mai ist da mit seinen goldnen Lichtern
Und seidnen Lüften und gewürzten Düften,
Und freundlich lockt er mit den weißen Blüten,
Und grüßt aus tausend blauen Veilchenaugen,
Und breitet aus den blumreich grünen Teppich,
Durchwebt mit Sonnenschein und Morgentau,
Und ruft herbei die lieben Menschenkinder.
Das blöde Volk gehorcht dem ersten Ruf.
Die Männer ziehn die Nankinhosen an
Und Sonntagsröck mit goldnen Spiegelknöpfen;
Die Frauen kleiden sich in Unschuldweiß;
Jünglinge kräuseln sich den Frühlingsschnurrbart;
Jungfrauen lassen ihre Busen wallen;
Die Stadtpoeten stecken in die Tasche
Papier und Bleistift und Lorgnett; – und jubelnd
Zieht nach dem Tor die krausbewegte Schar,

Those flames have gone out, and my heart is cold and sad, and this little book is the urn with the ashes of my love.

Twilight of the Gods

MAY is there with his golden lights and silky breezes and spiced scents, and in a friendly way he tempts us with white blossoms, and greets us with a thousand blue violet-eyes, and spreads out his flowery green carpet, interwoven with sunshine and morning dew, and summons to him God's dear children. The stupid people obey his first summons. The men put on their nankeen trousers and Sunday coats with golden, shining buttons; the women dress themselves in the white of innocence; young men curl their spring moustaches; maidens let their bosoms swell; the town's poets put into their pockets paper and pencil and lorgnette; – and the milling throng makes its way rejoicing towards the

Und lagert draußen sich auf grünem Rasen,
Bewundert, wie die Bäume fleißig wachsen,
Spielt mit den bunten, zarten Blümelein,
Horcht auf den Sang der lustgen Vögelein,
Und jauchzt hinauf zum blauen Himmelszelt.

Zu mir kam auch der Mai. Er klopfte dreimal
An meine Tür und rief: Ich bin der Mai,
Du bleicher Träumer, komm, ich will dich küssen!
Ich hielt verriegelt meine Tür, und rief:
Vergebens lockst du mich, du schlimmer Gast.
Ich habe dich durchschaut, ich hab durchschaut
Den Bau der Welt, und hab zu viel geschaut,
Und viel zu tief, und hin ist alle Freude,
Und ewge Qualen zogen in mein Herz.
Ich schaue durch die steinern harten Rinden
Der Menschenhäuser und der Menschenherzen,
Und schau in beiden Lug und Trug und Elend.
Auf den Gesichtern les ich die Gedanken,
Viel schlimme. In der Jungfrau Schamerröten
Seh ich geheime Lust begehrlich zittern;

gate, and settles down outside on the green grass, admiring the way in which
the trees grow so busily, playing with the brightly coloured, delicate little
flowers, listening to the song of the merry little birds, and sending its exulta-
tions up to the blue vault of heaven.

May came to me too. He knocked three times at my door and cried: I am
May, you pale dreamer, come, I want to kiss you! I kept my door bolted
and cried: You tempt me in vain, you rogue. I've seen right through you, I've
seen through the whole world order, and have seen too much, and much too
deeply, and all joy is gone, and everlasting torments have made their way into
my heart. I see through the hard stone shell of men's houses and men's hearts
and see in both lies and deception and wretchedness. In their faces I read their
many wicked thoughts. In the maiden's modest blush I see secret lust tremble

Auf dem begeistert stolzen Jünglingshaupt
Seh ich die lachend bunte Schellenkappe;
Und Fratzenbilder nur und sieche Schatten
Seh ich auf dieser Erde, und ich weiß nicht,
Ist sie ein Tollhaus oder Krankenhaus.
Ich sehe durch den Grund der alten Erde,
Als sei sie von Kristall, und seh das Grausen,
Das mit dem freudgen Grüne zu bedecken
Der Mai vergeblich strebt. Ich seh die Toten;
Sie liegen unten in den schmalen Särgen,
Die Händ gefaltet und die Augen offen,
Weiß das Gewand und weiß das Angesicht,
Und durch die Lippen kriechen gelbe Würmer.
Ich seh, der Sohn setzt sich mit seiner Buhle
Zur Kurzweil nieder auf des Vaters Grab; –
Spottlieder singen rings die Nachtigallen; –
Die sanften Wiesenblümchen lachen hämisch; –
Der tote Vater regt sich in dem Grab; –
Und schmerzhaft zuckt die alte Mutter Erde.

Du arme Erde, deine Schmerzen kenn ich!
Ich seh die Glut in deinem Busen wühlen,
Und deine tausend Adern seh ich bluten,
Und seh, wie deine Wunde klaffend aufreißt,

with desire; on the enthusiastic and proud youth's head I see laughing the many-coloured cap and bells of the fool; and caricatures and sick shadows are all I see on this earth, and I don't know whether it is a madhouse or a hospital. I see through the very foundations of old earth as if they were of crystal, and see the horror which May in vain tries to cover over with joyous green. I see the dead; they lie below in their narrow coffins, their hands folded and their eyes open, their dress and their faces alike white, and yellow worms crawl through their lips. I see the son sit down with his mistress to pass the time on his father's grave; – all around the nightingales sing mocking songs; – the gentle meadow-flowers laugh maliciously; – the dead father turns in his grave; – and old mother earth twitches in pain.

Poor earth, I know your pains! I see the glow rage in your bosom, and I see your thousand veins bleed, and see your wound burst wide open, and flames

Und wild hervorströmt Flamm und Rauch und Blut.
Ich sehe deine trotzgen Riesensöhne,
Uralte Brut, aus dunkeln Schlünden steigend,
Und rote Fackeln in den Händen schwingend; –
Sie legen ihre Eisenleiter an,
Und stürmen wild hinauf zur Himmelsfeste; –
Und schwarze Zwerge klettern nach; – und knisternd
Zerstieben droben alle goldnen Sterne.
Mit frecher Hand reißt man den goldnen Vorhang
Vom Zelte Gottes, heulend stürzen nieder,
Aufs Angesicht, die frommen Engelscharen.
Auf seinem Throne sitzt der bleiche Gott,
Reißt sich vom Haupt die Kron, zerrauft sein Haar –
Und näher drängt heran die wilde Rotte.
Die Riesen werfen ihre roten Fackeln
Ins weite Himmelreich, die Zwerge schlagen
Mit Flammengeißeln auf der Englein Rücken; –
Die winden sich und krümmen sich vor Qualen,
Und werden bei den Haaren fortgeschleudert; –
Und meinen eignen Engel seh ich dort,
Mit seinen blonden Locken, süßen Zügen,
Und mit der ewgen Liebe um den Mund,
Und mit der Seligkeit im blauen Auge –
Und ein entsetzlich häßlich schwarzer Kobold

and smoke and blood stream wildly forth. I see your huge defiant sons, prime-
val brood, climbing up out of their dark abysses, brandishing red torches in
their hands; – they set up their iron ladder and charge wildly up to heaven's
citadel; – and black dwarfs clamber after them – and higher still all the golden
stars burn themselves out with a crackling sound. With impious hand the
golden curtain of God's tent is torn away, and the hosts of good angels fall
howling on their faces. God sits pale on his throne, snatches the crown from
his head, tears his hair – and the wild horde presses nearer. The giants hurl
their red torches into heaven's broad kingdom, the dwarfs smite the little
angels' backs with flaming scourges; – they twist and writhe in pain, and are
tossed away by the hair; – and I see my own angel there, with her fair hair,
sweet features, and with everlasting love about her lips, and with blessedness
in her blue eye – and a hideously ugly black goblin jerks my pale angel from

Reißt ihn vom Boden, meinen bleichen Engel,
Beäugelt grinsend seine edlen Glieder,
Umschlingt ihn fest mit zärtlicher Umschlingung –
Und gellend dröhnt ein Schrei durchs ganze Weltall,
Die Säulen brechen, Erd und Himmel stürzen
Zusammen, und es herrscht die alte Nacht.

Nachlese

EINGEHÜLLT in graue Wolken,
Schlafen jetzt die großen Götter,
Und ich höre, wie sie schnarchen,
Und wir haben wildes Wetter.

Wildes Wetter! Sturmeswüten
Will das arme Schiff zerschellen –
Ach, wer zügelt diese Winde
Und die herrenlosen Wellen!

Kanns nicht hindern, daß es stürmet,
Daß da dröhnen Mast und Bretter,
Und ich hüll mich in den Mantel,
Um zu schlafen wie die Götter.

the ground, eyes her noble limbs mockingly, embraces her firmly with tender embrace – and a scream resounds piercingly through the entire universe, the columns break, earth and heaven crash together, and the old night reigns.

Supplementary Poem

WRAPPED in grey clouds the great gods now sleep, and I can hear them snoring, and we have wild weather.

Wild weather! The storm's rage threatens to shatter the poor ship – ah, who will curb these winds and the masterless waves?

Can't stop it raging, or mast and planks from groaning, and I wrap myself in my cloak to sleep like the gods.

AUS DER HARZREISE

BERGIDYLLE – I

Auf dem Berge steht die Hütte,
Wo der alte Bergmann wohnt;
Dorten rauscht die grüne Tanne,
Und erglänzt der goldne Mond.

In der Hütte steht ein Lehnstuhl,
Ausgeschnitzelt wunderlich,
Der darauf sitzt, der ist glücklich,
Und der Glückliche bin ich!

Auf dem Schemel sitzt die Kleine,
Stützt den Arm auf meinen Schoß;
Äuglein wie zwei blaue Sterne,
Mündlein wie die Purpurros.

Und die lieben, blauen Sterne
Schaun mich an so himmelgroß,
Und sie legt den Lilienfinger
Schalkhaft auf die Purpurros.

FROM THE HARZ JOURNEY

Mountain Idyll – I

On the mountain stands the hut where the old miner lives; there the green fir rustles and the golden moon shines.

In the hut stands an arm-chair, curiously carved; he who sits on it is happy, and I am the happy one!

On the foot-stool sits the little girl, rests her arm on my lap; little eyes like two blue stars, little mouth like the crimson rose.

And the dear, blue stars, as big as the heavens, look at me, and she places her lily finger mischievously on the crimson rose.

Nein, es sieht uns nicht die Mutter,
Denn sie spinnt mit großem Fleiß,
Und der Vater spielt die Zither,
Und er singt die alte Weis.

Und die Kleine flüstert leise,
Leise, mit gedämpftem Laut;
Manches wichtige Geheimnis
Hat sie mir schon anvertraut.

«Aber seit die Muhme tot ist,
Können wir ja nicht mehr gehn
Nach dem Schützenhof zu Goslar
Dorten ist es gar zu schön.

«Hier dagegen ist es einsam,
Auf der kalten Bergeshöh,
Und des Winters sind wir gänzlich
Wie begraben in dem Schnee.

«Und ich bin ein banges Mädchen,
Und ich fürcht mich wie ein Kind
Vor den bösen Bergesgeistern,
Die des Nachts geschäftig sind.»

No, mother is not looking at us, for she is spinning very busily, and father is playing the zither and singing his old song.

And the little girl whispers softly, softly, with muted tone; many an important secret has she already entrusted to me.

'But since my aunt died we can no longer go to the shooting-gallery at Goslar – it is very beautiful there.

'But here it is lonely on the cold mountain height, and in winter we are quite buried by the snow.

'And I am a timid girl, and I'm as frightened as a child of the evil mountain spirits who are active at night.'

Plötzlich schweigt die liebe Kleine,
Wie vom eignen Wort erschreckt,
Und sie hat mit beiden Händchen
Ihre Äugelein bedeckt.

Lauter rauscht die Tanne draußen,
Und das Spinnrad schnurrt und brummt,
Und die Zither klingt dazwischen,
Und die alte Weise summt:

«Fürcht dich nicht, du liebes Kindchen,
Vor der bösen Geister Macht;
Tag und Nacht, du liebes Kindchen,
Halten Englein bei dir Wacht!»

DER HIRTENKNABE

König ist der Hirtenknabe,
Grüner Hügel ist sein Thron;
Über seinem Haupt die Sonne
Ist die große, goldne Kron.

Suddenly the dear little girl is silent, as if frightened by her own words, and with both her little hands she has covered her little eyes.

Louder rustles the fir outside, and the spinning-wheel whirs and rumbles, and the zither is heard through it, and the old song hums on:

'Don't be frightened, dear little child, of the power of the evil spirits; day and night, dear little child, little angels keep watch over you!'

The Shepherd Boy

The shepherd boy is king, the green hill is his throne; the sun above his head is his great golden crown.

Ihm zu Füßen liegen Schafe,
Weiche Schmeichler, rotbekreuzt;
Kavaliere sind die Kälber,
Und sie wandeln stolzgespreizt.

Hofschauspieler sind die Böcklein;
Und die Vögel und die Küh,
Mit den Flöten, mit den Glöcklein,
Sind die Kammermusizi.

Und das klingt und singt so lieblich,
Und so lieblich rauschen drein
Wasserfall und Tannenbäume,
Und der König schlummert ein.

Unterdessen muß regieren
Der Minister, jener Hund,
Dessen knurriges Gebelle
Widerhallet in der Rund.

Schläfrig lallt der junge König:
« Das Regieren ist so schwer;
Ach, ich wollt, daß ich zu Hause
Schon bei meiner Köngin wär!

Sheep lie at his feet, soft flatterers with their red crosses. The calves are his
cavaliers, and they strut about proudly.

The little goats are his court actors; and the birds and the cows with their
flutes and little bells are his chamber musicians.

And the playing and singing is so charming, and so charmingly do waterfall
and fir-trees add their contribution, that the king falls asleep.

In the meantime his minister, the dog, must act as regent, his growling bark
echoes all around.

The young king murmurs sleepily: 'Ruling is so hard; ah, I wish I were
already at home again with my queen!

«In den Armen meiner Köngin
Ruht mein Königshaupt so weich,
Und in ihren schönen Augen
Liegt mein unermeßlich Reich!»

Nachlese

STEIGET auf, ihr alten Träume!
Öffne dich, du Herzenstor!
Liederwonne, Wehmutstränen
Strömen wunderbar hervor.

Durch die Tannen will ich schweifen,
Wo die muntre Quelle springt,
Wo die stolzen Hirsche wandeln,
Wo die liebe Drossel singt.

Auf die Berge will ich steigen,
Auf die schroffen Felsenhöhn,
Wo die grauen Schloßruinen
In dem Morgenlichte stehn.

'My royal head rests so softly in the arms of my queen, and in her lovely
eyes is my boundless kingdom!'

Supplementary Poem

ARISE, old dreams! Open up, door of the heart! The bliss of song and tears
of melancholy stream wonderfully forth.

Through the fir-trees will I wander, where the joyous source springs, where
the proud stags walk, where the dear thrush sings.

On to the mountains will I climb, on to the precipitous rocky heights, where
the grey castle ruins stand in the morning light.

Dorten setz ich still mich nieder
Und gedenke alter Zeit,
Alter blühender Geschlechter
Und versunkner Herrlichkeit.

Gras bedeckt jetzt den Turnierplatz,
Wo gekämpft der stolze Mann,
Der die Besten überwunden
Und des Kampfes Preis gewann.

Epheu rankt an dem Balkone,
Wo die schöne Dame stand,
Die den stolzen Überwinder
Mit den Augen überwand.

Ach! den Sieger und die Siegrin
Hat besiegt des Todes Hand –
Jener dürre Sensenritter
Streckt uns alle in den Sand!

There I shall sit down quietly and think of olden days, of old once-flourish-
ing families and vanished splendour.

Grass now covers the tilting-ground where the proud man fought who
conquered the champions and won the victor's prize.

Ivy climbs on the balcony where the fair lady stood who conquered the
proud conqueror with her eyes.

Ah, the hand of Death has defeated the victor and *his* fair victor – that bony
horseman with his scythe lays us all in the dust!

DIE NORDSEE

ABENDDÄMMERUNG

AM blassen Meeresstrande
Saß ich gedankenbekümmert und einsam.
Die Sonne neigte sich tiefer, und warf
Glührote Streifen auf das Wasser,
Und die weißen, weiten Wellen,
Von der Flut gedrängt,
Schäumten und rauschten näher und näher –
Ein seltsam Geräusch, ein Flüstern und Pfeifen,
Ein Lachen und Murmeln, Seufzen und Sausen,
Dazwischen ein wiegenliedheimliches Singen –
Mir war, als hört ich verschollne Sagen,
Uralte, liebliche Märchen,
Die ich einst, als Knabe,
Von Nachbarskindern vernahm,
Wenn wir am Sommerabend,
Auf den Treppensteinen der Haustür,
Zum stillen Erzählen niederkauerten,
Mit kleinen, horchenden Herzen

THE NORTH SEA

Evening Twilight

ON the pale sea-shore I sat alone troubled by my thoughts. The sun was sinking lower and cast glowing red streaks on the water, and the white, broad waves, urged on by the tide, foamed and roared nearer and nearer – a strange sound, a whispering and whistling, a laugh and a murmur, a sighing and soughing, and between, a lullaby-like mysterious singing – I seemed to be hearing forgotten legends, immemorial, lovely tales which, as a boy, I once learnt from neighbours' children when, on a summer's evening, we squatted on the stone steps of the front door for quiet story-telling with our little attentive hearts

Und neugierklugen Augen; –
Während die großen Mädchen,
Neben duftenden Blumentöpfen,
Gegenüber am Fenster saßen,
Rosengesichter,
Lächelnd und mondbeglänzt.

STURM

Es wütet der Sturm,
Und er peitscht die Wellen,
Und die Welln, wutschäumend und bäumend,
Türmen sich auf, und es wogen lebendig
Die weißen Wasserberge,
Und das Schifflein erklimmt sie,
Hastig mühsam,
Und plötzlich stürzt es hinab
In schwarze, weitgähnende Flutabgründe –

O Meer!
Mutter der Schönheit, der Schaumentstiegenen!
Großmutter der Liebe! schone meiner!
Schon flattert, leichenwitternd,
Die weiße, gespenstische Möwe,
Und wetzt an dem Mastbaum den Schnabel,
Und lechzt, voll Fraßbegier, nach dem Herzen,

and eyes sharpened by curiosity; – while the big girls sat at the window opposite by sweet-smelling pots of flowers, rosy faces, smiling and lit up by the moon.

Storm

THE storm rages, and it whips the waves, and the waves, foaming with anger and rearing, tower up, and the white mountains of water surge animatedly, and the little ship climbs them, hastily and laboriously, and suddenly it crashes down into the black, wide-yawning abysses of the flood –

O sea! Mother of Beauty, who rose from the foam! Grandmother of Love, spare me! The white, ghostly gull is already floating in the wind, smelling out corpses, sharpening its bill on the mast-head, hungering greedily for the heart

Das vom Ruhm deiner Tochter ertönt,
Und das dein Enkel, der kleine Schalk,
Zum Spielzeug erwählt.

Vergebens mein Bitten und Flehn!
Mein Rufen verhallt im tosenden Sturm,
Im Schlachtlärm der Winde.
Es braust und pfeift und prasselt und heult,
Wie ein Tollhaus von Tönen!
Und zwischendurch hör ich vernehmbar
Lockende Harfenlaute,
Sehnsuchtwilden Gesang,
Seelenschmelzend und seelenzerreißend,
Und ich erkenne die Stimme.

Fern an schottischer Felsenküste,
Wo das graue Schlößlein hinausragt
Über die brandende See,
Dort, am hochgewölbten Fenster,
Steht eine schöne, kranke Frau,
Zartdurchsichtig und marmorblaß,
Und sie spielt die Harfe und singt,
Und der Wind durchwühlt ihre langen Locken,
Und trägt ihr dunkles Lied
Über das weite, stürmende Meer.

which resounds with your daughter's fame, and which your grandson, the little rogue, chose for his plaything.

In vain my pleas and supplications! My cries are lost in the roaring storm, in the battle-din of the winds. There's a roaring and whistling and rattling and howling – like a madhouse of sounds! And in between I can clearly hear enticing harp-sounds, a singing wild with desire, melting and tearing the soul, and I recognize the voice.

Far away on a rocky Scottish coast, where the grey little castle juts out over the raging sea, there, at the high-vaulted window, stands a beautiful, ailing woman, delicately transparent and pale as marble, and she plays the harp and sings, and the wind rages through her long locks and carries her dark song over the broad, stormy sea.

SEEGESPENST

Icʜ aber lag am Rande des Schiffes,
Und schaute, träumenden Auges,
Hinab in das spiegelklare Wasser,
Und schaute tiefer und tiefer –
Bis tief, im Meeresgrunde,
Anfangs wie dämmernde Nebel,
Jedoch allmählich farbenbestimmter,
Kirchenkuppel und Türme sich zeigten,
Und endlich, sonnenklar, eine ganze Stadt,
Altertümlich niederländisch,
Und menschenbelebt.
Bedächtige Männer, schwarzbemäntelt,
Mit weißen Halskrausen und Ehrenketten
Und langen Degen und langen Gesichtern,
Schreiten über den wimmelnden Marktplatz
Nach dem treppenhohen Rathaus,
Wo steinerne Kaiserbilder
Wacht halten mit Zepter und Schwert.
Unferne, vor langen Häuserreihn,
Wo spiegelblanke Fenster
Und pyramidisch beschnittene Linden,
Wandeln seidenrauschende Jungfern,

Sea Ghost

Bᴜᴛ I lay at the side of the ship and gazed with dreamy eye down into the
mirror-clear water, and gazed deeper and deeper – until far down, at the
bottom of the sea, and looking at first like morning mists, but then growing
gradually clearer in colour, church domes and towers appeared, and at last,
as clear as the sun, a whole city, old and Netherlandish, and populated. Cir-
cumspect men with black cloaks, white ruffs and chains of office and long
swords and long faces, stride across the busy market-square to the town hall
with its high steps, where stone statues of emperors stand watch with sceptre
and sword. Not far away, in front of long rows of houses with mirror-bright
windows and lime-trees pruned to pyramid shapes, girls walk, rustling with

Schlanke Leibchen, die Blumengesichter
Sittsam umschlossen von schwarzen Mützchen
Und hervorquellendem Goldhaar.
Bunte Gesellen, in spanischer Tracht,
Stolzieren vorüber und nicken.
Bejahrte Frauen,
In braunen, verschollnen Gewändern,
Gesangbuch und Rosenkranz in der Hand,
Eilen, trippelnden Schritts,
Nach dem großen Dome,
Getrieben von Glockengeläute
Und rauschendem Orgelton.

Mich selbst ergreift des fernen Klangs
Geheimnisvoller Schauer!
Unendliches Sehnen, tiefe Wehmut
Beschleicht mein Herz,
Mein kaum geheiltes Herz; –
Mir ist, als würden seine Wunden
Von lieben Lippen aufgeküßt,
Und täten wieder bluten –
Heiße, rote Tropfen,
Die lang und langsam niederfalln
Auf ein altes Haus, dort unten

silk, slender-waisted, their flower-faces modestly enclosed by black caps and cascading golden hair. Gay young fellows, in Spanish costume, strut past and nod. Elderly ladies, in brown, outmoded dresses, hymn-book and rosary in hand, hasten with tripping steps towards the great cathedral, urged on by the ringing of bells and the swelling organ tones.

I too am seized by the mysterious thrill of the distant sound! Infinite longing, deep melancholy steals over my heart, my scarcely-healed heart; – I feel as if its wounds were being kissed open by dear lips, and were bleeding again – hot, red drops which fall long and slowly down on to an old house, down there

In der tiefen Meerstadt,
Auf ein altes, hochgegiebeltes Haus,
Das melancholisch menschenleer ist,
Nur daß am untern Fenster
Ein Mädchen sitzt,
Den Kopf auf den Arm gestützt,
Wie ein armes, vergessenes Kind –
Und ich kenne dich, armes, vergessenes Kind!

So tief, meertief also
Verstecktest du dich vor mir
Aus kindischer Laune,
Und konntest nicht mehr herauf,
Und saßest fremd unter fremden Leuten,
Jahrhundertelang,
Derweilen ich, die Seele voll Gram,
Auf der ganzen Erde dich suchte,
Und immer dich suchte,
Du Immergeliebte,
Du Längstverlorene,
Du Endlichgefundene –
Ich hab dich gefunden und schaue wieder
Dein süßes Gesicht,
Die klugen, treuen Augen,

in the deep sea-city, on to an old, high-gabled house which is sadly deserted,
apart from a girl sitting at a lower window, her head resting on her arm, like a
poor, forgotten child – and I know you, poor forgotten child!

So deep, sea-deep then did you hide from me in a childish whim, and you
couldn't get up again, and sat there, a stranger among strange people, for
centuries, while I, my soul full of grief, searched the whole earth for you,
constantly searched for you, eternally loved one, long ago lost one, finally
found one – I have found you and see again your sweet face, those wise, true

Das liebe Lächeln –
Und nimmer will ich dich wieder verlassen,
Und ich komme hinab zu dir,
Und mit ausgebreiteten Armen
Stürz ich hinab an dein Herz –

Aber zur rechten Zeit noch
Ergriff mich beim Fuß der Kapitän,
Und zog mich vom Schiffsrand,
Und rief, ärgerlich lachend:
Doktor, sind Sie des Teufels?

REINIGUNG

Bleib du in deiner Meerestiefe,
Wahnsinniger Traum,
Der du einst so manche Nacht
Mein Herz mit falschem Glück gequält hast,
Und jetzt, als Seegespenst,
Sogar am hellen Tag mich bedrohest –
Bleib du dort unten, in Ewigkeit,
Und ich werfe noch zu dir hinab
All meine Schmerzen und Sünden,
Und die Schellenkappe der Torheit,

eyes, that dear smile – and never again will I leave you, and I am coming down to you, and with arms outstretched I plunge down to your breast –

But just in time the captain seized me by the foot and pulled me back from the side of the ship, and cried, laughing angrily: Doctor, are you mad?

Purification

Stay in your sea-depths, mad dream which once so many nights tormented my heart with false happiness, and now, as a sea-ghost, threatens me even in broad daylight – stay down there for all time, and I shall throw down to you all my pains and sins, and the cap and bells of foolishness which have so long

Die so lange mein Haupt umklingelt,
Und die kalte, gleißende Schlangenhaut
Der Heuchelei,
Die mir so lang die Seele umwunden,
Die kranke Seele,
Die gottverleugnende, engelverleugnende,
Unselige Seele –
Hoiho! hoiho! Da kommt der Wind!
Die Segel auf! Sie flattern und schwelln!
Über die stillverderbliche Fläche
Eilet das Schiff,
Und es jauchzt die befreite Seele.

UNTERGANG DER SONNE

Die schöne Sonne
Ist ruhig hinabgestiegen ins Meer;
Die wogenden Wasser sind schon gefärbt
Von der dunkeln Nacht,
Nur noch die Abendröte
Überstreut sie mit goldnen Lichtern;
Und die rauschende Flutgewalt
Drängt ans Ufer die weißen Wellen,

tinkled about my head, and the cold, glittering snake-skin of hypocrisy which for so long was wound about my soul, my sick soul, my apostate and angel-denying, unhappy soul – Hoiho! hoiho! Here comes the wind! Hoist the sails! They flap and swell! The ship hastens over the silently destructive surface, and my soul rejoices in its freedom.

Sunset

THE beautiful sun has peacefully descended into the sea; the heaving waters are already coloured by dark night, only the evening glow still strews them with golden lights; and the murmuring force of the tide drives to the shore the

Die lustig und hastig hüpfen,
Wie wollige Lämmerherden,
Die abends der singende Hirtenjunge
Nach Hause treibt.

Wie schön ist die Sonne!
So sprach nach langem Schweigen der Freund,
Der mit mir am Strande wandelte,
Und scherzend halb und halb wehmütig
Versichert' er mir: die Sonne sei
Eine schöne Frau, die den alten Meergott
Aus Konvenienz geheiratet;
Des Tages über wandle sie freudig
Am hohen Himmel, purpurgeputzt
Und diamantenblitzend,
Und allgeliebt und allbewundert
Von allen Weltkreaturen,
Und alle Weltkreaturen erfreuend
Mit ihres Blickes Licht und Wärme;
Aber des Abends, trostlos gezwungen,
Kehre sie wieder zurück
In das nasse Haus, in die öden Arme
Des greisen Gemahls.

white waves which joyously and hurriedly skip like the woolly flocks of
lambs which in the evening the singing shepherd-boy drives homewards.

How beautiful the sun is! Thus after a long silence spoke the friend who was
wandering with me on the shore, and half jokingly and half sadly he assured
me: The sun is a beautiful woman who married the old sea-god out of con-
venience; all day long she walks joyfully in the high heavens, adorned in
purple and shining with diamonds, and universally loved and universally ad-
mired by every living creature, and gladdening every living creature with the
light and warmth of her glance; but in the evening, disconsolately compelled,
she returns again to the damp house and the arid arms of her ancient consort.

«Glaub mirs – setzte hinzu der Freund,
Und lachte und seufzte und lachte wieder –
Die führen dort unten die zärtlichste Ehe!
Entweder sie schlafen oder sie zanken sich,
Daß hoch aufbraust hier oben das Meer,
Und der Schiffer im Wellengeräusch es hört,
Wie der Alte sein Weib ausschilt:
‹Runde Metze des Weltalls!
Strahlenbuhlende!
Den ganzen Tag glühst du für andre,
Und nachts, für mich, bist du frostig und müde!›
Nach solcher Gardinenpredigt,
Versteht sich! bricht dann aus in Tränen
Die stolze Sonne und klagt ihr Elend,
Und klagt so jammerlang, daß der Meergott
Plötzlich verzweiflungsvoll aus dem Bett springt,
Und schnell nach der Meeresfläche heraufschwimmt,
Um Luft und Besinnung zu schöpfen.

«So sah ich ihn selbst, verflossene Nacht,
Bis an die Brust dem Meer enttauchen.
Er trug eine Jacke von gelbem Flanell,
Und eine lilienweiße Schlafmütz,
Und ein abgewelktes Gesicht.»

‘Believe me,’ my friend added, and laughed, and sighed, and laughed again, ‘they lead the most charming married life down there! Either they're asleep or they're quarrelling so much that the sea rages up here on the surface, and the sailor hears in the noise of the waves the old man scolding his wife: "Plump prostitute of the universe! Beaming whore! All day long you glow for others, and at night, for me, you are frosty and tired!" After a curtain-lecture like that, of course, the proud sun bursts into tears and laments her wretchedness, and laments so long in her grief that the sea-god suddenly in desperation jumps out of bed and swims swiftly up to the surface of the sea to take breath and counsel.

‘That's how I saw him myself last night, raising his head and shoulders out of the sea. He had a yellow flannel jacket on, and a lily-white night-cap, and a wizened face.’

DIE GÖTTER GRIECHENLANDS

VOLLBLÜHENDER Mond! In deinem Licht,
Wie fließendes Gold, erglänzt das Meer;
Wie Tagesklarheit, doch dämmrig verzaubert,
Liegts über der weiten Strandesfläche;
Und am hellblaun, sternlosen Himmel
Schweben die weißen Wolken,
Wie kolossale Götterbilder
Von leuchtendem Marmor.

Nein, nimmermehr, das sind keine Wolken!
Das sind sie selber, die Götter von Hellas,
Die einst so freudig die Welt beherrschten,
Doch jetzt, verdrängt und verstorben,
Als ungeheure Gespenster dahinziehn
Am mitternächtlichen Himmel.

Staunend, und seltsam geblendet, betracht ich
Das luftige Pantheon,
Die feierlich stummen, graunhaften bewegten
Riesengestalten.
Der dort ist Kronion, der Himmelskönig,
Schneeweiß sind die Locken des Haupts,

The Gods of Greece

FULL-BLOOMING moon! In your light the sea gleams like molten gold; like the clear light of day, though transformed in twilight enchantment, it lies upon the broad surface of the shore; and in the light blue, starless sky the white clouds hover like colossal statues of the gods made of shining marble.

No, it cannot be, those are not clouds! It is they themselves, the gods of Hellas, who once so joyously ruled the world, but now, expelled and extinct, they move across the midnight sky as giant ghosts.

With amazement, and strangely dazzled, I gaze at this airy Pantheon, the solemnly silent, frighteningly animated giant figures. That one is Kronos, King of Heaven, snowy white are the locks of his head, those famous Olyn-

Die berühmten, Olympos-erschütternden Locken.
Er hält in der Hand den erloschenen Blitz,
In seinem Antlitz liegt Unglück und Gram,
Und doch noch immer der alte Stolz.
Das waren bessere Zeiten, o Zeus,
Als du dich himmlisch ergötztest
An Knaben und Nymphen und Hekatomben;
Doch auch die Götter regieren nicht ewig,
Die jungen verdrängen die alten,
Wie du einst selber den greisen Vater
Und deine Titanen-Öhme verdrängt hast,
Jupiter Parricida!
Auch dich erkenn ich, stolze Juno!
Trotz all deiner eifersüchtigen Angst
Hat doch eine andre das Zepter gewonnen,
Und du bist nicht mehr die Himmelskönigin,
Und dein großes Aug ist erstarrt,
Und deine Lilienarme sind kraftlos,
Und nimmermehr trifft deine Rache
Die gottbefruchtete Jungfrau
Und den wundertätigen Gottessohn.
Auch dich erkenn ich, Pallas Athene!
Mit Schild und Weisheit konntest du nicht
Abwehren das Götterverderben?

pus-shaking locks. He holds in his hand the extinguished thunder-bolt, in his face there are misfortune and grief, and yet the old pride is still there. Those were better days, o Zeus, when you had your divine pleasure in boys and nymphs and hecatombs; but even the gods do not rule for ever, the young drive out the old, as you yourself once drove out your ancient father and your Titan uncles, Jupiter Parricida! You too I recognize, proud Juno! Despite all your jealous anxiety another woman nevertheless won the sceptre, and you are no longer the Queen of Heaven, and your great eye has grown stiff, and your lily arms are impotent, and never again shall your vengeance strike the maiden whom the God has made fruitful, or the God's wonder-working son. You too I recognize, Pallas Athene! With your shield and wisdom could you not prevent the destruction of the gods? You too I recognize,

Auch dich erkenn ich, auch dich, Aphrodite,
Einst die goldene! jetzt die silberne!
Zwar schmückt dich noch immer des Gürtels Liebreiz,
Doch graut mir heimlich vor deiner Schönheit,
Und wollt mich beglücken dein gütiger Leib,
Wie andere Helden, ich stürbe vor Angst –
Als Leichengöttin erscheinst du mir,
Venus Libitina!
Nicht mehr mit Liebe blickt nach dir,
Dort, der schreckliche Ares.
Es schaut so traurig Phöbos Apollo,
Der Jüngling. Es schweigt seine Leir,
Die so freudig erklungen beim Göttermahl.
Noch trauriger schaut Hephaistos,
Und wahrlich, der Hinkende! nimmermehr
Fällt er Heben ins Amt,
Und schenkt geschäftig, in der Versammlung,
Den lieblichen Nektar – Und längst ist erloschen
Das unauslöschliche Göttergelächter.

Ich hab euch niemals geliebt, ihr Götter!
Denn widerwärtig sind mir die Griechen,
Und gar die Römer sind mir verhaßt.
Doch heilges Erbarmen und schauriges Mitleid

you too, Aphrodite, once golden, now silver! It is true, the girdle's charm still adorns you, but I am filled with secret horror at your beauty, and if your generous body were to make me, like other heroes, happy, I would die of fright – as the Goddess of Corpses you appear to me, Venus Libitina! No longer with love does the terrible Ares gaze after you there. Phoebus Apollo, the youth, looks so sad. His lyre is silent which once rang out so joyously at the banquet of the gods. And Hephaestus looks sadder still, and indeed, never again shall the Lame One take over Hebe's office and busily pour out the lovely nectar in the assembly – and the inextinguishable laughter of the gods has long since been extinguished.

I have never loved you, Gods! For the Greeks are repugnant to me, and even the Romans I hate. But holy compassion and awful pity flow into my

Durchströmt mein Herz,
Wenn ich euch jetzt da droben schaue,
Verlassene Götter,
Tote, nachtwandelnde Schatten,
Nebelschwache, die der Wind verscheucht –
Und wenn ich bedenke, wie feig und windig
Die Götter sind, die euch besiegten,
Die neuen, herrschenden, tristen Götter,
Die schadenfrohen im Schafspelz der Demut –
O, da faßt mich ein düsterer Groll,
Und brechen möcht ich die neuen Tempel,
Und kämpfen für euch, ihr alten Götter,
Für euch und euer gutes, ambrosisches Recht,
Und vor euren hohen Altären,
Den wiedergebauten, den opferdampfenden,
Möcht ich selber knieen und beten,
Und flehend die Arme erheben –

Denn immerhin, ihr alten Götter,
Habt ihrs auch ehmals, in Kämpfen der Menschen,
Stets mit der Partei der Sieger gehalten,
So ist doch der Mensch großmütger als ihr,
Und in Götterkämpfen halt ich es jetzt
Mit der Partei der besiegten Götter.

*   *

*

heart when I see you up there now, abandoned Gods, dead shades, wandering at night as insubstantial as mists which the wind disperses – and when I reflect how cowardly and shifty the gods are who defeated you, the new, ruling, sad gods – malicious ones in the sheep's skin of humility – ah, then dark resentment comes over me, and I should like to break the new temples and fight for you, old Gods, for you and your good, ambrosial rights; and I myself should like to kneel and pray before your high altars, rebuilt and steaming with sacrificial offerings, and raise my arms in supplication –

For after all, you old Gods, you always used to take sides with the victors in the wars of men, and man is therefore more magnanimous than you, and in the wars of gods I now take the side of the defeated gods.

Also sprach ich, und sichtbar erröteten
Droben die blassen Wolkengestalten,
Und schauten mich an wie Sterbende,
Schmerzenverklärt, und schwanden plötzlich.
Der Mond verbarg sich eben
Hinter Gewölk, das dunkler heranzog;
Hoch aufrauschte das Meer,
Und siegreich traten hervor am Himmel
Die ewigen Sterne.

FRAGEN

Am Meer, am wüsten, nächtlichen Meer
Steht ein Jüngling-Mann,
Die Brust voll Wehmut, das Haupt voll Zweifel,
Und mit düstern Lippen fragt er die Wogen:

«O löst mir das Rätsel des Lebens,
Das qualvoll uralte Rätsel,
Worüber schon manche Häupter gegrübelt,
Häupter in Hieroglyphenmützen,
Häupter in Turban und schwarzem Barett,
Perückenhäupter und tausend andre

Thus I spoke, and the pale cloud-figures up there visibly blushed, and looked at me like dying men, transfigured by pain, and suddenly vanished. Just then the moon hid itself behind clouds which had banked up more darkly; the sea roared high, and in the heavens the eternal stars came forth victoriously.

Questions

By the sea, the desolate, night-time sea stands someone, half-youth, half-man, his heart full of melancholy, his mind full of doubts, and with sad lips he asks the waves:

'Oh, solve for me the riddle of life, the agonizing, immemorial puzzle over which so many heads have brooded – heads in magicians' caps, heads in turbans and black birettas, periwigged heads and thousands of other poor, per-

Arme, schwitzende Menschenhäupter –
Sagt mir, was bedeutet der Mensch?
Woher ist er kommen? Wo geht er hin?
Wer wohnt dort oben auf goldenen Sternen?»

Es murmeln die Wogen ihr ewges Gemurmel,
Es wehet der Wind, es fliehen die Wolken,
Es blinken die Sterne, gleichgültig und kalt,
Und ein Narr wartet auf Antwort.

spiring men's heads – tell me, what is the meaning of Man? Whence did he
come? Whither does he go? Who dwells up there on the golden stars?'
    The waves murmur their eternal murmur, the wind blows, the clouds fly,
the stars twinkle, indifferent and cold, and a fool waits for an answer.

NEUE GEDICHTE

NEW POEMS

NEUER FRÜHLING

PROLOG

In Gemäldegalerieen
Siehst du oft das Bild des Manns,
Der zum Kampfe wollte ziehen,
Wohlbewehrt mit Schild und Lanz.

Doch ihn necken Amoretten,
Rauben Lanze ihm und Schwert,
Binden ihn mit Blumenketten,
Wie er auch sich mürrisch wehrt.

So, in holden Hindernissen,
Wind ich mich in Lust und Leid,
Während andre kämpfen müssen
In dem großen Kampf der Zeit.

NEW SPRING

Prologue

In picture galleries you often see the picture of the man who was about to go off to battle, well armed with shield and lance.

But amoretti tease him, steal his lance and sword, bind him with chains of flowers, however sullenly he may resist.

Similarly, in charming fetters I writhe in joy and pain, while others have to fight in the great battle of the age.

HEINE

Untern weißen Baume sitzend,
Hörst du fern die Winde schrillen,
Siehst, wie oben stumme Wolken
Sich in Nebeldecken hüllen;

Siehst, wie unten ausgestorben
Wald und Flur, wie kahl geschoren; –
Um dich Winter, in dir Winter,
Und dein Herz ist eingefroren.

Plötzlich fallen auf dich nieder
Weiße Flocken, und verdrossen
Meinst du schon, mit Schneegestöber
Hab der Baum dich übergossen.

Doch es ist kein Schneegestöber,
Merkst es bald mit freudgem Schrecken;
Duftge Frühlingsblüten sind es,
Die dich necken und bedecken.

Welch ein schauersüßer Zauber!
Winter wandelt sich in Maie,
Schnee verwandelt sich in Blüten,
Und dein Herz es liebt aufs neue.

Sitting beneath a white tree you can hear the winds howling far away and see the silent clouds above wrap themselves in blankets of mist;

you can see down below how forest and meadow have died, as if shorn bare; –winter around you, winter inside you, and your heart is frozen up.

Suddenly white flakes are falling on you, and in your vexation you think the tree has sprinkled a flurry of snow on top of you.

But it isn't a flurry of snow, you soon notice with joyous dread; it is sweet-smelling spring blossom that teases and covers you.

How awful and yet sweet this magic! Winter is turning into May, snow is changing into blossom, and your heart is in love again.

Iᴄʜ lieb eine Blume, doch weiß ich nicht welche;
Das macht mir Schmerz.
Ich schau in alle Blumenkelche,
Und such ein Herz.

Es duften die Blumen im Abendscheine,
Die Nachtigall schlägt.
Ich such ein Herz so schön wie das meine,
So schön bewegt.

Die Nachtigall schlägt, und ich verstehe
Den süßen Gesang;
Uns beiden ist so bang und wehe,
So weh und bang.

Dᴇʀ Schmetterling ist in die Rose verliebt,
Umflattert sie tausendmal,
Ihn selber aber, goldig zart,
Umflattert der liebende Sonnenstrahl.

I'ᴍ in love with a flower, but I don't know which; that gives me pain. I gaze into the cups of all the flowers, looking for a heart.

The flowers smell sweet in the evening light, the nightingale sings. I'm looking for a heart as beautiful as my own, as beautifully moved.

The nightingale sings, and I understand the sweet song; we are both so afraid and sore, so sore and afraid.

Tʜᴇ butterfly is in love with the rose, flutters around her a thousand times, but he himself, golden and delicate, is surrounded by the fluttering of the loving sunbeam.

Jedoch, in wen ist die Rose verliebt?
Das wüßt ich gar zu gern.
Ist es die singende Nachtigall?
Ist es der schweigende Abendstern?

Ich weiß nicht, in wen die Rose verliebt;
Ich aber lieb euch all:
Rose, Schmetterling, Sonnenstrahl,
Abendstern und Nachtigall.

Es erklingen alle Bäume,
Und es singen alle Nester –
Wer ist der Kapellenmeister
In dem grünen Waldorchester?

Ist es dort der graue Kiebitz,
Der beständig nickt so wichtig?
Oder der Pedant, der dorten
Immer kuckuckt, zeitmaßrichtig?

Ist es jener Storch, der ernsthaft
Und als ob er dirigieret',
Mit dem langen Streckbein klappert,
Während alles musizieret?

But – with whom is the rose in love? I should dearly like to know. Is it the singing nightingale? Is it the silent evening star?

I don't know with whom the rose is in love; but I love you all: rose, butterfly, sunbeam, evening star and nightingale.

ALL the trees resound and all the nests sing – who is the Kapellmeister of the green forest orchestra?

Is it that grey peewit who is constantly nodding so importantly? Or that pedant over there who is forever cuckooing in time with the music?

Is it that stork who, as if he were conducting, solemnly taps with his long, outstretched leg while all the others are making music?

Nein, in meinem eignen Herzen
Sitzt des Walds Kapellenmeister,
Und ich fühl, wie er den Takt schlägt,
Und ich glaube, Amor heißt er.

"Im Anfang war die Nachtigall
Und sang das Wort: Züküht! Züküht!
Und wie sie sang, sproß überall
Grüngras, Violen, Apfelblüt.

«Sie biß sich in die Brust, da floß
Ihr rotes Blut, und aus dem Blut
Ein schöner Rosenbaum entsproß;
Dem singt sie ihre Liebesglut.

«Uns Vögel all in diesem Wald
Versöhnt das Blut aus jener Wund;
Doch wenn das Rosenlied verhallt,
Geht auch der ganze Wald zu Grund.»

So spricht zu seinem Spätzelein
Im Eichennest der alte Spatz;
Die Spätzin piepet manchmal drein,
Sie hockt auf ihrem Ehrenplatz.

No, the forest's Kapellmeister sits in my own heart, and I can feel him beating time, and I believe his name is Amor.

'In the beginning was the nightingale, and sang the word: jug! jug! And as she sang, green grass, violets, apple-blossom sprang up everywhere.

'She bit her own breast, and her red blood flowed, and a beautiful rose-tree sprang up from the blood; she sings of her passion to it.

'The blood from that wound is a propitiation for all of us birds in this forest; but when the rose-song shall cease to be heard, the whole forest too shall perish.'

That is what the old cock-sparrow tells his little son in their oak-tree nest; the hen-sparrow occasionally adds a peep as she perches in her place of honour;

HEINE

Sie ist ein häuslich gutes Weib
Und brütet brav und schmollet nicht;
Der Alte gibt zum Zeitvertreib
Den Kindern Glaubensunterricht.

Es hat die warme Frühlingsnacht
Die Blumen hervorgetrieben,
Und nimmt mein Herz sich nicht in acht,
So wird es sich wieder verlieben.

Doch welche von den Blumen alln
Wird mir das Herz umgarnen?
Es wollen die singenden Nachtigalln
Mich vor der Lilie warnen.

Die blauen Frühlingsaugen
Schaun aus dem Gras hervor;
Das sind die lieben Veilchen,
Die ich zum Strauß erkor.

she is a good, homely wife and broods properly and does not sulk; the old cock is passing the time by giving his children religious instruction.

The warm spring night has brought forth the flowers, and if my heart doesn't take care, it will fall in love again.
But which of all the flowers will ensnare my heart? The singing nightingales are trying to warn me against the lily.

The blue eyes of spring look up from the grass; they are the dear violets which I chose for a posy.

Ich pflücke sie und denke,
Und die Gedanken all,
Die mir im Herzen seufzen,
Singt laut die Nachtigall.

Ja, was ich denke, singt sie
Lautschmetternd, daß es schallt;
Mein zärtliches Geheimnis
Weiß schon der ganze Wald.

DIE schlanke Wasserlilie
Schaut träumend hervor aus dem See;
Da grüßt der Mond herunter
Mit lichtem Liebesweh.

Verschämt senkt sie das Köpfchen
Wieder hinab zu den Welln –
Da sieht sie zu ihren Füßen
Den armen blassen Geselln.

I pluck them and think, and all the thoughts which sigh in my heart are
sung out aloud by the nightingale.

Yes, whatever I think she sings out so loud that it resounds; the whole forest
already knows my tender secret.

THE slender water-lily gazes dreamily up from the lake; the moon nods his
greeting, bright with the pain of love.

She bashfully lowers her little head down towards the waves again – there
at her feet she sees her poor, pale companion.

Die Rose duftet – doch ob sie empfindet
Das was sie duftet, ob die Nachtigall
Selbst fühlt, was sich durch unsre Seele windet
Bei ihres Liedes süßem Widerhall; –

Ich weiß es nicht. Doch macht uns gar verdrießlich
Die Wahrheit oft! Und Ros und Nachtigall,
Erlögen sie auch das Gefühl, ersprießlich
Wär solche Lüge, wie in manchem Fall –

Es haben unsre Herzen
Geschlossen die heilge Allianz;
Sie lagen fest aneinander,
Und sie verstanden sich ganz.

Ach, nur die junge Rose,
Die deine Brust geschmückt,
Die arme Bundesgenossin,
Sie wurde fast zerdrückt.

The rose smells sweet – but if she is aware of her scent, if the nightingale her-self feels what makes its way through our hearts at the sweet echo of her song –
I don't know. But truth often makes us very cross! And rose and nightingale, even if they were fabricating their feeling, – such a lie would be beneficial, as in so many cases –

Our hearts have formed a holy alliance; they lay close together and com-pletely understood each other.
Ah, only the young rose which adorned your breast – that poor confederate was practically flattened.

Sag mir, wer einst die Uhren erfund,
Die Zeitabteilung, Minuten und Stund?
Das war ein frierend trauriger Mann.
Er saß in der Winternacht und sann,
Und zählte der Mäuschen heimliches Quicken
Und des Holzwurms ebenmäßiges Picken.

Sag mir, wer einst das Küssen erfund?
Das war ein glühend glücklicher Mund;
Er küßte und dachte nichts dabei.
Es war im schönen Monat Mai,
Die Blumen sind aus der Erde gesprungen,
Die Sonne lachte, die Vögel sungen.

Hab ich nicht dieselben Träume
Schon geträumt von diesem Glücke?
Warens nicht dieselben Bäume,
Blumen, Küsse, Liebesblicke?

Schien der Mond nicht durch die Blätter
Unsrer Laube hier am Bache?
Hielten nicht die Marmorgötter
Vor dem Eingang stille Wache?

Tell me, who invented clocks, division of time, minutes and hours? It was a freezing-cold, sad man. He sat and thought in a winter's night, and counted the furtive squeakings of mice and the woodworm's regular ticking.

Tell me, who invented kissing? It was a glowing, happy mouth; it kissed, and did not think at all. It was in the lovely month of May, the flowers have sprung from the earth, the sun laughed, the birds sang.

Have I not already dreamt the same dreams about this happiness? Were they not the same trees, flowers, kisses, loving glances?

Did not the moon shine through the leaves of our bower here by the stream? Did not the marble gods keep silent watch before the entrance?

Ach! ich weiß, wie sich verändern
Diese allzuholden Träume,
Wie mit kalten Schneegewändern
Sich umhüllen Herz und Bäume;

Wie wir selber dann erkühlen
Und uns fliehen und vergessen,
Wir, die jetzt so zärtlich fühlen,
Herz an Herz so zärtlich pressen.

Es war ein alter König,
Sein Herz war schwer, sein Haupt war grau;
Der arme alte König,
Er nahm eine junge Frau.

Es war ein schöner Page,
Blond war sein Haupt, leicht war sein Sinn;
Er trug die seidne Schleppe
Der jungen Königin.

Kennst du das alte Liedchen?
Es klingt so süß, es klingt so trüb!
Sie mußten beide sterben,
Sie hatten sich viel zu lieb.

Ah, I know how these all-too-dear dreams change, how heart and trees
wrap themselves round with cold garments of snow;
   how we ourselves then grow cold and flee from and forget each other, we
who now feel so tenderly, press heart to heart so tenderly.

There was an old king, his heart was heavy, his head was grey; the poor old
king took a young wife.
   There was a handsome page, his hair was blond, his mind was carefree;
he bore the silken train of the young queen.
   Do you know the old song? It sounds so sweet, it sounds so sad! They both
had to die, they loved each other much too much.

"MONDSCHEINTRUNKNE Lindenblüten,
Sie ergießen ihre Düfte,
Und von Nachtigallenliedern
Sind erfüllet Laub und Lüfte.

«Lieblich läßt es sich, Geliebter,
Unter dieser Linde sitzen,
Wenn die goldnen Mondeslichter
Durch des Baumes Blätter blitzen.

«Sieh dies Lindenblatt! du wirst es
Wie ein Herz gestaltet finden;
Darum sitzen die Verliebten
Auch am liebsten unter Linden.

«Doch du lächelst, wie verloren
In entfernten Sehnsuchtträumen –
Sprich, Geliebter, welche Wünsche
Dir im lieben Herzen keimen?»

Ach, ich will es dir, Geliebte,
Gern bekennen, ach, ich möchte,
Daß ein kalter Nordwind plötzlich
Weißes Schneegestöber brächte;

'LIME blossoms drunk with moonlight pour forth their scents, and leaves and breezes are filled with the songs of nightingales.

'How lovely it is, beloved, to sit beneath this lime-tree when the golden light of the moon shines through the tree's leaves.

'Look at this lime leaf! You will find it shaped like a heart; that's why lovers like sitting beneath lime-trees best.

'But you are smiling, as if lost in distant dreams of longing – say, beloved, what wishes are forming in your dear heart?'

Ah, I will gladly tell you, my love, ah, I wish a cold north wind would suddenly bring a white flurry of snow;

Und daß wir, mit Pelz bedecket
Und im buntgeschmückten Schlitten,
Schellenklingelnd, peitschenknallend,
Über Fluß und Fluren glitten.

DURCH den Wald, im Mondenscheine,
Sah ich jüngst die Elfen reuten;
Ihre Hörner hört ich klingen,
Ihre Glöckchen hört ich läuten.

Ihre weißen Rößlein trugen
Güldnes Hirschgeweih und flogen
Rasch dahin, wie wilde Schwäne
Kam es durch die Luft gezogen.

Lächelnd nickte mir die Köngin,
Lächelnd, im Vorüberreuten.
Galt das meiner neuen Liebe,
Oder soll es Tod bedeuten?

and that we, wrapped in furs and sitting in a gaily-coloured sledge, with
jingling bells and cracking whip, were gliding over river and meadows.

I RECENTLY saw the elves riding through the woods in the moonlight; I
heard their horns ring out and I heard their little bells jingle.

Their little white horses had golden antlers and flew rapidly past, they came
flying through the air like wild swans.

The queen nodded to me with a smile as she rode past. Was that because of
my new love, or does it mean death?

Morgens send ich dir die Veilchen,
Die ich früh im Wald gefunden,
Und des Abends bring ich Rosen,
Die ich brach in Dämmrungstunden.

Weißt du was die hübschen Blumen
Dir Verblümtes sagen möchten?
Treu sein sollst du mir am Tage
Und mich lieben in den Nächten.

Ernst ist der Frühling, seine Träume
Sind traurig, jede Blume schaut
Von Schmerz bewegt, es bebt geheime
Wehmut im Nachtigallenlaut.

O lächle nicht, geliebte Schöne,
So freundlich heiter, lächle nicht!
O, weine lieber, eine Träne
Küß ich so gern dir vom Gesicht.

In the morning I send you the violets which I found in the wood early, and
in the evening I bring roses which I plucked in the twilight hours.

Do you know what flowery things the pretty flowers would like to say to
you? You must be true to me by day and love me at night.

Spring is serious, its dreams are sad, every flower seems moved by pain,
secret melancholy quivers in the nightingale's song.

Oh do not smile, beloved beauty, in that friendly, cheerful manner, do not
smile! Oh, I'd rather you cried, I so love kissing tears from your face.

Verdroßnen Sinn im kalten Herzen hegend,
Reis ich verdrießlich durch die kalte Welt,
Zu Ende geht der Herbst, ein Nebel hält
Feuchteingehüllt die abgestorbne Gegend.

Die Winde pfeifen, hin und her bewegend
Das rote Laub, das von den Bäumen fällt,
Es seufzt der Wald, es dampft das kahle Feld,
Nun kommt das Schlimmste noch, es regent.

Himmel grau und wochentäglich!
Auch die Stadt ist noch dieselbe!
Und noch immer blöd und kläglich
Spiegelt sie sich in der Elbe.

Lange Nasen, noch langweilig
Werden sie wie sonst geschneuzet,
Und das duckt sich noch scheinheilig,
Oder bläht sich, stolz gespreizet.

Nurturing a bad temper in a cold heart I travel crossly through the cold world, autumn is drawing near its end, a mist holds the dead region in its damp mantle.

The winds whistle, tossing the red leaves hither and thither as they fall from the trees, the forest sighs, the bare field steams – and now, worst of all, it is raining.

It is a grey, week-day sky! The town, too, is still the same! And in the same stupid and pitiful way it is still reflected in the Elbe.

Long noses are blown just as monotonously as ever, and people hypocritically bow their heads, or puff themselves up, proudly strutting.

Schöner Süden! wie verehr ich
Deinen Himmel, deine Götter,
Seit ich diesen Menschenkehricht
Wiederseh, und dieses Wetter!

Beautiful South! How I venerate your skies, your Gods, since I see again these dregs of humanity, and this weather!

VERSCHIEDENE

from SERAPHINE

AUF diesem Felsen bauen wir
Die Kirche von dem dritten,
Dem dritten neuen Testament;
Das Leid ist ausgelitten.

Vernichtet ist das Zweierlei,
Das uns so lang betöret;
Die dumme Leiberquälerei
Hat endlich aufgehöret.

Hörst du den Gott im finstern Meer?
Mit tausend Stimmen spricht er.
Und siehst du über unserm Haupt
Die tausend Gotteslichter?

Der heilge Gott der ist im Licht
Wie in den Finsternissen;
Und Gott ist alles was da ist;
Er ist in unsern Küssen.

VARIOUS WOMEN

from SERAPHINE

ON this rock we build the church of the third New Testament; there is an end
to suffering.

The dichotomy which so long bemused us is destroyed; the stupid morti-
fication of our bodies has finally ceased.

Do you hear God in the dark sea? He speaks with a thousand voices. And
do you see above our heads the thousand divine lights?

The Lord God is in the light and also in the darkness; and God is everything
that exists; he is in our kisses.

Das Fräulein stand am Meere
Und seufzte lang und bang,
Es rührte sie so sehre
Der Sonnenuntergang.

Mein Fräulein! sein Sie munter,
Das ist ein altes Stück;
Hier vorne geht sie unter
Und kehrt von hinten zurück.

from ANGELIQUE

Wie rasch du auch vorüberschrittest,
Noch einmal schautest du zurück,
Der Mund, wie fragend, kühngeöffnet,
Stürmischer Hochmut in dem Blick.

O, daß ich nie zu fassen suchte
Das weiße, flüchtige Gewand!
Die holde Spur der kleinen Füße,
O, daß ich nie sie wiederfand!

The young lady stood on the sea-shore and sighed long and anxiously, so deeply did the sunset move her.

Young lady, cheer up, that is an old tale; it goes down in front of us here, and comes back again behind.

from ANGELIQUE

Quickly though you walked past, you did look behind you again, your mouth open boldly as if asking a question, stormy pride in your glance.

Oh, that I had never tried to grasp your white, elusive dress! Would that I had never again found the lovely print of your little feet.

Verschwunden ist ja deine Wildheit,
Bist wie die andern zahm und klar,
Und sanft und unerträglich gütig,
Und ach! nun liebst du mich sogar!

WENN ich, beseligt von schönen Küssen,
In deinen Armen mich wohl befinde,
Dann mußt du mir nie von Deutschland reden; –
Ich kanns nicht vertragen – es hat seine Gründe.

Ich bitte dich, laß mich mit Deutschland in Frieden!
Du mußt mich nicht plagen mit ewigen Fragen
Nach Heimat, Sippschaft und Lebensverhältnis; –
Es hat seine Gründe – ich kanns nicht vertragen.

Die Eichen sind grün, und blau sind die Augen
Der deutschen Frauen; sie schmachten gelinde
Und seufzen von Liebe, Hoffnung und Glauben; –
Ich kanns nicht vertragen – es hat seine Gründe.

Your fierceness has vanished, like other girls you are tractable and limpid, and gentle, and unbearably kind, and ah! now you are even in love with me!

WHEN, made happy by beautiful kisses, I lie comfortably in your arms, you must never speak to me about Germany; – I can't bear it – there are reasons why.

I beg you, don't bother me with Germany! You mustn't torment me with everlasting questions about fatherland, family and living conditions; – there are reasons why – I can't bear it.

The oaks are green, and the eyes of German women are blue; they languish gently and sigh of love, hope and belief; – I can't bear it – there are reasons why.

JA freilich, du bist mein Ideal,
Habs dir ja oft bekräftigt
Mit Küssen und Eiden sonder Zahl;
Doch heute bin ich beschäftigt.

Komm morgen zwischen zwei und drei,
Dann sollen neue Flammen
Bewähren meine Schwärmerei;
Wir essen nachher zusammen.

Wenn ich Billete bekommen kann,
Bin ich sogar kapabel
Dich in die Oper zu führen alsdann:
Man gibt Robert-le-Diable.

Es ist ein großes Zauberstück
Voll Teufelslust und Liebe;
Von Meyerbeer ist die Musik,
Der schlechte Text von Scribe.

DIESER Liebe toller Fasching,
Dieser Taumel unsrer Herzen,
Geht zu Ende, und ernüchtert
Gähnen wir einander an!

YES, of course you are my ideal, I've often corroborated it for you with kisses
and oaths without number; but today I'm busy.

Come tomorrow between two and three, then new flames shall prove my
passion; we'll eat together afterwards.

If I can get tickets I'm even capable of taking you to the opera then: they're
doing *Robert le Diable*.

It's a great magic work, full of devilish pleasures and love; the music is by
Meyerbeer and the wretched text by Scribe.

THE mad carnival of this love, this giddiness of our hearts is coming to an end
and, sobered, we yawn at each other!

Ausgetrunken ist der Kelch,
Der mit Sinnenrausch gefüllt war,
Schäumend, lodernd, bis am Rande;
Ausgetrunken ist der Kelch.

Es verstummen auch die Geigen,
Die zum Tanze mächtig spielten,
Zu dem Tanz der Leidenschaft;
Auch die Geigen, sie verstummen.

Es erlöschen auch die Lampen,
Die das wilde Licht ergossen
Auf den bunten Mummenschanz;
Auch die Lampen, sie erlöschen.

Morgen kommt der Aschenmittwoch,
Und ich zeichne deine Stirne
Mit dem Aschenkreuz und spreche:
Weib, bedenke, daß du Staub bist.

Ach, wie schön bist du, wenn traulich
Dein Gemüt sich mir erschließet,
Und von nobelster Gesinnung
Deine Rede überfließet!

Emptied is the cup which was filled with intoxication of the senses, foaming, glowing, up to the brim; emptied is the cup.

The violins, too, fall silent which played boldly for the dance, the dance of passion; the violins, too, fall silent.

The lamps, too, are going out which shed their wild light on the gay masquerade; the lamps, too, are going out.

Tomorrow is Ash Wednesday, and I shall mark your brow with the ashen cross, and say: Woman, remember thou art dust.

Ah, how beautiful you are when your mind unlocks all its confidences and your speech overflows with the noblest sentiments!

Wenn du mir erzählst, wie immer
Du so groß und würdig dachtest,
Wie dem Stolze deines Herzens
Du die größten Opfer brachtest!

Wie man dich für Millionen
Nicht vermöchte zu erwerben –
Eh du dich für Geld verkauftest,
Lieber würdest du ja sterben!

Und ich steh vor dir und höre,
Und ich höre dich zu Ende;
Wie ein stummes Bild des Glaubens
Falt ich andachtsvoll die Hände.

Fürchte nichts, geliebte Seele,
Übersicher bist du hier;
Fürchte nicht, daß man uns stehle,
Ich verriegle schon die Tür.

Wie der Wind auch wütend wehe,
Er gefährdet nicht das Haus;
Daß auch nicht ein Brand entstehe,
Lösch ich unsre Lampe aus.

When you tell me how grand and worthy your thoughts always were, how great the sacrifices were which you made to the pride of your heart!

How you weren't to be bought for millions – you would rather have died than sell yourself for money!

And I stand before you and listen, and I shall hear you out; like a silent statue of Faith I reverently fold my hands.

Fear nought, beloved soul, you are more than safe here; fear not that we'll be robbed, I'm just locking the door.

However angrily the wind blows it won't endanger the house; so that fire can't break out I'll put out the lamp.

Ach, erlaube, daß ich winde
Meinen Arm um deinen Hals;
Man erkältet sich geschwinde
In Ermanglung eines Schals.

from HORTENSE

EHMALS glaubt ich, alle Küsse,
Die ein Weib uns gibt und nimmt,
Seien uns, durch Schicksalsschlüsse,
Schon urzeitlich vorbestimmt.

Küsse nahm ich und ich küßte
So mit Ernst in jener Zeit,
Als ob ich erfüllen müßte
Taten der Notwendigkeit.

Jetzo weiß ich, überflüssig,
Wie so manches, ist der Kuß,
Und mit leichtern Sinnen küß ich,
Glaubenlos im Überfluß.

Ah, let me put my arm round your neck; one can easily catch cold when one hasn't got a shawl.

from HORTENSE

I ONCE believed that all the kisses a woman gives us and takes were predestined for us by fate's decree from the beginning of time.

I took kisses and gave them with such seriousness in those days, as though obliged to fulfil deeds of necessity.

I now know that the kiss is, like so much else, superfluous, and with lighter heart I kiss, unbelieving, to superfluity.

from SCHÖPFUNGSLIEDER

WARUM ich eigentlich erschuf
Die Welt, ich will es gern bekennen:
Ich fühlte in der Seele brennen,
Wie Flammenwahnsinn, den Beruf.

Krankheit ist wohl der letzte Grund
Des ganzen Schöpferdrangs gewesen;
Erschaffend konnte ich genesen,
Erschaffend wurde ich gesund.

from KATHARINA

DER Frühling schien schon an dem Tor
Mich freundlich zu erwarten.
Die ganze Gegend steht im Flor
Als wie ein Blumengarten.

Die Liebste sitzt an meiner Seit
Im rasch hinrollenden Wagen;
Sie schaut mich an voll Zärtlichkeit,
Ihr Herz, das fühl ich schlagen.

from SONGS OF CREATION

I WILL gladly confess why I actually created the world: I felt the call burning in my soul like the flames of madness.

Sickness was really the ultimate reason for the whole creative impulse; by creating I was able to recover, by creating I got well.

from KATHARINA

SPRING seemed to be waiting for me at the gate in friendly fashion. The whole region is in bloom, like a flower-garden.

My dearest sits at my side in the rapidly moving coach; she looks at me full of tenderness, I feel her heart beat.

Das trillert und duftet so sonnenvergnügt!
Das blinkt im grünen Geschmeide!
Sein weißes Blütenköpfchen wiegt
Der junge Baum mit Freude.

Die Blumen schaun aus der Erd hervor,
Betrachten, neugierigen Blickes,
Das schöne Weib, das ich erkor,
Und mich, den Mann des Glückes.

Vergängliches Glück! Schon morgen klirrt
Die Sichel über den Saaten,
Der holde Frühling verwelken wird,
Das Weib wird mich verraten.

GESANGLOS war ich und beklommen
So lange Zeit – nun dicht ich wieder!
Wie Tränen, die uns plötzlich kommen,
So kommen plötzlich auch die Lieder.

Melodisch kann ich wieder klagen
Von großem Lieben, größerm Leiden,
Von Herzen, die sich schlecht vertragen
Und dennoch brechen, wenn sie scheiden.

Songs and scents rejoice in the sunshine! Everything shines in its green finery! The young tree joyously nods its little white crown of blossoms.

The flowers gaze up from the earth, stare with curious eyes at the beautiful woman I have chosen, and at me, the happy man.

Transient happiness! Tomorrow the sickle will already be swishing over the crops, lovely spring will fade, the woman will betray me.

I WAS songless and oppressed for such a long time – now I am writing again! Like tears which come suddenly upon us, songs too come suddenly.

I can once again complain melodiously of great love and greater suffering, of hearts which don't get on well together and yet break when they part.

Manchmal ist mir, als fühlt ich wehen
Über dem Haupt die deutschen Eichen –
Sie flüstern gar von Wiedersehen –
Das sind nur Träume – sie verbleichen.

Manchmal ist mir, als hört ich singen
Die alten, deutschen Nachtigallen –
Wie mich die Töne sanft umschlingen! –
Das sind nur Träume – sie verhallen.

Wo sind die Rosen, deren Liebe
Mich einst beglückt? – All ihre Blüte
Ist längst verwelkt! – Gespenstisch trübe
Spukt noch ihr Duft mir im Gemüte.

Nachlese

from KITTY

Er ist so herzbeweglich,
Der Brief, den sie geschrieben:
Sie werde mich ewig lieben,
Ewig, unendlich, unsäglich.

Sometimes I seem to be feeling German oaks moving above my head – they
even whisper of another meeting – these are only dreams – they fade away.
Sometimes I seem to hear the old German nightingales singing – how gently
the sounds enfold me! – they are only dreams – they die away.
Where are the roses whose love once made me happy? – All their blossom
faded long ago! – Ghostlike and sadly their perfume still haunts my mind.

Supplementary Poems

from KITTY

How it moves my heart, that letter she wrote: she will always love me, always,
for ever, unutterably.

III

Sie ennuyiere sich täglich,
Ihr sei die Brust beklommen –
«Du mußt herüber kommen
Nach England, so bald als möglich.»

Es läuft dahin die Barke,
Wie eine flinke Gemse.
Bald sind wir auf der Themse,
Bald sind wir im Regentsparke.

Da wohnet meine Kitty,
Mein allerliebstes Weibchen;
Es gibt kein weißres Leibchen
Im West-End und in der City.

Schon meiner Ankunft gewärtig,
Füllt sie den Wasserkessel
Und rückt an den Herd den Sessel;
Den Tee, den find ich fertig.

She's bored every day, her heart is heavy – 'You must come across to England as soon as you can.'

THE bark hastens on like a nimble chamois. We'll soon be on the Thames, we'll soon be in Regent's Park.
   That's where my Kitty lives, my dearest little woman; there isn't a whiter bodice/little body in the West End and the City.
   Expecting my arrival she fills the kettle and moves the chair up to the fire; I'll find the tea all ready.

Das Glück, das gestern mich geküßt,
Ist heute schon zerronnen,
Und treue Liebe hab ich nie
Auf lange Zeit gewonnen.

Die Neugier hat wohl manches Weib
In meinen Arm gezogen;
Hat sie mir mal ins Herz geschaut,
Ist sie davon geflogen.

Die eine lachte, eh sie ging,
Die andre tät erblassen;
Nur Kitty weinte bitterlich,
Bevor sie mich verlassen.

AN JENNY

Ich bin nun fünfunddreißig Jahr alt,
Und du bist fünfzehnjährig kaum . . .
O Jenny, wenn ich dich betrachte,
Erwacht in mir der alte Traum!

The happiness that kissed me yesterday has dissolved by today, and I've never won true love for any length of time.

Curiosity has drawn many a woman to my arms; but when she's had a look into my heart she has fled.

One laughed before she went, another turned pale; only Kitty wept bitterly before she left me.

To Jenny

I am thirty-five years old and you are scarcely fifteen . . . O Jenny, when I look at you the old dream awakens within me!

Im Jahre achtzehnhundert siebzehn
Sah ich ein Mädchen, wunderbar
Dir ähnlich an Gestalt und Wesen,
Auch trug sie ganz wie du das Haar.

Ich geh auf Universitäten,
Sprach ich zu ihr, ich komm zurück
In kurzer Zeit, erwarte meiner.
Sie sprach: «Du bist mein einzges Glück.»

Drei Jahre schon hatt ich Pandekten
Studiert, als ich am ersten Mai
Zu Göttingen die Nachricht hörte,
Daß meine Braut vermählet sei.

Es war am ersten Mai! Der Frühling
Zog lachend grün durch Feld und Tal,
Die Vögel sangen, und es freute
Sich jeder Wurm im Sonnenstrahl.

Ich aber wurde blaß und kränklich,
Und meine Kräfte nahmen ab;
Der liebe Gott nur kann es wissen,
Was ich des Nachts gelitten hab.

In the year 1817 I saw a girl, wonderfully like you in appearance and in nature, and she wore her hair just as you do.

I'm off to the university, I told her, I'll come back soon, wait for me. She said: 'You are my only joy.'

I had been studying law for three years when, at Göttingen, on the first of May, I heard the news that my fiancée had got married.

It was on the first of May! Spring was making his laughing, green way through field and valley, the birds were singing, and every creeping thing was rejoicing in the sunbeams.

But I grew pale and sick, and my strength waned; only the dear Lord can know what I suffered at nights.

Doch ich genas. Meine Gesundheit
Ist jetzt so stark wie'n Eichenbaum . . .
O Jenny, wenn ich dich betrachte,
Erwacht in mir der alte Traum!

IN DER FRÜHE

MEINE gute, liebe Frau,
Meine gütge Frau Geliebte,
Hielt bereit den Morgenimbiß,
Braunen Kaffee, weiße Sahne.

Und sie schenkt ihn selber ein,
Scherzend, kosend, lieblich lächelnd.
In der ganzen Christenheit
Lächelt wohl kein Mund so lieblich!

Auch der Stimme Flötenton
Findet sich nur bei den Engeln,
Oder allenfalls hienieden
Bei den besten Nachtigallen.

But I got better. My health is now as strong as an oak-tree . . . O Jenny,
when I look at you the old dream awakens within me!

In the Early Morning

MY dear, good wife, my kind, wifely mistress had breakfast ready, brown
coffee, white cream.

And she pours it out herself, joking, flirting, smiling lovingly. In all Chris-
tendom surely no mouth smiles as lovingly!

The flute-like tones of her voice, too, are only found in angels, or perhaps
here below in the best nightingales.

Wie die Hände lilienweiß!
Wie das Haar sich träumend ringelt
Um das rosge Angesicht!
Ihre Schönheit ist vollkommen.

Heute nur bedünkt es mich
– Weiß nicht warum –, ein bißchen schmäler
Dürfte ihre Taille sein,
Nur ein kleines bißchen schmäler.

from IN DER FREMDE

ICH hatte einst ein schönes Vaterland.
Der Eichenbaum
Wuchs dort so hoch, die Veilchen nickten sanft.
Es war ein Traum.

Das küßte mich auf deutsch und sprach auf deutsch
(Man glaubt es kaum
Wie gut es klang) das Wort: «Ich liebe dich!»
Es war ein Traum.

How lily-white her hands are! How dreamily her hair curls around her rosy face! Her beauty is perfect.

Just today it occurs to me – I don't know why – that her figure could be a little bit more slender, just a tiny little bit more slender.

from IN A FOREIGN LAND

I ONCE had a beautiful fatherland. The oak-tree grew so tall there, the violets nodded gently. It was a dream.

I was kissed with a German kiss and addressed in German (you can scarcely believe how good it sounded): 'I love you!' It was a dream.

ROMANZEN

EIN WEIB

SIE hatten sich beide so herzlich lieb,
Spitzbübin war sie, er war ein Dieb.
Wenn er Schelmenstreiche machte,
Sie warf sich aufs Bett und lachte.

Der Tag verging in Freud und Lust,
Des Nachts lag sie an seiner Brust.
Als man ins Gefängnis ihn brachte,
Sie stand am Fenster und lachte.

Er ließ ihr sagen: O komm zu mir,
Ich sehne mich so sehr nach dir,
Ich rufe nach dir, ich schmachte –
Sie schüttelt' das Haupt und lachte.

Um sechse des Morgens ward er gehenkt,
Um sieben ward er ins Grab gesenkt;
Sie aber schon um achte
Trank roten Wein und lachte.

ROMANCES
A Woman

THEY loved each other so very dearly, she was a scoundrel, he was a thief.
When he got up to his knavish tricks she threw herself on to the bed and
laughed.

The days passed in joy and delight, at night she lay on his breast. When
they took him off to prison she stood at the window and laughed.

He sent her a message: Oh come to me, I long for you so much, I cry out
for you, I languish – she shook her head and laughed.

At six in the morning he was hanged, at seven he was lowered into his grave;
but at eight she was drinking red wine and laughing.

CHILDE HAROLD

Eine starke, schwarze Barke
Segelt trauervoll dahin.
Die vermummten und verstummten
Leichenhüter sitzen drin.

Toter Dichter, stille liegt er,
Mit entblößtem Angesicht;
Seine blauen Augen schauen
Immer noch zum Himmelslicht.

Aus der Tiefe klingts, als riefe
Eine kranke Nixenbraut,
Und die Wellen, sie zerschellen
An dem Kahn, wie Klagelaut.

ANNO 1839

O, Deutschland, meine ferne Liebe,
Gedenk ich deiner, wein ich fast!
Das muntre Frankreich scheint mir trübe,
Das leichte Volk wird mir zur Last.

Childe Harold

A stout, black bark sails sadly along. In it sit the masked and silent pall-watchers.

The dead poet lies still, his face unshrouded; his blue eyes still gaze up at the light of heaven.

Sounds rise from the deep, as if a water-sprite's ailing bride were calling, and the waves break against the bark, like lamentations.

Anno 1839

O Germany my distant love, when I think of you I almost weep! Gay France seems to me sad, her frivolous people weigh me down.

Nur der Verstand, so kalt und trocken,
Herrscht in dem witzigen Paris –
O, Narrheitsglöcklein, Glaubensglocken,
Wie klingelt ihr daheim so süß!

Höfliche Männer! Doch verdrossen
Geb ich den artgen Gruß zurück. –
Die Grobheit, die ich einst genossen
Im Vaterland, das war mein Glück!

Lächelnde Weiber! Plappern immer,
Wie Mühlenräder stets bewegt!
Da lob ich Deutschlands Frauenzimmer,
Das schweigend sich zu Bette legt.

Und alles dreht sich hier im Kreise,
Mit Ungestüm, wie'n toller Traum!
Bei uns bleibt alles hübsch im Gleise,
Wie angenagelt, rührt sich kaum.

Mir ist, als hört ich fern erklingen
Nachtwächterhörner, sanft und traut;
Nachtwächterlieder hör ich singen,
Dazwischen Nachtigallenlaut.

Reason alone, so cold and dry, reigns in witty Paris – O fool's bells, great bells of faith, how sweetly you ring out at home!

Polite men! But sullenly I return their courteous greeting. – The rudeness I once enjoyed in my fatherland was happiness to me!

Smiling women! They chatter away like steadily turning mill-wheels! I praise Germany's girls who go quietly to bed.

And everything spins round here impetuously, as in a mad dream! At home everything follows its accustomed course, as if fixed, and scarcely bestirs itself.

I seem to hear, far away, night-watchmen's horns ring out, soft and familiar; I hear night-watchmen's songs, and in between, the sound of the nightingale.

Dem Dichter war so wohl daheime,
In Schildas teurem Eichenhain!
Dort wob ich meine zarten Reime
Aus Veilchenduft und Mondenschein.

DIE NIXEN

Am einsamen Strande plätschert die Flut,
Der Mond ist aufgegangen,
Auf weißer Düne der Ritter ruht,
Von bunten Träumen befangen.

Die schönen Nixen, im Schleiergewand,
Entsteigen der Meerestiefe.
Sie nahen sich leise dem jungen Fant,
Sie glaubten wahrhaftig, er schliefe.

Die eine betastet mit Neubegier
Die Federn auf seinem Barette.
Die andre nestelt am Bandelier
Und an der Waffenkette.

Die dritte lacht, und ihr Auge blitzt,
Sie zieht das Schwert aus der Scheide,
Und auf dem blanken Schwert gestützt
Beschaut sie den Ritter mit Freude.

The poet was so content at home, in Gotham's beloved oak-grove! There I wove my tender rhymes from the scent of violets and from moonshine.

The Nixies

The tide murmurs on the lonely shore, the moon has risen, the knight rests on the white dune, engrossed in happy dreams.

The lovely nixies, dressed in veils, emerge from the depths of the sea. They softly approach the young man, they really thought he was asleep.

In her curiosity one fingers the feathers on his cap. Another fumbles with his bandoleer and sword-belt.

The third laughs and her eye sparkles, she draws the sword from its sheath, and leaning on the shining sword she gazes at the knight with pleasure.

Die vierte tänzelt wohl hin und her
Und flüstert aus tiefem Gemüte:
«O, daß ich doch dein Liebchen wär,
Du holde Menschenblüte!»

Die fünfte küßt des Ritters Händ,
Mit Sehnsucht und Verlangen;
Die sechste zögert und küßt am End
Die Lippen und die Wangen.

Der Ritter ist klug, es fällt ihm nicht ein,
Die Augen öffnen zu müssen;
Er läßt sich ruhig im Mondenschein
Von schönen Nixen küssen.

DIE UNBEKANNTE

MEINER goldgelockten Schönen
Weiß ich täglich zu begegnen,
In dem Tuileriengarten,
Unter den Kastanienbäumen.

The fourth dances to and fro and whispers feelingly: 'Oh, if only I were your darling, fair flower of men!'

The fifth kisses the knight's hands with desire and longing; the sixth hesitates and finally kisses his lips and cheeks.

The knight is sensible, the need to open his eyes doesn't occur to him; he quietly lets himself be kissed in the moonlight by lovely nixies.

The Unknown Lady

I CAN be sure of meeting my golden-haired beauty each day in the Tuileries gardens beneath the chestnut-trees.

Täglich geht sie dort spazieren,
Mit zwei häßlich alten Damen –
Sind es Tanten? Sinds Dragoner,
Die vermummt in Weiberröcken?

Niemand konnt mir Auskunft geben,
Wer sie sei? Bei allen Freunden
Frug ich nach, und stets vergebens!
Ich erkrankte fast vor Sehnsucht.

Eingeschüchtert von dem Schnurrbart
Ihrer zwei Begleiterinnen,
Und von meinem eignen Herzen
Noch viel strenger eingeschüchtert,

Wagt ich nie ein seufzend Wörtchen
Im Vorübergehn zu flüstern,
Und ich wagte kaum mit Blicken
Meine Flamme zu bekunden.

Heute erst hab ich erfahren
Ihren Namen. Laura heißt sie,
Wie die schöne Provenzalin,
Die der große Dichter liebte.

Each day she walks there with two ugly old ladies – are they aunts? Are they dragoons disguised in women's clothes?

No one could tell me who she was. I inquired of all my friends, and always in vain! I was almost sick from desire.

Intimidated by the moustaches of her two companions, and intimidated much more strongly still by my own heart,

I never dared to whisper a single sighing word as I went past, and I scarcely dared to show my ardour by my glances.

Only today have I learnt her name. She is called Laura, like the beautiful maid of Provence whom the great poet loved.

Laura heißt sie! Nun da bin ich
Just so weit wie einst Petrarcha,
Der das schöne Weib gefeiert
In Kanzonen und Sonetten.

Laura heißt sie! Wie Petrarcha
Kann ich jetzt platonisch schwelgen
In dem Wohllaut dieses Namens –
Weiter hat ers nie gebracht.

WECHSEL

MIT Brünetten hats ein Ende!
Ich gerate dieses Jahr
Wieder in die blauen Augen,
Wieder in das blonde Haar.

Die Blondine, die ich liebe,
Ist so fromm, so sanft, so mild!
In der Hand den Lilienstengel
Wäre sie ein Heilgenbild.

She is called Laura! So now I have got as far as Petrarch once did, who celebrated the beautiful woman in canzonas and sonnets.

She is called Laura! Like Petrarch I can now bask platonically in the euphony of this name – he never got any farther.

Change

BRUNETTES are out! This year I'm falling for blue eyes again, and fair hair.

The blonde I love is so good, so gentle, so mild! With a lily in her hand she would be the image of a saint.

Schlanke, schwärmerische Glieder,
Wenig Fleisch, sehr viel Gemüt;
Und für Liebe, Hoffnung, Glaube
Ihre ganze Seele glüht.

Sie behauptet, sie verstünde
Gar kein Deutsch – ich glaub es nicht.
Niemals hättest du gelesen
Klopstocks himmlisches Gedicht?*

BEGEGNUNG

WOHL unter der Linde erklingt die Musik,
Da tanzen die Burschen und Mädel,
Da tanzen zwei, die niemand kennt,
Sie schaun so schlank und edel.

Sie schweben auf, sie schweben ab,
In seltsam fremder Weise,
Sie lachen sich an, sie schütteln das Haupt,
Das Fräulein flüstert leise:

Slender, passionate limbs, not much flesh, plenty of spirit; and her whole soul glows for love, hope, faith.

She claims she doesn't understand any German – I don't believe it. You don't mean to say you've never read Klopstock's heavenly poem? *

Meeting

MUSIC rings out under the lime-tree, and the boys and girls are dancing; there are two dancers whom no one knows, they look so slender and noble.

They bob up and down in a strange, unfamiliar way, they look laughingly at each other, they shake their heads, the girl whispers softly:

---

* *Der Messias* (The Messiah), a vast and in its time popular epic, published between 1748 and 1773.

«Mein schöner Junker, auf Eurem Hut
Schwankt eine Neckenlilie,
Die wächst nur tief in Meeresgrund –
Ihr stammt nicht aus Adams Familie.

«Ihr seid der Wassermann, Ihr wollt
Verlocken des Dorfes Schönen.
Ich hab Euch erkannt, beim ersten Blick,
An Euren fischgrätigen Zähnen.»

Sie schweben auf, sie schweben ab,
In seltsam fremder Weise,
Sie lachen sich an, sie schütteln das Haupt,
Der Junker flüstert leise:

«Mein schönes Fräulein, sagt mir, warum
So eiskalt Eure Hand ist?
Sagt mir, warum so naß der Saum
An Eurem weißen Gewand ist?

«Ich hab Euch erkannt, beim ersten Blick,
An Eurem spöttischen Knixe –
Du bist kein irdisches Menschenkind,
Du bist mein Mühmchen, die Nixe.»

'My handsome sir knight, a nixie's lily waves on your hat, such as only grows deep at the bottom of the sea – you are not of Adam's brood.

'You are the water-sprite, you want to seduce the village beauties. I recognized you at a glance by your fish-bone teeth.'

They bob up and down in a strange, unfamiliar way, they look laughingly at each other, they shake their heads, the knight whispers softly:

'My fair young lady, tell me why your hand is so ice-cold? Tell me why the hem of your white garment is so wet?

'I recognized you at a glance by your mocking curtsy – you are no mortal child, you are my kinswoman the nixie.'

Die Geigen verstummen, der Tanz ist aus,
Es trennen sich höflich die beiden.
Sie kennen sich leider viel zu gut,
Suchen sich jetzt zu vermeiden.

The violins fall silent, the dance is over, the two take leave of each other politely. Alas, they know each other much too well, and now try to avoid each other.

ZUR OLLEA

WINTER

Die Kälte kann wahrlich brennen
Wie Feuer. Die Menschenkinder
Im Schneegestöber rennen
Und laufen immer geschwinder.

O, bittre Winterhärte!
Die Nasen sind erfroren,
Und die Klavierkonzerte
Zerreißen uns die Ohren.

Weit besser ist es im Summer,
Da kann ich im Walde spazieren
Allein mit meinem Kummer
Und Liebeslieder skandieren.

OLLA PODRIDA

Winter

The cold can really burn like fire. Mortals run in a snow-storm and rush along
ever faster.

O, bitter severity of winter! Noses are frozen, and piano recitals tear at our
ears.

It is much better in summer, then I can walk in the forest, alone with my
grief, and scan love-songs.

HEINE

ALTES KAMINSTÜCK

Draußen ziehen weiße Flocken
Durch die Nacht, der Sturm ist laut;
Hier im Stübchen ist es trocken,
Warm und einsam, stillvertraut.

Sinnend sitz ich auf dem Sessel,
An dem knisternden Kamin,
Kochend summt der Wasserkessel
Längst verklungne Melodien.

Und ein Kätzchen sitzt daneben,
Wärmt die Pfötchen an der Glut;
Und die Flammen schweben, weben,
Wundersam wird mir zu Mut.

Dämmernd kommt heraufgestiegen
Manche längst vergeßne Zeit,
Wie mit bunten Maskenzügen
Und verblichner Herrlichkeit.

Schöne Fraun, mit kluger Miene,
Winken süßgeheimnisvoll,
Und dazwischen Harlekine
Springen, lachen, lustigtoll.

The Old Chimney-Corner

Outside, white flakes blow through the night, the storm is loud; here in the little chamber it is dry, warm and secluded, quietly familiar.

I sit in my chair thinking by the crackling fireplace, the boiling kettle hums melodies which died away long ago.

And a little cat sits near by, warming its little paws in the glow; and the flames flicker and interweave, and a strange feeling comes over me.

Many a long-forgotten age rises up in the twilight, as if with colourful masquerades and faded splendour.

Beautiful women with knowing expressions beckon sweetly and mysteriously, and, in between, Harlequins jump and laugh with gay abandon.

Ferne grüßen Marmorgötter,
Traumhaft neben ihnen stehn
Märchenblumen, deren Blätter
In dem Mondenlichte wehn.

Wackelnd kommt herbeigeschwommen
Manches alte Zauberschloß;
Hintendrein geritten kommen
Blanke Ritter, Knappentroß.

Und das alles zieht vorüber,
Schattenhastig übereilt –
Ach! da kocht der Kessel über,
Und das nasse Kätzchen heult.

DIE ENGEL

FREILICH, ein ungläubger Thomas,
Glaub ich an den Himmel nicht,
Den die Kirchenlehre Romas
Und Jerusalems verspricht.

In the distance marble gods give greeting, near them grow dreamlike fairy-tale flowers whose leaves stir in the moonlight.

Many an old magic castle swims uncertainly into view; behind come shining knights on horseback, with their attendant pages.

And all this passes by, hurrying with the speed of shadows – Ah, the kettle's boiling over, and the wet little cat howls.

The Angels

OF course, as a doubting Thomas I don't believe in the Heaven which the doctrine of Rome and Jerusalem promises.

Doch die Existenz der Engel,
Die bezweifelte ich nie;
Lichtgeschöpfe sonder Mängel,
Hier auf Erden wandeln sie.

Nur, genädge Frau, die Flügel
Sprech ich jenen Wesen ab;
Engel gibt es ohne Flügel,
Wie ich selbst gesehen hab.

Lieblich mit den weißen Händen,
Lieblich mit dem schönen Blick
Schützen sie den Menschen, wenden
Von ihm ab das Mißgeschick.

Ihre Huld und ihre Gnaden
Trösten jeden, doch zumeist
Ihn, der doppelt qualbeladen,
Ihn, den man den Dichter heißt.

But I have never doubted the existence of angels; immaculate creatures of light, they walk here on earth.

Only, Madam, I would deny that these creatures have wings; there are angels without wings, as I have seen for myself.

With their white hands and their beautiful gaze they lovingly protect man, and turn ill fortune from him.

Their grace and favour comfort every man, but especially him who bears a double burden of torment, him whom men call poet.

ZEITGEDICHTE

ADAM DER ERSTE

Du schicktest mit dem Flammenschwert
Den himmlischen Gendarmen,
Und jagtest mich aus dem Paradies,
Ganz ohne Recht und Erbarmen!

Ich ziehe fort mit meiner Frau
Nach andren Erdenländern;
Doch daß ich genossen des Wissens Frucht,
Das kannst du nicht mehr ändern.

Du kannst nicht ändern, daß ich weiß,
Wie sehr du klein und nichtig,
Und machst du dich auch noch so sehr
Durch Tod und Donnern wichtig.

O Gott! wie erbärmlich ist doch dies
Consilium abeundi!
Das nenne ich ein Magnifikus
Der Welt, ein Lumen Mundi!

POEMS OF THE TIMES

Adam the First

You sent the divine gendarme with his flaming sword and chased me out of
Paradise entirely without justice and mercy!

I'm making my way with my wife towards other lands; but you can't alter
the fact that I have enjoyed the fruit of Knowledge.

You can't alter the fact that I know how small and insignificant you are,
however important you make yourself out to be with death and thunder.

O God! How pitiful this Consilium abeundi is! That's what I call a real
Magnificus of the world, a Lumen mundi!

131

Vermissen werde ich nimmermehr
Die paradiesischen Räume;
Das war kein wahres Paradies –
Es gab dort verbotene Bäume.

Ich will mein volles Freiheitsrecht!
Find ich die gringste Beschränknis,
Verwandelt sich mir das Paradies
In Hölle und Gefängnis.

WARNUNG

SOLCHE Bücher läßt du drucken!
Teurer Freund, du bist verloren!
Willst du Geld und Ehre haben,
Mußt du dich gehörig ducken.

Nimmer hätt ich dir geraten
So zu sprechen vor dem Volke,
So zu sprechen von den Pfaffen
Und von hohen Potentaten!

I shall certainly never miss the realms of Paradise; it wasn't a true Paradise –
there were forbidden trees there.
I want my full rights of freedom! If I find the slightest restriction, Paradise
turns into a hell and prison for me.

Warning

YOU have books like that printed! Dear friend, you are lost! If you want
money and honour, you must knuckle under in the proper way.
I should never have advised you to speak like that in front of the people, to
speak like that about the priests and the mighty potentates!

Teurer Freund, du bist verloren!
Fürsten haben lange Arme,
Pfaffen haben lange Zungen,
Und das Volk hat lange Ohren!

ENTARTUNG

HAT die Natur sich auch verschlechtert,
Und nimmt sie Menschenfehler an?
Mich dünkt, die Pflanzen und die Tiere,
Sie lügen jetzt wie jedermann.

Ich glaub nicht an der Lilie Keuschheit,
Es buhlt mit ihr der bunte Geck,
Der Schmetterling; der küßt und flattert
Am End mit ihrer Unschuld weg.

Von der Bescheidenheit der Veilchen
Halt ich nicht viel. Die kleine Blum,
Mit den koketten Düften lockt sie,
Und heimlich dürstet sie nach Ruhm.

Dear friend, you are lost! Princes have long arms, priests have long tongues and the people have long ears!

Degeneration

HAS nature too grown bad, and is she adopting human faults? It seems to me that plants and animals now tell lies like everyone else.

I don't believe in the lily's chastity, that gay coxcomb the butterfly plays the wanton with her; he kisses her, and in the end flutters off with her innocence.

I haven't much of an opinion of the violet's modesty. This little flower allures with her coquettish scent, and secretly she's thirsting for renown.

Ich zweifle auch, ob sie empfindet,
Die Nachtigall, das was sie singt;
Sie übertreibt und schluchzt und trillert
Nur aus Routine, wie mich dünkt.

Die Wahrheit schwindet von der Erde,
Auch mit der Treu ist es vorbei.
Die Hunde wedeln noch und stinken
Wie sonst, doch sind sie nicht mehr treu.

DIE TENDENZ

Deutscher Sänger! sing und preise
Deutsche Freiheit, daß dein Lied
Unsrer Seelen sich bemeistre
Und zu Taten uns begeistre,
In Marseillerhymnenweise.

Girre nicht mehr wie ein Werther,
Welcher nur für Lotten glüht –
Was die Glocke hat geschlagen
Sollst du deinem Volke sagen,
Rede Dolche, rede Schwerter!

I'm also doubtful whether the nightingale feels what she's singing about; she exaggerates and sobs and trills away purely out of routine, it seems to me.

Truth is disappearing from the world, and loyalty too is a thing of the past. Dogs still wag their tails and stink, as before, but they are no longer loyal.

Tendentiousness

German singer! sing and praise German freedom, let your song take possession of our souls and inspire us to deeds as the Marseillaise does.

Stop cooing like a Werther, glowing only for his Lotte – you must tell your people what hour has struck, speak daggers, speak swords!

Sei nicht mehr die weiche Flöte,
Das idyllische Gemüt –
Sei des Vaterlands Posaune,
Sei Kanone, sei Kartaune,
Blase, schmettre, donnre, töte!

Blase, schmettre, donnre täglich,
Bis der letzte Dränger flieht –
Singe nur in dieser Richtung,
Aber halte deine Dichtung
Nur so allgemein als möglich.

DER KAISER VON CHINA

MEIN Vater war ein trockner Taps,
Ein nüchterner Duckmäuser,
Ich aber trinke meinen Schnaps
Und bin ein großer Kaiser.

Das ist ein Zaubertrank! Ich habs
Entdeckt in meinem Gemüte:
Sobald ich getrunken meinen Schnaps,
Steht China ganz in Blüte.

Cease to be a gentle flute, idyllic temperament, be your fatherland's trumpet, be a cannon, be a siege-piece, blow, ring out, thunder, kill!

Blow, ring out, thunder daily, until the last oppressor flees – point your song in this direction, but keep your words as general as possible.

The Emperor of China

MY father was a dry old stick, an abstemious dodger, but I drink my schnaps and am a great emperor.

It is a magic potion! I have discovered in my mind that as soon as I've drunk my schnaps, all China is in bloom.

Das Reich der Mitte verwandelt sich dann
In einen Blumenanger,
Ich selber werde fast ein Mann
Und meine Frau wird schwanger.

Allüberall ist Überfluß,
Und es gesunden die Kranken;
Mein Hofweltweiser Confusius
Bekömmt die klarsten Gedanken.

Der Pumpernickel des Soldats
Wird Mandelkuchen – O Freude!
Und alle Lumpen meines Staats
Spazieren in Samt und Seide.

Die Mandarinenritterschaft,
Die invaliden Köpfe,
Gewinnen wieder Jugendkraft
Und schütteln ihre Zöpfe.

Die große Pagode, Symbol und Hort
Des Glaubens, ist fertig geworden;
Die letzten Juden taufen sich dort
Und kriegen den Drachenorden.

The Middle Kingdom then changes to a flowery pasture, I myself almost become a man, and my wife becomes pregnant.

Everywhere there is plenty, and the sick get well again; my court sage Confuse-ius has very clear thoughts.

The soldiers' pumpernickel becomes almond cake – what joy! And all the ragamuffins in my state walk out in velvet and silk.

The mandarin knights, the old invalids, regain their youthful vigour and shake their pigtails.

The great pagoda, symbol and shield of faith, is completed; the last of the Jews get baptized there and are awarded the Order of the Dragon.

Es schwindet der Geist der Revolution
Und es rufen die edelsten Mandschu:
Wir wollen keine Konstitution,
Wir wollen den Stock, den Kantschu!*

Wohl haben die Schüler Äskulaps
Das Trinken mir widerraten,
Ich aber trinke meinen Schnaps
Zum Besten meiner Staaten.

Und noch einen Schnaps, und noch einen Schnaps!
Das schmeckt wie lauter Manna!
Mein Volk ist glücklich, hats auch den Raps,
Und jubelt: Hosianna!

ZUR BERUHIGUNG

WIR schlafen ganz, wie Brutus schlief –
Doch jener erwachte und bohrte tief
In Cäsars Brust das kalte Messer!
Die Römer waren Tyrannenfresser.

The spirit of revolution is vanishing, and the noblest Manchus shout: we
don't want a constitution, we want the rod, the whip!

Aesculapius's pupils have certainly advised me to give up drink, but I drink
my schnaps to the welfare of my states.

And one more schnaps, and yet another! It tastes like the purest manna!
My people are happy even if they suffer from sudden accesses of madness, and
shout 'Hosannah!' for joy.

To Set Your Mind at Rest

WE sleep just as Brutus slept – but he awoke and buried the cold knife deep in
Caesar's breast! The Romans were great devourers of tyrants.

---

* From the Turkish Kamchi, a whip.

Wir sind keine Römer, wir rauchen Tabak.
Ein jedes Volk hat seinen Geschmack,
Ein jedes Volk hat seine Größe;
In Schwaben kocht man die besten Klöße.

Wir sind Germanen, gemütlich und brav,
Wir schlafen gesunden Pflanzenschlaf,
Und wenn wir erwachen, pflegt uns zu dürsten,
Doch nicht nach dem Blute unserer Fürsten.

Wir sind so treu wie Eichenholz,
Auch Lindenholz, drauf sind wir stolz;
Im Land der Eichen und der Linden
Wird niemals sich ein Brutus finden.

Und wenn auch ein Brutus unter uns wär,
Den Cäsar fänd er nimmermehr,
Vergeblich würd er den Cäsar suchen;
Wir haben gute Pfefferkuchen.

Wir haben sechsunddreißig Herrn
(Ist nicht zu viel!), und einen Stern
Trägt jeder schützend auf seinem Herzen,
Und er braucht nicht zu fürchten die Iden des Märzen.

We aren't Romans, we smoke tobacco. Every nation has its own tastes, every nation has its own greatness; in Swabia they cook the best dumplings.

We are Germans, easy-going and worthy, we sleep a sound, vegetable sleep, and when we awake, we are usually thirsty, but not for the blood of our princes.

We are as trusty as oak, as lime-wood too, and we're proud of it; in the land of oaks and limes there will never be a Brutus.

And if there did happen to be a Brutus among us, he would never find his Caesar, he would search for Caesar in vain; we have good ginger-bread.

We have thirty-six rulers (that's not too many!), and each of them wears a protecting star on his breast and need not fear the Ides of March.

Wir nennen sie Väter, und Vaterland
Benennen wir dasjenige Land,
Das erbeigentümlich gehört den Fürsten;
Wir lieben auch Sauerkraut mit Würsten.

Wenn unser Vater spazieren geht,
Ziehn wir den Hut mit Pietät;
Deutschland, die fromme Kinderstube,
Ist keine römische Mördergrube.

WARTET NUR

Weil ich so ganz vorzüglich blitze,
Glaubt Ihr, daß ich nicht donnern könnt!
Ihr irrt Euch sehr, denn ich besitze
Gleichfalls fürs Donnern ein Talent.

Es wird sich grausenhaft bewähren,
Wenn einst erscheint der rechte Tag;
Dann sollt Ihr meine Stimme hören,
Das Donnerwort, den Wetterschlag.

We call them fathers, and fatherland is the name we give to the land which
by hereditary right belongs to the princes; we're also very fond of sauerkraut
and sausages.

When our father goes for a walk we take off our hats with reverence; Germany, that pious nursery, is no Roman cut-throats' den.

Just Wait

Because I'm so good at making lightning you think I couldn't thunder!
You're very much mistaken, for I've also got a gift for thundering.

This will be proved frighteningly true when the right day dawns; then you
shall hear my voice, the mighty word, the thunderclap.

Gar manche Eiche wird zersplittern
An jenem Tag der wilde Sturm,
Gar mancher Palast wird erzittern
Und stürzen mancher Kirchenturm!

NACHTGEDANKEN

Denk ich an Deutschland in der Nacht,
Dann bin ich um den Schlaf gebracht,
Ich kann nicht mehr die Augen schließen,
Und meine heißen Tränen fließen.

Die Jahre kommen und vergehn!
Seit ich die Mutter nicht gesehn,
Zwölf Jahre sind schon hingegangen;
Es wächst mein Sehnen und Verlangen.

Mein Sehnen und Verlangen wächst.
Die alte Frau hat mich behext,
Ich denke immer an die alte,
Die alte Frau, die Gott erhalte!

The raging storm will that day cleave many an oak, many a palace will tremble and many a church-tower crash!

Night Thoughts

When at night my thoughts turn to Germany there is no chance of sleep, I cannot close my eyes, and my hot tears flow.

The years come and go. Since I last saw my mother, twelve years have gone by; my longing and desire increase.

My longing and desire increase. The old lady has bewitched me, I constantly think of the old lady, whom God preserve!

Die alte Frau hat mich so lieb,
Und in den Briefen, die sie schrieb,
Seh ich, wie ihre Hand gezittert,
Wie tief das Mutterherz erschüttert.

Die Mutter liegt mir stets im Sinn.
Zwölf lange Jahre flossen hin,
Zwölf lange Jahre sind verflossen,
Seit ich sie nicht ans Herz geschlossen.

Deutschland hat ewigen Bestand,
Es ist ein kerngesundes Land,
Mit seinen Eichen, seinen Linden,
Werd ich es immer wiederfinden.

Nach Deutschland lechzt ich nicht so sehr,
Wenn nicht die Mutter dorten wär;
Das Vaterland wird nie verderben,
Jedoch die alte Frau kann sterben.

Seit ich das Land verlassen hab,
So viele sanken dort ins Grab,
Die ich geliebt – wenn ich sie zähle,
So will verbluten meine Seele.

The old lady loves me so much, and from her letters I can see how her hand shook, how deeply her maternal heart was moved.

My mother is constantly in my mind. Twelve long years have slipped by, twelve long years have slipped away since I last held her to my heart.

Germany will last for ever, it is a thoroughly healthy land, I will always find it again with its oaks and its lime-trees.

I wouldn't long for Germany so much if my mother were not there; my fatherland will never perish, but the old lady may die.

Since I left the country so many people whom I loved have died and been buried there – when I count them, my soul bleeds.

Und zählen muß ich – Mit der Zahl
Schwillt immer höher meine Qual,
Mir ist, als wälzten sich die Leichen
Auf meine Brust – Gottlob! sie weichen!

Gottlob! durch meine Fenster bricht
Französisch heitres Tageslicht;
Es kommt mein Weib, schön wie der Morgen,
Und lächelt fort die deutschen Sorgen.

Nachlese

DEUTSCHLAND
(Geschrieben im Sommer 1840)

DEUTSCHLAND ist noch ein kleines Kind,
Doch die Sonne ist seine Amme;
Sie säugt es nicht mit stiller Milch,
Sie säugt es mit wilder Flamme.

And yet I must count them – as the number rises, my grief grows ever greater; I feel as if the corpses were being heaped on my chest – thank God, they yield!
Thank God! cheerful French daylight breaks through my windows; my wife comes, as fair as the morning, and smiles away my German cares.

Supplementary Poems

Germany

(Written in the Summer of 1840)

GERMANY is still a small child, but the sun is his nurse, she suckles him not with peaceful milk, but with a wild flame.

Bei solcher Nahrung wächst man schnell
Und kocht das Blut in den Adern.
Ihr Nachbarskinder, hütet euch
Mit dem jungen Burschen zu hadern!

Es ist ein täppisches Rieselein,
Reißt aus dem Boden die Eiche,
Und schlägt euch damit den Rücken wund
Und die Köpfe windelweiche.

Dem Siegfried gleicht er, dem edlen Fant,
Von dem wir singen und sagen;
Der hat, nachdem er geschmiedet sein Schwert,
Den Amboß entzwei geschlagen!

Ja, du wirst einst wie Siegfried sein
Und töten den häßlichen Drachen,
Heisa! wie freudig vom Himmel herab
Wird deine Frau Amme lachen!

Du wirst ihn töten, und seinen Hort,
Die Reichskleinodien, besitzen.
Heisa! wie wird auf deinem Haupt
Die goldne Krone blitzen!

With nourishment like that one grows fast and blood pulses in the veins. Neighbours' children, take care not to quarrel with the young boy!

He's an awkward little giant, he tears the oak-tree out of the earth, and beats your back with it till you're sore, and smashes your head in.

He's like Siegfried, the noble stripling of whom we sing and tell tales; after he had forged his sword he cut the anvil in two.

Yes, one day you'll be like Siegfried and kill the ugly dragon; hurrah! how joyously your nurse will laugh down at you from the heavens!

You will kill it, and own its hoard, the imperial jewels. Hurrah! how the golden crown will sparkle on your head!

AN GEORG HERWEGH

HERWEGH, du eiserne Lerche,
Mit klirrendem Jubel steigst du empor
Zum heiligen Sonnenlichte!
Ward wirklich der Winter zu nichte?
Steht wirklich Deutschland im Frühlingsflor?

Herwegh, du eiserne Lerche,
Weil du so himmelhoch dich schwingst,
Hast du die Erde aus dem Gesichte
Verloren – Nur in deinem Gedichte
Lebt jener Lenz, den du besingst.

LOBGESÄNGE AUF KÖNIG LUDWIG

I

DAS ist Herr Ludwig von Bayerland,
Desgleichen gibt es wenig;
Das Volk der Bavaren verehrt in ihm
Den angestammelten König.

To Georg Herwegh

HERWEGH, you iron lark, with what rattling jubilation do you rise up into the holy sunlight! Has Winter really been overcome? Is Germany really decked in Spring blossom?

Herwegh, you iron lark, because you are soaring so high in the heavens you have quite lost sight of the earth – only in your poem does the Spring live of which you sing.

Songs in Praise of King Ludwig

I

THAT is Herr Ludwig of Bavaria, there aren't many like him; the Bavarian people honour in him their stuttering, hereditary king.

Er liebt die Kunst, und die schönsten Fraun
Die läßt er porträtieren;
Er geht in diesem gemalten Serail
Als Kunst-Eunuch spazieren.

Bei Regensburg läßt er erbaun
Eine marmorne Schädelstätte,
Und er hat höchstselbst für jeden Kopf
Verfertigt die Etikette.

«Walhallagenossen», ein Meisterwerk,
Worin er jedweden Mannes
Verdienste, Charakter und Taten gerühmt,
Von Teut bis Schinderhannes.*

Nur Luther, der Dickkopf, fehlt in Walhall,
Und es feiert ihn nicht der Walhall-Wisch;
In Naturaliensammlungen fehlt
Oft unter den Fischen der Walfisch.

Herr Ludwig ist ein großer Poet,
Und singt er, so stürzt Apollo
Vor ihm auf die Kniee und bittet und fleht:
Halt ein! ich werde sonst toll, o!

He is an art-lover, and he has the greatest beauties sit for their portraits; he walks about in this painted seraglio as an art-eunuch.

He has had a marble Golgotha built near Regensburg, and with his very own hand he has made the label for each skull.

'The Companions of Valhalla' – a master-work in which he praises the merits, character and deeds of everyone from Teut to Schinderhannes.*

Only that stubborn fellow Luther is missing from Valhalla, the Valhalla records don't celebrate him; in natural history collections the whale is often missing from the fish section.

Herr Ludwig is a great poet, and when he sings Apollo falls on his knees before him and entreats and prays: 'Stop! or I shall go mad!'

* Captain of a Rhineland robber band, executed in 1803.

Herr Ludwig ist ein mutiger Held,
Wie Otto, das Kind, sein Söhnchen;
Der kriegte den Durchfall zu Athen,
Und hat dort besudelt sein Thrönchen.

Stirbt einst Herr Ludwig, so kanonisiert
Zu Rom ihn der heilige Vater –
Die Glorie paßt für ein solches Gesicht,
Wie Manschetten für unseren Kater!

Sobald auch die Affen und Känguruhs
Zum Christentum sich bekehren,
Sie werden gewiß Sankt Ludewig
Als Schutzpatron verehren.

III

Zu München in der Schloßkapell
Steht eine schöne Madonne;
Sie trägt in den Armen ihr Jesulein,
Der Welt und des Himmels Wonne.

Herr Ludwig is a bold hero, like little Otto, his son; he got diarrhoea at Athens and dirtied his little throne.

If Herr Ludwig should one day die, then the Holy Father in Rome will canonize him – the halo suits a face like that as cuffs would our tom-cat!

As soon as monkeys and kangaroos are converted to Christianity, they will surely honour St Ludwig as their patron saint.

III

In the castle chapel in Munich there stands a beautiful Madonna; she carries her little Jesus, joy of the world and of heaven, in her arms.

Als Ludewig von Bayerland
Das Heiligenbild erblicket,
Da kniete er nieder andachtsvoll
Und stotterte selig verzücket:

«Maria, Himmelskönigin,
Du Fürstin sonder Mängel!
Aus Heilgen besteht dein Hofgesind
Und deine Diener sind Engel.

«Geflügelte Pagen warten dir auf,
Sie flechten dir Blumen und Bänder
Ins goldene Haar, sie tragen dir nach
Die Schleppe deiner Gewänder.

«Maria, reiner Morgenstern,
Du Lilie sonder Makel,
Du hast so manches Wunder getan,
So manches fromme Mirakel –

«O, laß aus deiner Gnaden Born
Auch mir ein Tröpflein gleiten!
Gib mir ein Zeichen deiner Huld,
Der hochgebenedeiten!» –

When Ludwig of Bavaria saw the statue of the saint he knelt down devoutly and stuttered in blissful rapture:
'Mary, Queen of Heaven, immaculate Sovereign Lady! Your household consists of saints and your servants are angels.
'Winged pages wait upon you, they bind flowers and ribbons into your golden hair, they carry behind you the train of your garments.
'Mary, pure morning star, lily without blemish, you have wrought so many wonders, so many holy miracles –
'Oh, let me too receive a drop from the well of your grace! Give me a sign of your favour, which all men praise!' –

Die Muttergottes bewegt sich alsbald,
Sichtbar bewegt sich ihr Mündchen,
Sie schüttelt ungeduldig das Haupt
Und spricht zu ihrem Kindchen:

«Es ist ein Glück, daß ich auf dem Arm
Dich trage und nicht mehr im Bauche,
Ein Glück, daß ich vor dem Versehn
Mich nicht mehr zu fürchten brauche.

«Hätt ich in meiner Schwangerschaft
Erblickt den häßlichen Toren,
Ich hätte gewiß einen Wechselbalg
Statt eines Gottes geboren.»

DIE SCHLESISCHEN WEBER

Im düstern Auge keine Träne,
Sie sitzen am Webstuhl und fletschen die Zähne:
Deutschland, wir weben dein Leichentuch,
Wir weben hinein den dreifachen Fluch –
    Wir weben, wir weben!

The Mother of God at once moves, her little mouth moves visibly, she shakes her head impatiently and says to her little child:

'It's lucky that I'm carrying you in my arms and not in my belly any longer, lucky that I need no longer fear a miscarriage.

'If I'd seen this ugly idiot during my pregnancy I would surely have given birth to a changeling instead of a God.'

The Silesian Weavers

No tears in their sombre eyes, they sit at the loom and bare their teeth: Germany, we are weaving your shroud, we are weaving into it the threefold curse – we are weaving, we are weaving!

Ein Fluch dem Gotte, zu dem wir gebeten
In Winterskälte und Hungersnöten;
Wir haben vergebens gehofft und geharrt,
Er hat uns geäfft und gefoppt und genarrt —
   Wir weben, wir weben!

Ein Fluch dem König, dem König der Reichen,
Den unser Elend nicht konnte erweichen,
Der den letzten Groschen von uns erpreßt
Und uns wie Hunde erschießen läßt —
   Wir weben, wir weben!

Ein Fluch dem falschen Vaterlande,
Wo nur gedeihen Schmach und Schande,
Wo jede Blume früh geknickt,
Wo Fäulnis und Moder den Wurm erquickt —
   Wir weben, wir weben!

Das Schiffchen fliegt, der Webstuhl kracht,
Wir weben emsig Tag und Nacht —
Altdeutschland, wir weben dein Leichentuch,
Wir weben hinein den dreifachen Fluch,
   Wir weben, wir weben!

A curse on the God to whom we prayed in the winter's cold and in time of famine; we have hoped and waited in vain, he has mocked and fooled and deluded us — we are weaving, we are weaving!

A curse on the king, the king of the rich, whom our wretchedness could not soften, who has extorted our last penny from us, and has us shot like dogs — we are weaving, we are weaving!

A curse on our false fatherland where only disgrace and shame flourish, where every flower is soon broken, where putrefaction and decay refresh the worm — we are weaving, we are weaving!

The shuttle flies, the loom creaks, we are weaving busily day and night — old Germany, we are weaving your shroud, we are weaving into it the three-fold curse, we are weaving, we are weaving!

ZUR NOTIZ

Die Philister, die Beschränkten,
Diese geistig Eingeengten,
Darf man nie und nimmer necken.
Aber weite, kluge Herzen
Wissen stets in unsren Scherzen
Lieb und Freundschaft zu entdecken.

GUTER RAT

Gib ihren wahren Namen immer
In deiner Fabel ihren Helden.
Wagst du es nicht, ergehts dir schlimmer:
Zu deinem Eselbilde melden
Sich gleich ein Dutzend graue Toren —
«Das sind ja meine langen Ohren!»
Ruft jeder, «dieses gräßlich grimme
Gebreie ist ja meine Stimme!
Der Esel bin ich! Obgleich nicht genannt,

Nota Bene

The Philistines, those bigoted, narrow-minded people, may never, never be teased. But generous, wise hearts always know how to discover love and friendship in our jokes.

Good Advice

Always give their proper names to the heroes in your fables. If you don't dare to, it'll be all the worse for you: a dozen grey fools will promptly claim to be the original of your ass's portrait — 'Those are my long ears!' they all cry, 'that hideous, angry braying is my voice! That donkey is me! Although I'm

Erkennt mich doch mein Vaterland,
Mein Vaterland Germania!
Der Esel bin ich! I-A! I-A!» –
Hast einen Dummkopf schonen wollen,
Und zwölfe sind es, die dir grollen.

not named my native land will recognize me at once, Germany, my native
land! That donkey is me! Hee-haw! Hee-haw!' – You wanted to spare one
fool, and there are twelve who bear you a grudge.

ATTA TROLL. EIN SOMMERNACHTSTRAUM

ATTA TROLL. A MIDSUMMER-NIGHT'S
DREAM

Aus dem sonngen Goldgrund lachen
Violette Bergeshöhen,
Und am Abhang klebt ein Dörfchen,
Wie ein keckes Vogelnest.

Als ich dort hinaufklomm, fand ich,
Daß die Alten ausgeflogen
Und zurückgeblieben nur
Junge Brut, die noch nicht flügge.

Hübsche Bübchen, kleine Mädchen,
Fast vermummt in scharlachroten
Oder weißen wollnen Kappen;
Spielten Brautfahrt, auf dem Marktplatz.

Ließen sich im Spiel nicht stören,
Und ich sah, wie der verliebte
Mäuseprinz pathetisch kniete
Vor der Katzenkaiserstochter.

Caput XIV

From the sunny, golden background violet mountain-heights laugh, and on the slopes hangs a little village, like a bold bird's nest.

When I climbed up to it I found that the old birds had flown off, and only the young who were not yet fully fledged had remained behind.

Pretty little boys, small girls, almost hidden inside scarlet-red or white woollen caps; they were playing at weddings on the market-place.

They refused to be disturbed in their game, and I watched the enamoured mouse-prince kneel with due solemnity before the cat-emperor's daughter.

Armer Prinz! Er wird vermählt
Mit der Schönen. Mürrisch zankt sie,
Und sie beißt ihn, und sie frißt ihn;
Tote Maus, das Spiel ist aus.

Fast den ganzen Tag verweilt ich
Bei den Kindern, und wir schwatzten
Sehr vertraut. Sie wollten wissen,
Wer ich sei und was ich triebe?

Lieben Freunde, – sprach ich – Deutschland
Heißt das Land, wo ich geboren;
Bären gibt es dort in Menge,
Und ich wurde Bärenjäger.

Manchem zog ich dort das Fell
Über seine Bärenohren.
Wohl mitunter ward ich selber
Stark gezaust von Bärentatzen.

Doch mit schlechtgeleckten Tölpeln
Täglich mich herumzubalgen
In der teuren Heimat, dessen
Ward ich endlich überdrüssig.

Poor prince! He is being married to the beauty. She scolds sullenly, and
she bites him and she eats him up; dead mouse, the game is over.

I stayed on almost the whole day with the children, and we chatted very
intimately. They wanted to know who I was and what I did.

Dear friends, I said, Germany is the name of the land where I was born;
there are plenty of bears there, and I became a bear-hunter.

I pulled the skin over more than one bear's ears. And from time to time I
was myself badly torn by a bear's claws.

But in the end I grew tired of scuffling daily in my beloved homeland
with louts who had not yet been licked into shape.

Und ich bin hierhergekommen,
Bessres Weidwerk aufzusuchen;
Meine Kraft will ich versuchen
An dem großen Atta Troll.

Dieser ist ein edler Gegner,
Meiner würdig. Ach! in Deutschland
Hab ich manchen Kampf bestanden,
Wo ich mich des Sieges schämte. ‒ ‒

Als ich Abschied nahm, da tanzten
Um mich her die kleinen Wesen
Eine Ronde, und sie sangen:
Girofflino, Giroflette!

Keck und zierlich trat zuletzt
Vor mir hin die Allerjüngste,
Knickste zweimal, dreimal, viermal,
Und sie sang mit feiner Stimme:

«Wenn der König mir begegnet,
Mach ich ihm zwei Reverenzen,
Und begegnet mir die Köngin,
Mach ich Reverenzen drei.

And I've come here to seek better sport; I want to try my strength with the great Atta Troll.

He is a noble opponent, worthy of me. Ah! in Germany I have come through many a fight where I was ashamed of my victory. ‒ ‒

When I took my leave the little creatures danced a round-dance all about me, and they sang: Girofflino, Giroflette!

Boldly and daintily the youngest of all the girls at last stepped up to me, curtsied twice, thrice, four times, and she sang with a pretty voice:

'When the King meets me, I make him two obeisances, and when the Queen meets me I make three obeisances.

«Aber kommt mir gar der Teufel
In den Weg mit seinen Hörnern,
Knicks ich zweimal, dreimal, viermal –
Girofflino, Giroflette!»

Girofflino, Giroflette!
Wiederholt' das Chor, und neckend
Wirbelte um meine Beine
Sich der Ringeltanz und Singsang.

Während ich ins Tal hinabstieg,
Scholl mir nach, verhallend lieblich,
Immerfort, wie Vogelzwitschern:
Girofflino, Giroflette!

'But if the devil himself with his horns should cross my path I curtsy twice,
thrice, four times – Girofflino, Giroflette!'
Girofflino, Giroflette! the chorus repeated, and teasingly the round-dance
and sing-song twisted about my legs.
As I made my way down into the valley there constantly rang after me,
dying away charmingly, like the twittering of birds: Girofflino, Giroflette!

DEUTSCHLAND. EIN WINTERMÄRCHEN

GERMANY. A WINTER'S TALE

Ein feuchter Wind, ein kahles Land,
Die Chaise wackelt im Schlamme,
Doch singt es und klingt es in meinem Gemüt:
Sonne, du klagende Flamme!

Das ist der Schlußreim des alten Lieds,
Das oft meine Amme gesungen –
«Sonne, du klagende Flamme!» das hat
Wie Waldhornruf geklungen.

Es kommt im Lied ein Mörder vor,
Der lebt' in Lust und Freude;
Man findet ihn endlich im Walde gehenkt,
An einer grauen Weide.

Des Mörders Todesurteil war
Genagelt am Weidenstamme;
Das haben die Rächer der Feme* getan –
Sonne, du klagende Flamme!

Caput XIV

A DAMP wind, a bare land, the post-chaise lurches in the mud, but in my mind there is a singing and a ringing: Sun, thou accusing flame!

That is the final rhyme of the old song which my nurse often sang – 'Sun, thou accusing flame!' – it rang out like a horn-call.

A murderer appears in the song who lived in pleasure and joy; they finally find him in the forest, hanging from a grey willow.

The murderer's death-sentence was nailed to the willow's stem; that was the work of the avengers of the secret court – sun, thou accusing flame!

* A secret tribunal in the middle ages, especially powerful in Westphalia.

Die Sonne war Kläger, sie hatte bewirkt,
Daß man den Mörder verdamme.
Ottilie hatte sterbend geschrien:
Sonne, du klagende Flamme!

Und denk ich des Liedes, so denk ich auch
Der Amme, der lieben Alten;
Ich sehe wieder ihr braunes Gesicht,
Mit allen Runzeln und Falten.

Sie war geboren im Münsterland,
Und wußte, in großer Menge,
Gespenstergeschichten, grausenhaft,
Und Märchen und Volksgesänge.

Wie pochte mein Herz, wenn die alte Frau
Von der Königstochter erzählte,
Die einsam auf der Heide saß
Und die goldnen Haare strählte.

Die Gänse mußte sie hüten dort
Als Gänsemagd, und trieb sie
Am Abend die Gänse wieder durchs Tor,
Gar traurig stehen blieb sie.

The sun was the accuser, she brought about the sentence of the murderer.
Ottilie had cried with her dying breath: Sun, thou accusing flame!

And when I think of the song, I also think of my dear old nurse; I see again
her brown face with all its wrinkles and folds.

She was born in the Münster region and knew a great number of terrifying
ghost-stories, and fairy-tales and folksongs.

How my heart beat when the old woman told of the king's daughter who
sat alone on the heath and combed her golden hair.

As goose-girl she had to mind the geese there, and in the evening when she
drove the geese back through the gate she stood there very sadly.

Denn angenagelt über dem Tor
Sah sie ein Roßhaupt ragen,
Das war der Kopf des armen Pferds,
Das sie in die Fremde getragen.

Die Königstochter seufzte tief:
O, Falada, daß du hangest!
Der Pferdekopf herunter rief:
O wehe, daß du gangest!

Die Königstochter seufzte tief:
Wenn das meine Mutter wüßte!
Der Pferdekopf herunter rief:
Ihr Herze brechen müßte!

Mit stockendem Atem horchte ich hin,
Wenn die Alte ernster und leiser
Zu sprechen begann und vom Rotbart sprach,
Von unserem heimlichen Kaiser.

Sie hat mir versichert, er sei nicht tot,
Wie da glauben die Gelehrten,
Er hause versteckt in einem Berg
Mit seinen Waffengefährten.

For, nailed above the gate, she saw a horse's head sticking out, it was the head of the poor horse which had carried her into a foreign land.

The king's daughter sighed deeply: O Falada, that you should hang there! The horse's head called down to her: Alack, that you went away!

The king's daughter sighed deeply: If my mother only knew! The horse's head called down to her: Her heart would break!

With bated breath I listened attentively as the old woman began to speak more gravely and quietly, and spoke of Redbeard, our secret emperor.

She assured me he is not dead, as the scholars believe, he lives hidden away in a mountain with his comrades-in-arms.

Kyffhäuser ist der Berg genannt,
Und drinnen ist eine Höhle;
Die Ampeln erhellen so geisterhaft
Die hochgewölbten Säle.

Ein Marstall ist der erste Saal,
Und dorten kann man sehen
Viel tausend Pferde, blankgeschirrt,
Die an den Krippen stehen.

Sie sind gesattelt und gezäumt,
Jedoch von diesen Rossen
Kein einziges wiehert, kein einziges stampft,
Sind still, wie aus Eisen gegossen.

Im zweiten Saale, auf der Streu,
Sieht man Soldaten liegen,
Viel tausend Soldaten, bärtiges Volk,
Mit kriegerisch trotzigen Zügen.

Sie sind gerüstet von Kopf bis Fuß,
Doch alle diese Braven,
Sie rühren sich nicht, bewegen sich nicht,
Sie liegen fest und schlafen.

Kyffhäuser is the name of the mountain, and inside there is a cave; the hanging-lamps light up the high-vaulted halls so spookily.

A royal stable is the first hall, and you can see there many thousands of horses, with shining harness, standing at the mangers.

They are saddled and bridled, yet not one of these horses whinnies, not one of them stamps, they are as motionless as if cast in iron.

In the second hall you can see soldiers lying in the straw, many thousands of soldiers, bearded men, with warlike, defiant features.

They are armed from head to foot, but all these gallant men do not move, do not stir, they lie tight and sleep.

Hochaufgestapelt im dritten Saal
Sind Schwerter, Streitäxte, Speere,
Harnische, Helme, von Silber und Stahl,
Altfränkische Feuergewehre.

Sehr wenig Kanonen, jedoch genug
Um eine Trophäe zu bilden.
Hoch ragt daraus eine Fahne hervor,
Die Farbe ist schwarz-rot-gülden.

Der Kaiser bewohnt den vierten Saal.
Schon seit Jahrhunderten sitzt er
Auf steinernem Stuhl, am steinernen Tisch,
Das Haupt auf den Armen stützt er.

Sein Bart, der bis zur Erde wuchs,
Ist rot wie Feuerflammen,
Zuweilen zwinkert er mit dem Aug,
Zieht manchmal die Braunen zusammen.

Schläft er oder denkt er nach?
Man kanns nicht genau ermitteln;
Doch wenn die rechte Stunde kommt,
Wird er gewaltig sich rütteln.

Piled up high in the third hall are swords, battle-axes, spears, suits of armour, helmets of silver and steel, old-fashioned fire-arms.

Very few cannon, yet enough to form a trophy. A banner towers high above it, the colour is black, red and gold.

The emperor lives in the fourth hall. For centuries now he has been sitting there on a stone seat at a stone table, he rests his head on his arms.

His beard, which has grown to the floor, is red like flames of fire, at times he blinks his eyes, and sometimes he puckers his brows.

Is he asleep, or is he meditating? You can't exactly tell; but when the right hour comes, he will shake himself mightily.

Die gute Fahne ergreift er dann
Und ruft: Zu Pferd! zu Pferde!
Sein reisiges Volk erwacht und springt
Lautrasselnd empor von der Erde.

Ein jeder schwingt sich auf sein Roß,
Das wiehert und stampft mit den Hufen!
Sie reiten hinaus in die klirrende Welt,
Und die Trompeten rufen.

Sie reiten gut, sie schlagen gut,
Sie haben ausgeschlafen.
Der Kaiser hält ein strenges Gericht,
Er will die Mörder bestrafen –

Die Mörder, die gemeuchelt einst
Die teure, wundersame,
Goldlockigte Jungfrau Germania –
Sonne, du klagende Flamme!

Wohl mancher, der sich geborgen geglaubt,
Und lachend auf seinem Schloß saß,
Er wird nicht entgehen dem rächenden Strang,
Dem Zorne Barbarossas! – – –

He will then grasp his trusty banner and call: To horse! to horse! His war-like men will then awake and leap up from the floor, clattering loudly.

Every man will leap on to his horse, which will whinny and stamp its hooves! They will ride out into the noisy world, and the trumpets will call.

They ride well, they strike good blows, they have slept their fill. The emperor sits in strict judgement, he will punish the murderers –

The murderers who once assassinated the dear, strange, golden-haired maiden Germania – sun, thou accusing flame!

Many a man indeed who thought himself safe and sat laughing in his castle will not escape the avenging rope and Barbarossa's anger! – –

Wie klingen sie lieblich, wie klingen sie süß,
Die Märchen der alten Amme!
Mein abergläubisches Herze jauchzt:
Sonne, du klagende Flamme!

CAPUT XV

EIN feiner Regen prickelt herab,
Eiskalt, wie Nähnadelspitzen.
Die Pferde bewegen traurig den Schwanz,
Sie waten im Kot und schwitzen.

Der Postillon stößt in sein Horn,
Ich kenne das alte Getute –
«Es reiten drei Reiter zum Tor hinaus!» –
Es wird mir so dämmrig zu Mute.

Mich schläferte und ich entschlief,
Und siehe! mir träumte am Ende,
Daß ich mich in dem Wunderberg
Beim Kaiser Rotbart befände.

How lovely and sweet they sound, my old nurse's tales! My superstitious
heart shouts with joy: Sun, thou accusing flame!

Caput XV

A FINE rain comes stinging down, ice-cold, like needle-points. The horses
shake their tails sadly, they wade through the mud and are sweating.

The postillion blows his horn, I know the old song he's tooting: 'Three
horsemen ride out of the gate.' – A twilight feeling comes over me.

I was sleepy and I fell asleep, and behold! I dreamt in the end that I was in
the magic mountain with the Emperor Barbarossa.

Er saß nicht mehr auf steinernem Stuhl,
Am steinernen Tisch, wie ein Steinbild;
Auch sah er nicht so ehrwürdig aus,
Wie man sich gewöhnlich einbildt.

Er watschelte durch die Säle herum
Mit mir im trauten Geschwätze.
Er zeigte wie ein Antiquar
Mir seine Kuriosa und Schätze.

Im Saale der Waffen erklärte er mir,
Wie man sich der Kolben bediene,
Von einigen Schwertern rieb er den Rost
Mit seinem Hermeline.

Er nahm ein Pfauenwedel zur Hand,
Und reinigte vom Staube
Gar manchen Harnisch, gar manchen Helm,
Auch manche Pickelhaube.

Die Fahne stäubte er gleichfalls ab,
Und er sprach: «Mein größter Stolz ist,
Daß noch keine Motte die Seide zerfraß,
Und auch kein Wurm im Holz ist.»

He no longer sat on his stone seat at the stone table, like a stone statue; and he did not look as venerable as one usually imagines him to be.

He was waddling about in the halls, in intimate conversation with me. He showed me his curiosities and treasures like an antique dealer.

In the armoury he explained to me how you wield a mace; he rubbed the rust from some swords with his ermine.

He took a fan of peacock's feathers in his hand and wiped the dust from full many a suit of armour, full many a head-piece, and many a spiked helmet too.

He also dusted the banner and he said: 'My proudest boast is that the moth has not yet eaten away the silk, and there are no worms in the wood.'

Und als wir kamen in den Saal,
Wo schlafend am Boden liegen
Viel tausend Krieger, kampfbereit,
Der Alte sprach mit Vergnügen:

«Hier müssen wir leiser reden und gehn,
Damit wir nicht wecken die Leute;
Wieder verflossen sind hundert Jahr,
Und Löhnungstag ist heute.»

Und siehe! der Kaiser nahte sich sacht
Den schlafenden Soldaten,
Und steckte heimlich in die Tasch
Jedwedem einen Dukaten.

Er sprach mit schmunzelndem Gesicht,
Als ich ihn ansah verwundert:
«Ich zahle einen Dukaten per Mann,
Als Sold, nach jedem Jahrhundert.»

Im Saale, wo die Pferde stehn
In langen, schweigenden Reihen,
Da rieb der Kaiser sich die Händ,
Schien sonderbar sich zu freuen.

And when we came to the hall where many thousand warriors lie sleeping
on the floor, ready for battle, the old boy said with satisfaction:
    'We must talk and walk more softly here so we don't wake up the men;
another hundred years have passed, and today is pay-day.'
    And behold! The Kaiser silently approached the sleeping soldiers and
stealthily slipped a ducat into the pocket of each one of them.
    He said with a self-satisfied expression when I looked at him in wonder: 'I
give a ducat to each man as pay after every hundred years.'
    In the hall where the horses stand in long, silent lines the Kaiser rubbed his
hands, seemed to be strangely pleased.

Er zählte die Gäule, Stück vor Stück,
Und klätschelte ihnen die Rippen;
Er zählte und zählte, mit ängstlicher Hast
Bewegten sich seine Lippen.

«Das ist noch nicht die rechte Zahl» –
Sprach er zuletzt verdrossen –
«Soldaten und Waffen hab ich genung,
Doch fehlt es noch an Rossen.

«Roßkämme habe ich ausgeschickt
In alle Welt, die kaufen
Für mich die besten Pferde ein,
Hab schon einen guten Haufen.

«Ich warte, bis die Zahl komplett,
Dann schlag ich los und befreie
Mein Vaterland, mein deutsches Volk,
Das meiner harret mit Treue.»

So sprach der Kaiser, ich aber rief:
Schlag los, du alter Geselle,
Schlag los, und hast du nicht Pferde genug,
Nimm Esel an ihrer Stelle.

He counted the steeds one by one, and smacked them in the ribs; he counted and counted, his lips moving in nervous haste.

'I've not got the right number yet,' he said finally in vexation – 'I have enough soldiers and arms, but I'm still short of horses.

'I've sent dealers out all over the world to buy the best horses for me; I've got quite a lot already.

'I'm waiting till I've got the number I need, then I'll attack and free my fatherland, my German people, who are loyally waiting for me.'

Thus spoke the Kaiser, but I cried: 'Attack, old boy, attack, and if you've not got enough horses, use asses instead.'

Der Rotbart erwiderte lächelnd: «Es hat
Mit dem Schlagen gar keine Eile,
Man baute nicht Rom in einem Tag,
Gut Ding will haben Weile.

«Wer heute nicht kommt, kommt morgen gewiß,
Nur langsam wächst die Eiche,
Und chi va piano, va sano, so heißt
Das Sprichwort im römischen Reiche.»

CAPUT XVII

ICH habe mich mit dem Kaiser gezankt
Im Traum, im Traum versteht sich, –
Im wachenden Zustand sprechen wir nicht
Mit Fürsten so widersetzig.

Nur träumend, im idealen Traum,
Wagt ihnen der Deutsche zu sagen
Die deutsche Meinung, die er so tief
Im treuen Herzen getragen.

Redbeard replied, smiling: 'There's no hurry about the fighting, they
didn't build Rome in a day, nothing good is done in a hurry.
'He who doesn't come today is sure to come tomorrow, the oak only grows
slowly, and "chi va piano, va sano" is the proverb in the Roman Empire.'

Caput XVI, which has been omitted, is an account of happenings and per-
sonalities since the Seven Years War – the last time any news of life above
ground reached Barbarossa. The poet tells the king about the guillotine, offends
him with his familiar tone, and then seizes the chance to tell him to stay under-
ground: 'We have no further need for emperors.'

Caput XVII

I QUARRELLED with the Emperor in my dreams – in my dreams, of course,
for when awake we don't speak so insubordinately with sovereigns.
Only dreaming, in an ideal dream, does the German dare to tell them his
German opinion, which he has kept so deep in his loyal heart.

Als ich erwacht', fuhr ich einem Wald
Vorbei, der Anblick der Bäume,
Der nackten hölzernen Wirklichkeit,
Verscheuchte meine Träume.

Die Eichen schüttelten ernsthaft das Haupt,
Die Birken und Birkenreiser
Sie nickten so warnend – und ich rief:
Vergib mir, mein teurer Kaiser!

Vergib mir, o Rotbart, das rasche Wort!
Ich weiß, du bist viel weiser
Als ich, ich habe so wenig Geduld –
Doch komme du bald, mein Kaiser!

Behagt dir das Guillotinieren nicht,
So bleib bei den alten Mitteln:
Das Schwert für Edelleute, der Strick
Für Bürger und Bauern in Kitteln.

Nur manchmal wechsle ab, und laß
Den Adel hängen, und köpfe
Ein bißchen die Bürger und Bauern, wir sind
Ja alle Gottesgeschöpfe.

When I awoke I was driving past a wood, and the sight of the trees, of bare,
wooden reality, chased away my dreams.

The oaks gravely shook their heads, the birches and birch-twigs nodded
so warningly – and I cried: Forgive me, my dear Emperor!

Forgive, o Redbeard, my hasty words! I know you are much wiser than
me, I have so little patience – but come soon, my Emperor!

If you don't like guillotining, keep to the old measures: the sword for the
nobility, the rope for burghers and besmocked peasants.

But make a change sometimes, and let nobles be hanged, and chop off a
few burghers' and peasants' heads, we are all God's creatures.

Stell wieder her das Halsgericht,
Das peinliche Karls des Fünften,
Und teile wieder ein das Volk
Nach Ständen, Gilden und Zünften.

Das alte heilige römische Reich,
Stells wieder her, das ganze,
Gib uns den modrigsten Plunder zurück
Mit allem Firlefanze.

Das Mittelalter, immerhin,
Das wahre, wie es gewesen,
Ich will es ertragen – erlöse uns nur
Von jenem Zwitterwesen,

Von jenem Kamaschenrittertum,
Das ekelhaft ein Gemisch ist
Von gotischem Wahn und modernem Lug,
Das weder Fleisch noch Fisch ist.

Jag fort das Komödiantenpack,
Und schließe die Schauspielhäuser,
Wo man die Vorzeit parodiert –
Komme du bald, o Kaiser!

Revive the criminal court of Charles V, that capital institution, and divide up all the people again according to classes, guilds and companies.

Restore the old Holy Roman Empire, restore it complete, give us back the mustiest old lumber and all that frippery.

In spite of everything, I will gladly put up with the Middle Ages as they really were – just free us from that mongrel state,

from that martinetism which is a nauseating mixture of Gothic illusion and modern deceit, which is neither flesh nor fish.

Chase off the rabble of comedians and close the theatres where they parody the olden days – come soon, o Emperor!

ROMANZERO

ROMANCERO

ERSTES BUCH

HISTORIEN

RHAMPSENIT

Als der König Rhampsenit
Eintrat in die goldne Halle
Seiner Tochter, lachte diese,
Lachten ihre Zofen alle.

Auch die Schwarzen, die Eunuchen,
Stimmten lachend ein, es lachten
Selbst die Mumien, selbst die Sphinxe,
Daß sie schier zu bersten dachten.

Die Prinzessin sprach: Ich glaubte
Schon den Schatzdieb zu erfassen,
Der hat aber einen toten
Arm in meiner Hand gelassen.

Jetzt begreif ich, wie der Schatzdieb
Dringt in deine Schatzhauskammern
Und die Schätze dir entwendet,
Trotz den Schlössern, Riegeln, Klammern.

FIRST BOOK. HISTORIES

Rhampsinitus

When King Rhampsinitus entered his daughter's golden hall, she was laughing, and all her maids were laughing too.

The black men, the eunuchs, joined in the laughter, even the mummies were laughing so much, even the sphinxes, that they thought they would burst.

The Princess said: I thought I had caught the thief, but he left a dead arm in my hand.

Now I understand how the thief forces his way into your treasure-chambers and removes your treasure, despite the locks, bolts and bars.

Einen Zauberschlüssel hat er,
Der erschließet allerorten
Jede Türe, widerstehen
Können nicht die stärksten Pforten.

Ich bin keine starke Pforte
Und ich hab nicht widerstanden,
Schätzehütend diese Nacht
Kam ein Schätzlein mir abhanden.

So sprach lachend die Prinzessin
Und sie tänzelt im Gemache,
Und die Zofen und Eunuchen
Hoben wieder ihre Lache.

An demselben Tag ganz Memphis
Lachte, selbst die Krokodile
Reckten lachend ihre Häupter
Aus dem schlammig gelben Nile,

Als sie Trommelschlag vernahmen
Und sie hörten an dem Ufer
Folgendes Reskript verlesen
Von dem Kanzelei-Ausrufer:

He has a magic key which everywhere opens every door, the strongest gates
cannot withstand him.

I am no strong gate, and I haven't withstood him, while guarding treasure
last night a little treasure of mine got lost.

Thus spoke the Princess, laughing, and she skips about in her room, and
the maids and eunuchs began to laugh again.

On that day all Memphis laughed, even the crocodiles in their laughter
thrust their jaws up out of the muddy yellow Nile

when they noticed the drum-beats and heard the following proclamation
read out by the court herald on the river-bank:

Rhampsenit von Gottes Gnaden
König zu und in Ägypten,
Wir entbieten Gruß und Freundschaft
Unsern Vielgetreun und Liebden.

In der Nacht vom dritten zu dem
Vierten Junius des Jahres
Dreizehnhundertvierundzwanzig
Vor Christi Geburt, da war es,

Daß ein Dieb aus unserm Schatzhaus
Eine Menge von Juwelen
Uns entwendet; es gelang ihm
Uns auch später zu bestehlen.

Zur Ermittelung des Täters
Ließen schlafen wir die Tochter
Bei den Schätzen – doch auch jene
Zu bestehlen schlau vermocht er.

Um zu steuern solchem Diebstahl
Und zu gleicher Zeit dem Diebe
Unsre Sympathie zu zeigen,
Unsre Ehrfurcht, unsre Liebe,

We, Rhampsinitus, by God's grace King of and in Egypt, offer greetings
and goodwill to our subjects loyal and dear.

It was in the night of the 3rd to the 4th of June in the year 1324 B.C.
that a thief removed a quantity of jewels from our treasure-house; and he
succeeded later in robbing us further.

In order to discover the identity of the culprit we let our daughter sleep by
the treasure – but he was able cunningly to rob her too.

To put a stop to these thefts, and at the same time to show the thief our
sympathy, our respect and love,

Wollen wir ihm zur Gemahlin
Unsre einzge Tochter geben
Und ihn auch als Thronnachfolger
In den Fürstenstand erheben.

Sintemal uns die Adresse
Unsres Eidams noch zur Stunde
Unbekannt, soll dies Reskript ihm
Bringen Unsrer Gnade Kunde.

So geschehn den dritten Jenner
Dreizehnhundert zwanzig sechs
Vor Christi Geburt. – Signieret
Von Uns: Rhampsenitus Rex.

Rhampsenit hat Wort gehalten,
Nahm den Dieb zum Schwiegersohne,
Und nach seinem Tode erbte
Auch der Dieb Ägyptens Krone.

Er regierte wie die andern,
Schützte Handel und Talente;
Wenig, heißt es, ward gestohlen
Unter seinem Regimente.

it is our will to give him our only daughter to be his wife, and to ennoble him as heir to the throne.

Whereas the address of our son-in-law is at present unknown to us, this proclamation shall bring him knowledge of our favour.

Enacted this 3rd day of January 1326 B.C. – Signed with our hand: Rhampsinitus rex.

Rhampsinitus kept his word, took the thief as his son-in-law, and after his death the thief succeeded to the crown of Egypt.

He ruled as others do, encouraged trade and the arts; there was, it is said, very little thieving in his reign.

KÖNIG RICHARD

Wohl durch der Wälder einödige Pracht
Jagt ungestüm ein Reiter;
Er bläst ins Horn, er singt und lacht
Gar seelenvergnügt und heiter.

Sein Harnisch ist von starkem Erz,
Noch stärker ist sein Gemüte,
Das ist Herr Richard Löwenherz,
Der christlichen Ritterschaft Blüte.

Willkommen in England! rufen ihm zu
Die Bäume mit grünen Zungen –
Wir freuen uns, o König, daß du
Östreichischer Haft entsprungen.

Dem König ist wohl in der freien Luft,
Er fühlt sich wie neugeboren,
Er denkt an Östreichs Festungsduft –
Und gibt seinem Pferde die Sporen.

King Richard

A horseman gallops impetuously through the forest's deserted splendour;
he blows his horn, he sings and laughs very gaily and with a contented heart.

His armour is of strong metal, and his spirit is even stronger; it is Richard
the Lion-heart, flower of Christian chivalry.

'Welcome to England!' the trees shout to him with their green tongues –
'We are glad, o King, that you have escaped from Austrian captivity.'

The king rejoices in the fresh air, he feels himself new-born, he thinks of the
air in Austria's dungeons – and spurs on his horse.

DER ASRA

TÄGLICH ging die wunderschöne
Sultanstochter auf und nieder
Um die Abendzeit am Springbrunn,
Wo die weißen Wasser plätschern.

Täglich stand der junge Sklave
Um die Abendzeit am Springbrunn,
Wo die weißen Wasser plätschern;
Täglich ward er bleich und bleicher.

Eines Abends trat die Fürstin
Auf ihn zu mit raschen Worten:
Deinen Namen will ich wissen,
Deine Heimat, deine Sippschaft!

Und der Sklave sprach: ich heiße
Mohamet, ich bin aus Jemen,
Und mein Stamm sind jene Asra,
Welche sterben, wenn sie lieben.

The Asra

EVERY day at evening the Sultan's wonderfully beautiful daughter walked up and down by the fountain in which the white waters murmur.

Every day at evening the young slave stood by the fountain where the white waters murmur; every day he grew more and more pale.

One evening the princess came up to him with rapid words: I wish to know your name, your home, your kin!

And the slave said: I am called Mohamet, I come from the Yemen, and my tribe are the Asras who die when they love.

DER MOHRENKÖNIG

I N S Exil der Alpujarren*
Zog der junge Mohrenkönig;
Schweigsam und das Herz voll Kummer
Ritt er an des Zuges Spitze.

Hinter ihm auf hohen Zeltern
Oder auch in güldnen Sänften
Saßen seines Hauses Frauen;
Schwarze Mägde trägt das Maultier.

Hundert treue Diener folgen
Auf arabisch edlen Rappen;
Stolze Gäule, doch die Reiter
Hängen schlottrig in den Sätteln.

Keine Zymbel, keine Pauke,
Kein Gesangeslaut ertönte;
Nur des Maultiers Silberglöckchen
Wimmern schmerzlich in der Stille.

The Moorish King

THE young Moorish king was making his way into exile in the Alpujarras;*
silent and with a heart full of grief he rode at the head of the column.

Behind him on high palfreys or in golden litters sat the women of his house;
mules bear black waiting-women.

A hundred loyal servants follow on noble Arab horses; proud steeds –
but their riders hang limply in the saddle.

No cymbals, no drums, no singing rang out; only the mules' little silver
bells whimper painfully in the silence.

---

* Las Alpujarras: a chain of valleys on the southern slopes of the Sierra
Nevada.

Auf der Höhe, wo der Blick
Ins Duero-Tal hinabschweift,
Und die Zinnen von Granada
Sichtbar sind zum letzten Male:

Dorten stieg vom Pferd der König
Und betrachtete die Stadt,
Die im Abendlichte glänzte,
Wie geschmückt mit Gold und Purpur.

Aber, Allah! Welch ein Anblick!
Statt des vielgeliebten Halbmonds,
Prangen Spaniens Kreuz und Fahnen
Auf den Türmen der Alhambra.

Ach, bei diesem Anblick brachen
Aus des Königs Brust die Seufzer,
Tränen überströmten plötzlich
Wie ein Sturzbach seine Wangen.

Düster von dem hohen Zelter
Schaut' herab des Königs Mutter,
Schaut' auf ihres Sohnes Jammer,
Und sie schalt ihn stolz und bitter.

On the height, from where the eye strays downwards into the Duero valley
and the battlements of Granada are visible for the last time –
  there the king dismounted from his horse and gazed at the city, which
gleamed in the evening light as if adorned with gold and purple.
  But Allah! What a sight! In place of the much-loved half-moon Spain's
cross and banners flaunt from the towers of the Alhambra.
  Ah, at this sight sighs broke from the king's breast, tears like a torrent
suddenly flooded his cheeks.
  The king's mother looked down sombrely from her high palfrey, looked
at her son's misery, and she chided him proudly and bitterly.

«Boabdil el Chico,» sprach sie,
«Wie ein Weib beweinst du jetzo
Jene Stadt, die du nicht wußtest
Zu verteidgen wie ein Mann.»

Als des Königs liebste Kebsin
Solche harte Rede hörte,
Stürzte sie aus ihrer Sänfte
Und umhalste den Gebieter.

«Boabdil el Chico,» sprach sie,
«Tröste dich, mein Heißgeliebter,
Aus dem Abgrund deines Elends
Blüht hervor ein schöner Lorbeer.

«Nicht allein der Triumphator,
Nicht allein der sieggekrönte
Günstling jener blinden Göttin,
Auch der blutge Sohn des Unglücks,

«Auch der heldenmütge Kämpfer,
Der dem ungeheuren Schicksal
Unterlag, wird ewig leben
In der Menschen Angedenken.»

'Boabdil el Chico,' she said, 'like a woman you are now mourning that city which you did not know how to defend like a man.'

When the king's favourite concubine heard such a harsh speech she threw herself from her litter and embraced her master.

'Boabdil el Chico,' she said, 'take comfort, my dearly loved one, from the abyss of your wretchedness a beautiful laurel will blossom forth.

'Not just the man who triumphed, not just the victory-crowned favourite of that blind goddess – the bloody son of misfortune too,

'the heroic warrior who succumbed to a monstrous fate, will live eternally in the memory of men.'

«Berg des letzten Mohrenseufzers»
Heißt bis auf den heutgen Tag
Jene Höhe, wo der König
Sah zum letztenmal Granada.

Lieblich hat die Zeit erfüllet
Seiner Liebsten Prophezeiung,
Und des Mohrenkönigs Name
Ward verherrlicht und gefeiert.

Nimmer wird sein Ruhm verhallen,
Ehe nicht die letzte Saite
Schnarrend losspringt von der letzten
Andalusischen Gitarre.

GEOFFROY RUDÈL UND MELISANDE VON TRIPOLI

In dem Schlosse Blay erblickt man
Die Tapete an den Wänden,
So die Gräfin Tripolis
Einst gestickt mit klugen Händen.

'Mount of the last Moorish sigh' is to this day the name of that height where the king saw Granada for the last time.

Kindly has time fulfilled the prophecy of his beloved, and the name of the Moorish king was glorified and celebrated.

Never will his fame die away before the last string breaks jarringly on the last Andalusian guitar.

Geoffroy Rudèl and Melisande of Tripoli

At Blay Castle you can see on the walls the tapestry which the Countess of Tripoli once stitched with skilful hands.

Ihre ganze Seele stickte
Sie hinein, und Liebesträne
Hat gefeit das seidne Bildwerk,
Welches darstellt jene Szene:

Wie die Gräfin den Rudèl
Sterbend sah am Strande liegen,
Und das Urbild ihrer Sehnsucht
Gleich erkannt' in seinen Zügen.

Auch Rudèl hat hier zum ersten
Und zum letzten Mal erblicket
In der Wirklichkeit die Dame,
Die ihn oft im Traum entzücket.

Über ihn beugt sich die Gräfin,
Hält ihn liebevoll umschlungen,
Küßt den todesbleichen Mund,
Der so schön ihr Lob gesungen!

Ach! der Kuß des Willkomms wurde
Auch zugleich der Kuß des Scheidens,
Und so leerten sie den Kelch
Höchster Lust und tiefsten Leidens.

She stitched her whole soul into it, and tears of love have put a spell on the
silken picture, which represents this scene:

The Countess finding Rudèl as he lay dying on the shore, and at once re-
cognizing in his features the object of her longing.

Rudèl, too, saw here in real life for the first and last time the lady who had
often enchanted him in his dreams.

The Countess bends over him, holds him in a loving embrace, kisses the
deathly pale mouth which so beautifully sang her praises!

Alas! the kiss of welcome became at the same time the kiss of parting, and
thus they drained the cup of highest joy and deepest suffering.

HEINE

In dem Schlosse Blay allnächtlich
Gibts ein Rauschen, Knistern, Beben,
Die Figuren der Tapete
Fangen plötzlich an zu leben.

Troubadour und Dame schütteln
Die verschlafnen Schattenglieder,
Treten aus der Wand und wandeln
Durch die Säle auf und nieder.

Trautes Flüstern, sanftes Tändeln,
Wehmutsüße Heimlichkeiten,
Und posthume Galantrie
Aus des Minnesanges Zeiten:

«Geoffroy! Mein totes Herz
Wird erwärmt von deiner Stimme,
In den längst erloschnen Kohlen
Fühl ich wieder ein Geglimme!»

«‹Melisande! Glück und Blume!
Wenn ich dir ins Auge sehe,
Leb ich auf – gestorben ist
Nur mein Erdenleid und -Wehe.›»

At Blay Castle each night there is a swishing, a rustling, a quivering, the
figures in the tapestry suddenly come to life.

Troubadour and damsel shake their sleepy, shadowy limbs, step from the
wall and walk up and down through the halls.

Intimate whispering, gentle dalliance, sad-sweet secrets and posthumous
galanterie from the days of minstrelsy:

'Geoffroy! My dead heart is warmed by your voice, in the long-extinguished
embers I feel a new glow!'

'"Melisande! Joy and flower! When I gaze into your eyes I live again –
only my earthly suffering and woe are dead."'

«Geoffroy! Wir liebten uns
Einst im Traume, und jetzunder
Lieben wir uns gar im Tode –
Gott Amur tat dieses Wunder!»

«‹Melisande! Was ist Traum?
Was ist Tod? Nur eitel Töne.
In der Liebe nur ist Wahrheit,
Und dich lieb ich, ewig Schöne.› »

«Geoffroy! Wie traulich ist es
Hier im stillen Mondscheinsaale,
Möchte nicht mehr draußen wandeln
In des Tages Sonnenstrahle.»

«‹Melisande! teure Närrin,
Du bist selber Licht und Sonne,
Wo du wandelst, blüht der Frühling,
Sprossen Lieb und Maienwonne!›»

Also kosen, also wandeln
Jene zärtlichen Gespenster
Auf und ab, derweil das Mondlicht
Lauschet durch die Bogenfenster.

‘Geoffroy! We once loved each other in a dream, and now we love each other even in death – God Amor wrought this wonder!’
‘“Melisande! What is a dream? What is death? Just empty sounds. In love alone is truth, and I love you, eternally beautiful one.”’
‘Geoffroy! How pleasant it is here in the silent moonlit hall, I should no longer wish to walk outside in the sunlight of day.’
‘“Melisande! dear foolish one, you yourself are light and sun, wherever you walk, spring blossoms, love and May joys burst forth!”’
Thus do those tender ghosts talk amorously and walk up and down, while the moonlight peeps in through the arched windows.

Doch den holden Spuk vertreibend,
Kommt am End die Morgenröte –
Jene huschen scheu zurück
In die Wand, in die Tapete.

But the morning glow at last comes and drives away these gentle ghosts –
they slip shyly back into the wall, into the tapestry.

ZWEITES BUCH

LAMENTATIONEN

MYTHOLOGIE

JA, Europa ist erlegen –
Wer kann Ochsen widerstehen?
Wir verzeihen auch Danäen –
Sie erlag dem goldnen Regen!

Semele ließ sich verführen –
Denn sie dachte: eine Wolke,
Ideale Himmelswolke,
Kann uns nicht kompromittieren.

Aber tief muß uns empören
Was wir von der Leda lesen –
Welche Gans bist du gewesen,
Daß ein Schwan dich konnt betören!

SECOND BOOK. LAMENTATIONS

Mythology

YES, Europa succumbed – who can resist bulls? We forgive Danae too – she succumbed to golden rain!

Semele let herself be seduced – for, she thought, a cloud, an ideal cloud from heaven, cannot compromise us.

But what we read of Leda cannot but shock us deeply – what a goose you were that a swan could fool you!

JETZT WOHIN?

Jetzt wohin? Der dumme Fuß
Will mich gern nach Deutschland tragen;
Doch es schüttelt klug das Haupt
Mein Verstand und scheint zu sagen:

Zwar beendigt ist der Krieg,
Doch die Kriegsgerichte blieben,
Und es heißt, du habest einst
Viel Erschießliches geschrieben.

Das ist wahr, unangenehm
Wär mir das Erschossenwerden;
Bin kein Held, es fehlen mir
Die pathetischen Gebärden.

Gern würd ich nach England gehn,
Wären dort nicht Kohlendämpfe
Und Engländer – schon ihr Duft
Gibt Erbrechen mir und Krämpfe.

Whither Now?

Whither now? My stupid foot is eager to take me to Germany; but my
reason wisely shakes its head and seems to say:

The war is over, to be sure, but courts-martial remain, and it is said you once
wrote much that would bring you before the firing-squad.

That is true, I should find it unpleasant to be shot; I'm no hero, I quite lack
the tragic gesture.

I'd gladly go to England if there weren't coal-smoke and Englishmen there –
their very smell sickens and convulses me.

Manchmal kommt mir in den Sinn
Nach Amerika zu segeln,
Nach dem großen Freiheitstall,
Der bewohnt von Gleichheitsflegeln –

Doch es ängstet mich ein Land,
Wo die Menschen Tabak käuen,
Wo sie ohne König kegeln,
Wo sie ohne Spucknapf speien.

Rußland, dieses schöne Reich,
Würde mir vielleicht behagen,
Doch im Winter könnte ich
Dort die Knute nicht ertragen.

Traurig schau ich in die Höh,
Wo viel tausend Sterne nicken –
Aber meinen eignen Stern
Kann ich nirgends dort erblicken.

Hat im güldnen Labyrinth
Sich vielleicht verirrt am Himmel,
Wie ich selber mich verirrt
In dem irdischen Getümmel. –

I sometimes think I'll go to America, that huge freedom-stall inhabited by churls who believe in equality –

But I'm put off by a country where people chew tobacco, where they play skittles without a king, where they spit without a spittoon.

Russia, that beautiful empire, would perhaps please me, but in winter I shouldn't be able to bear the knout.

I sadly gaze up into the sky, where many thousands of stars nod – but nowhere there can I see my own star.

Perhaps it has got lost in the golden labyrinth of the heavens, as I myself have got lost in the turmoil on earth. –

HEINE

from LAZARUS

GEDÄCHTNISFEIER

Keine Messe wird man singen,
Keinen Kadosch wird man sagen,
Nichts gesagt und nichts gesungen
Wird an meinen Sterbetagen.

Doch vielleicht an solchem Tage,
Wenn das Wetter schön und milde,
Geht spazieren auf Montmartre
Mit Paulinen Frau Mathilde.

Mit dem Kranz von Immortellen
Kommt sie mir das Grab zu schmücken,
Und sie seufzet: Pauvre homme!
Feuchte Wehmut in den Blicken.

Leider wohn ich viel zu hoch,
Und ich habe meiner Süßen
Keinen Stuhl hier anzubieten;
Ach! sie schwankt mit müden Füßen.

from LAZARUS

Memorial Service

No mass will be sung, no kaddish said, nothing will be said or sung in the days following my death.

But perhaps on a day when the weather is mild and good, Frau Mathilde will go for a walk on Montmartre with Pauline.

She will come and adorn my grave with a wreath of everlasting flowers, and sigh: Pauvre homme!, a misty sadness in her eye.

Alas, I live much too far up, and I've no chair here to offer my sweet one; alas, she totters on weary feet.

194

Süßes, dickes Kind, du darfst
Nicht zu Fuß nach Hause gehen;
An dem Barrieregitter
Siehst du die Fiaker stehen.

AN DIE ENGEL

Das ist der böse Thanatos,
Er kommt auf einem fahlen Roß;
Ich hör den Hufschlag, hör den Trab,
Der dunkle Reiter holt mich ab –
Er reißt mich fort, Mathilden soll ich lassen,
O, den Gedanken kann mein Herz nicht fassen!

Sie war mir Weib und Kind zugleich,
Und geh ich in das Schattenreich,
Wird Witwe sie und Waise sein!
Ich laß in dieser Welt allein
Das Weib, das Kind, das, trauend meinem Mute,
Sorglos und treu an meinem Herzen ruhte.

Sweet fat child, you mustn't walk home; you'll see the cabs standing at the gate.

To the Angels

THAT is evil Thanatos, he comes on a dun horse; I hear the hoof-beats, hear his trot, the dark horseman is coming for me – he tears me away, I must leave Mathilde, oh, my heart cannot grasp the thought!

She was at once wife and child to me, and when I go into the land of shadows, she will be widow and orphan! I leave alone in this world the wife and child who, trusting in my courage, rested carefree and loyal on my breast.

Ihr Engel in den Himmelshöhn,
Vernehmt mein Schluchzen und mein Flehn:
Beschützt, wenn ich im öden Grab,
Das Weib, das ich geliebet hab;
Seid Schild und Vögte eurem Ebenbilde,
Beschützt, beschirmt mein armes Kind, Mathilde.

Bei allen Tränen, die ihr je
Geweint um unser Menschenweh,
Beim Wort, das nur der Priester kennt
Und niemals ohne Schauder nennt,
Bei eurer eignen Schönheit, Huld und Milde,
Beschwör ich euch, ihr Engel, schützt Mathilde.

SIE ERLISCHT

Der Vorhang fällt, das Stück ist aus,
Und Herrn und Damen gehn nach Haus.
Ob ihnen auch das Stück gefallen?
Ich glaub, ich hörte Beifall schallen.
Ein hochverehrtes Publikum
Beklatschte dankbar seinen Dichter.
Jetzt aber ist das Haus so stumm,
Und sind verschwunden Lust und Lichter.

You angels in the heavenly heights, hear my sobbing and entreaties: when I am in my bleak grave, protect the wife I have loved; be shield and guard to your own image, protect, shelter my poor child Mathilde.

By all the tears you have ever shed for our human woe, by the word which only the priest knows and never uses without awe, by your own beauty, graciousness and mildness – I entreat you, angels, protect Mathilde.

It Goes Out

The curtain falls, the play is over, and the ladies and gentlemen are going home. Did they like the play? I think I heard the sound of applause. The highly respected audience was gratefully clapping its poet. But now the theatre is so quiet, and joy and lights have disappeared.

Doch horch! ein schollernd schnöder Klang
Ertönt unfern der öden Bühne; –
Vielleicht daß eine Saite sprang
An einer alten Violine.
Verdrießlich rascheln im Parterr
Etwelche Ratten hin und her,
Und alles riecht nach ranzgem Öle.
Die letzte Lampe ächzt und zischt
Verzweiflungsvoll, und sie erlischt.
Das arme Licht war meine Seele.

ENFANT PERDU

VERLORNER Posten in dem Freiheitskriege,
Hielt ich seit dreißig Jahren treulich aus.
Ich kämpfe ohne Hoffnung, daß ich siege,
Ich wußte, nie komm ich gesund nach Haus.

Ich wachte Tag und Nacht – Ich konnt nicht schlafen,
Wie in dem Lagerzelt der Freunde Schar –
(Auch hielt das laute Schnarchen dieser Braven
Mich wach, wenn ich ein bißchen schlummrig war).

But hark! there sounds a heavy, discordant twang not far from the deserted stage; – perhaps it was a string breaking on an old violin. Some rats scurry peevishly here and there in the stalls, and everything smells of rancid oil. The last lamp groans and splutters in despair, and it goes out. That poor light was my soul.

Enfant Perdu

A LOST sentry in the war of liberation, I have held out loyally for thirty years. I fight without hope of winning, I knew I should never get home unscathed.

I kept watch day and night – I couldn't sleep, as my crowd of friends in the tent could (and the loud snoring of these good fellows kept me awake when I was a bit tired).

HEINE

In jenen Nächten hat Langweil ergriffen
Mich oft, auch Furcht – (nur Narren fürchten nichts) –
Sie zu verscheuchen, hab ich dann gepfiffen
Die frechen Reime eines Spottgedichts.

Ja, wachsam stand ich, das Gewehr im Arme,
Und nahte irgend ein verdächtger Gauch,
So schoß ich gut und jagt ihm eine warme,
Brühwarme Kugel in den schnöden Bauch.

Mitunter freilich mocht es sich ereignen,
Daß solch ein schlechter Gauch gleichfalls sehr gut
Zu schießen wußte – ach, ich kanns nicht leugnen –
Die Wunden klaffen – es verströmt mein Blut.

Ein Posten ist vakant! – Die Wunden klaffen –
Der eine fällt, die andern rücken nach –
Doch fall ich unbesiegt, und meine Waffen
Sind nicht gebrochen – nur mein Herze brach.

In those nights boredom often took hold of me, fear too – (only fools fear
nothing) – and to banish them I then whistled the impudent rhymes of a
satirical poem.

Yes, I stood watchfully, my rifle in my arms, and if any suspicious fool came
near, I aimed true and sent a piping-hot bullet into his vile belly.

From time to time, of course, it happened that an evil fool of this sort was
also a good shot – ah, I can't deny it – my wounds gape – my blood flows fast.

One sentry is required! – My wounds gape – one man falls, the others close
up – but I fall unbeaten, and my weapons are not broken – only my heart broke.

DRITTES BUCH
HEBRÄISCHE MELODIEN

PRINZESSIN SABBATH

In Arabiens Märchenbuche
Sehen wir verwünschte Prinzen,
Die zuzeiten ihre schöne
Urgestalt zurückgewinnen:

Das behaarte Ungeheuer
Ist ein Königsohn geworden;
Schmuckreich glänzend angekleidet,
Auch verliebt die Flöte blasend.

Doch die Zauberfrist zerrinnt,
Und wir schauen plötzlich wieder
Seine königliche Hoheit
In ein Ungetüm verzottelt.

Einen Prinzen solchen Schicksals
Singt mein Lied. Er ist geheißen
Israel. Ihn hat verwandelt
Hexenspruch in einen Hund.

THIRD BOOK. HEBREW MELODIES

Princess Sabbath

In Arabia's book of fairy-stories we see enchanted princes who at certain
times win back their original beauty of form:

The hairy monster has become a king's son; resplendent in richly adorned
clothes, and playing the flute amorously.

But the magic term runs out, and we suddenly see his Royal Highness
turned back into a hairy monster.

My song tells of a prince whose fate this was. He was called Israel. A
witch's spell turned him into a dog.

199

Hund mit hündischen Gedanken,
Kötert er die ganze Woche
Durch des Lebens Kot und Kehricht,
Gassenbuben zum Gespötte.

Aber jeden Freitag Abend,
In der Dämmrungstunde, plötzlich
Weicht der Zauber, und der Hund
Wird aufs neu ein menschlich Wesen.

Mensch mit menschlichen Gefühlen,
Mit erhobnem Haupt und Herzen,
Festlich, reinlich schier gekleidet,
Tritt er in des Vaters Halle.

«Sei gegrüßt, geliebte Halle
Meines königlichen Vaters!
Zelte Jakobs, eure heilgen
Eingangspfosten küßt mein Mund!»

Durch das Haus geheimnisvoll
Zieht ein Wispern und ein Weben,
Und der unsichtbare Hausherr
Atmet schaurig in der Stille.

A dog with doggy thoughts, all through the week he sniffs his way through the filth and refuse of life, the laughing-stock of the street urchins.

But every Friday evening, at dusk, the magic suddenly yields, and the dog becomes a human being again.

A human with human feelings, with head and heart held high, and festively, thoroughly neatly attired, he enters his father's hall.

'I greet you, well-loved hall of my kingly father! Tents of Jacob, my mouth kisses your sacred door-posts!'

Through the house a whispering and a stirring passes mysteriously, and the invisible master of the house breathes awesomely in the silence.

Stille! Nur der Seneschall,
(Vulgo Synagogendiener)
Springt geschäftig auf und nieder,
Um die Lampen anzuzünden.

Trostverheißend goldne Lichter,
Wie sie glänzen, wie sie glimmern!
Stolz aufflackern auch die Kerzen
Auf der Brüstung des Almemors.*

Vor dem Schreine, der die Thora
Aufbewahret und verhängt ist
Mit der kostbar seidnen Decke,
Die von Edelsteinen funkelt –

Dort an seinem Betpultständer
Steht schon der Gemeindesänger;
Schmuckes Männchen, das sein schwarzes
Mäntelchen kokett geachselt.

Um die weiße Hand zu zeigen,
Haspelt er am Halse, seltsam
An die Schläf den Zeigefinger,
An die Kehl den Daumen drückend.

Silence! Only the seneschal (*vulgo* synagogue attendant) hops busily up and down lighting the lamps.

Golden lights, promising solace, how they shine, how they glimmer! The candles too flicker proudly upwards on the balustrade of the almemor.*

Before the shrine in which the Torah is kept, and which is hung with its costly silken cover sparkling with precious stones –

there at his prayer-desk stands the cantor, all ready; a neat little man who shrugs his little black coat coquettishly on his shoulders.

To show his white hand he fingers his neck, pressing his index-finger to his forehead with a strange gesture, and his thumb to his throat.

* The pulpit in the centre of a synagogue.

Trällert vor sich hin ganz leise,
Bis er endlich lautaufjubelnd
Seine Stimm erhebt und singt:
Lecho Daudi likras Kalle!

Lecho Daudi likras Kalle –
Komm, Geliebter, deiner harret
Schon die Braut, die dir entschleiert
Ihr verschämtes Angesicht!

Dieses hübsche Hochzeitkarmen
Ist gedichtet von dem großen,
Hochberühmten Minnesinger
Don Jehuda ben Halevy.

In dem Liede wird gefeiert
Die Vermählung Israels
Mit der Frau Prinzessin Sabbath,
Die man nennt die stille Fürstin.

Perl und Blume aller Schönheit
Ist die Fürstin. Schöner war
Nicht die Königin von Saba,
Salomonis Busenfreundin,

He hums quite quietly to himself until he at last raises his voice in an out-
burst of jubilation and sings: Lecha dodi, likrath kallah!

Lecha dodi, likrath kallah – come, beloved, thy bride already awaits thee,
unveiling for thee her bashful face!

This pretty wedding song was written by the great and highly renowned
Minnesinger Don Jehuda ben Halevy.

In this song is celebrated Israel's marriage with Princess Sabbath, whom
men call the silent princess.

The princess is the pearl and flower of all beauty. The Queen of Sheba was
not more beautiful, Solomon's bosom friend,

Die, ein Blaustrumpf Äthiopiens,
Durch Esprit brillieren wollte,
Und mit ihren klugen Rätseln
Auf die Länge fatigant ward.

Die Prinzessin Sabbath, welche
Ja die personifizierte
Ruhe ist, verabscheut alle
Geisteskämpfe und Debatten.

Gleich fatal ist ihr die trampelnd
Deklamierende Passion,
Jenes Pathos, das mit flatternd
Aufgelöstem Haar einherstürmt.

Sittsam birgt die stille Fürstin
In der Haube ihre Zöpfe;
Blickt so sanft wie die Gazelle,
Blüht so schlank wie eine Addas.

Sie erlaubt dem Liebsten alles,
Ausgenommen Tabakrauchen –
«Liebster! Rauchen ist verboten,
Weil es heute Sabbath ist.

an Ethiopian blue-stocking who wanted to dazzle with her wit, and who with her cunning riddles in the end became boring.

Princess Sabbath, the very personification of peace, detests all intellectual skirmishing and debates.

Equally odious to her is passion ploddingly declaimed, that pathos which storms in with hair waving in disarray.

The silent princess modestly hides her tresses in her cap; she has an eye as gentle as a gazelle, she blooms as slender as a myrtle-tree.

She allows her dearest everything except tobacco-smoking – 'Dearest! Smoking is forbidden because today is the Sabbath.

«Dafür aber heute mittag
Soll dir dampfen, zum Ersatz,
Ein Gericht, das wahrhaft göttlich –
Heute sollst du Schalet essen!»

Schalet, schöner Götterfunken,
Tochter aus Elysium!
Also klänge Schillers Hochlied,
Hätt er Schalet je gekostet.

Schalet ist die Himmelspeise,
Die der liebe Herrgott selber
Einst den Moses kochen lehrte
Auf dem Berge Sinai,

Wo der Allerhöchste gleichfalls
All die guten Glaubenslehren
Und die heilgen zehn Gebote
Wetterleuchtend offenbarte.

Schalet ist des wahren Gottes
Koscheres Ambrosia,
Wonnebrot des Paradieses,
Und mit solcher Kost verglichen

'But as compensation, a dish which is truly divine shall be steaming for you
at midday – today you shall eat shalet!'

Shalet, beautiful divine spark, daughter of Elysium! That's how Schiller's
anthem would have gone if he had ever tasted shalet.

Shalet is the heavenly food which our dear Lord God himself once taught
Moses to cook on the Mount of Sinai,

where the All-Highest similarly revealed with his lightning all the good pre-
cepts of religion and the ten holy commandments.

Shalet is the true God's kosher ambrosia, blissful bread of Paradise, and
compared with such food

Ist nur eitel Teufelsdreck
Das Ambrosia der falschen
Heidengötter Griechenlands,
Die verkappte Teufel waren.

Speist der Prinz von solcher Speise,
Glänzt sein Auge wie verkläret,
Und er knöpfet auf die Weste,
Und er spricht mit selgem Lächeln:

«Hör ich nicht den Jordan rauschen?
Sind das nicht die Brüßelbrunnen
In dem Palmental von Beth-El,
Wo gelagert die Kamele?

«Hör ich nicht die Herdenglöckchen?
Sind das nicht die fetten Hämmel,
Die vom Gileathgebirge
Abendlich der Hirt herabtreibt?»

Doch der schöne Tag verflittert;
Wie mit langen Schattenbeinen
Kommt geschritten der Verwünschung
Böse Stund – Es seufzt der Prinz.

the ambrosia of the false heathen gods of Greece, those devils in disguise, is mere devil's muck.

When the prince eats of such a dish his eye gleams as if transfigured, and he unbuttons his waistcoat and speaks with a happy smile:

'Do I not hear the Jordan murmur? Are those not the murmuring springs in the palmy valley of Bethel, where the camels lie?

'Do I not hear the little bells from the herds, are those not the fat wethers which the shepherd drives down from the Mount of Gileath at evening?'

But the beautiful day glimmers past; as if with long shadow-legs the evil hour of the spell comes striding – the prince sighs.

Ist ihm doch als griffen eiskalt
Hexenfinger in sein Herze.
Schon durchrieseln ihn die Schauer
Hündischer Metamorphose.

Die Prinzessin reicht dem Prinzen
Ihre güldne Nardenbüchse.
Langsam riecht er – Will sich laben
Noch einmal an Wohlgerüchen.

Es kredenzet die Prinzessin
Auch den Abschiedstrunk dem Prinzen –
Hastig trinkt er, und im Becher
Bleiben wenge Tropfen nur.

Er besprengt damit den Tisch,
Nimmt alsdann ein kleines Wachslicht.
Und er tunkt es in die Nässe,
Daß es knistert und erlischt.

He feels as if witch's fingers were probing ice-cold into his heart. Dread of the doggy metamorphosis shivers through him.

The princess passes the prince her golden nard-box. He slowly inhales – he wants to regale himself once more with pleasant odours.

The princess also pours the prince his parting drink – he drinks hastily, and in the goblet only a few drops remain.

He sprinkles the table with them, then takes a small wax candle, and he dips it into the moisture so that it splutters and goes out.

GEDICHTE. 1853 UND 1854

POEMS. 1853 AND 1854

ROTE PANTOFFELN

GAR böse Katze, so alt und grau,
Sie sagte, sie sei eine Schusterfrau;
Auch stand vor ihrem Fenster ein Lädchen,
Worin Pantoffeln für junge Mädchen,
Pantöffelchen von Maroquin,
Von Saffian und von Satin,
Von Samt, mit goldnen Borden garniert
Und buntgeblümten Bändern verziert.
Am lieblichsten dort zu schauen war
Ein scharlachrotes Pantöffelchenpaar;
Es hat mit seiner Farbenpracht
Gar manchem Dirnchen ins Herz gelacht.

Eine junge weiße Edelmaus,
Die ging vorbei dem Schusterhaus,
Kehrt' wieder um, dann blieb sie stehn,
Tät nochmals durch das Fenster sehn –
Sprach endlich: Ich grüß Euch, Frau Kitze, Frau Katze,
Gar schöne rote Pantöffelchen hat Sie;

Red Slippers

WHAT a very wicked cat, so old and grey, she said she was a cobbler's wife; and a little stall stood before her window, on which there were slippers for young girls, little slippers of morocco leather, of soft goat's hide and of satin, of velvet, trimmed with golden edges and adorned with bright, flowery ribbons. Prettiest of all to be seen there was a pair of little scarlet slippers; with its colourful splendour it ingratiated itself into full many a young girl's heart.

A young white noble-mouse walked past the cobbler's house, turned round again, and then stopped, gazed into the window once more – and finally said: Greetings, Madam Kitty, Madam Cat, you have very beautiful little red

Sind sie nicht teuer, ich kauf sie Euch ab,
Sagt mir, wieviel ich zu zahlen hab.

Die Katze rief: Mein Jüngferlein,
Ich bitte gehorsamst, treten Sie ein,
Geruhen Sie mein Haus zu beehren
Mit Dero Gegenwart; es verkehren
Mit mir die allerschönsten Madel
Und Herzoginnen, der höchste Adel –
Die Töffelchen will ich wohlfeil lassen –
Doch laßt uns sehn, ob sie Euch passen –
Ach, treten Sie ein und nehmen Sie Platz –

So flötet die boshaft listige Katz,
Und das weiße, unerfahrene Ding
In die Mördergrub, in die Falle ging –
Auf eine Bank setzt sich die Maus
Und streckt ihr kleines Beinchen aus,
Um anzuprobieren die roten Schuhe –
Sie war ein Bild von Unschuld und Ruhe –
Da packt sie plötzlich die böse Katze
Und würgt sie mit der grimmigen Tatze,
Und beißt ihr ab das arme Köpfchen,

slippers; if they aren't dear, I'll buy them from you, tell me how much I must pay.

The cat called: My dear young lady, I beg you most humbly, step inside, be so kind as to honour my house with your presence; the most beautiful girls are among my customers, duchesses too, the highest nobility – I'll let you have the slippers cheap – but let's see if they fit you – do please step inside and take a seat –

Thus warbles the wicked, cunning cat, and the inexperienced, white little thing walked into the assassin's den, into the trap – the mouse sits down on a seat and sticks out her tiny little leg in order to try on the red shoes – she was a picture of innocence and calm – then the wicked cat suddenly grabs her and strangles her with her fierce paw, and bites her poor little head off, and says:

Und spricht: Mein liebes, weißes Geschöpfchen,
Mein Mäuschen, du bist mausetot!
Jedoch die Pantöffelchen scharlachrot,
Die will ich stellen auf deine Gruft;
Und wenn die Weltposaune ruft
Zum jüngsten Tanz, o weiße Maus,
Aus deinem Grab steigst du heraus,
Ganz wie die andern, und sodann
Ziehst du die roten Pantöffelchen an.

MORAL

Ihr weißen Mäuschen, nehmt euch in acht,
Laßt euch nicht ködern von weltlicher Pracht!
Ich rat euch, lieber barfuß zu laufen
Als bei der Katze Pantoffeln zu kaufen.

DAS SKLAVENSCHIFF

I

DER Superkargo Mynheer van Koek
Sitzt rechnend in seiner Kajüte;
Er kalkuliert der Ladung Betrag
Und die probabeln Profite.

My dear little white creature, my little mouse, you are as dead as a dormouse! But I will put the little scarlet slippers on your grave; and when the Last Trumpet sounds for the Judgement Dance, o white mouse, you will step forth from your grave, just like the others, and at once put your little red slippers on.

MORAL

Little white mice, take care, don't be lured by worldly splendour! I advise you to go barefoot rather than buy slippers from the cat.

The Slave-Ship

I

THE supercargo Mynheer van Koek sits at his accounts in his cabin; he is calculating the sum total of the cargo and the probable profits.

211

HEINE

«Der Gummi ist gut, der Pfeffer ist gut,
Dreihundert Säcke und Fässer;
Ich habe Goldstaub und Elfenbein –
Die schwarze Ware ist besser.

«Sechshundert Neger tauschte ich ein
Spottwohlfeil am Senegalflusse.
Das Fleisch ist hart, die Sehnen sind stramm,
Wie Eisen vom besten Gusse.

«Ich hab zum Tausche Branntewein,
Glasperlen und Stahlzeug gegeben;
Gewinne daran achthundert Prozent,
Bleibt mir die Hälfte am Leben.

«Bleiben mir Neger dreihundert nur
Im Hafen von Rio-Janeiro,
Zahlt dort mir hundert Dukaten per Stück
Das Haus Gonzales Perreiro.»

Da plötzlich wird Mynheer van Koek
Aus seinen Gedanken gerissen;
Der Schiffschirurgius tritt herein,
Der Doktor van der Smissen.

'The rubber is good, the pepper is good, 300 sacks and barrels; I have gold-dust and ivory – the black merchandise is better.

'I got 600 niggers dirt-cheap on the river Senegal. Their flesh is firm, their muscles are hard, like iron of the best casting.

'I gave brandy, beads and steel goods in exchange; I'll make 800 per cent on them if half of them remain alive.

'If I have only 300 niggers left at Rio de Janeiro harbour, the firm of Gonzales Perreiro will pay me 100 ducats a head.'

Mynheer van Koek is suddenly torn from his thoughts; the ship's surgeon enters, Dr van der Smissen.

Das ist eine klapperdürre Figur,
Die Nase voll roter Warzen –
Nun, Wasserfeldscherer, ruft van Koek,
Wie gehts meinen lieben Schwarzen?

Der Doktor dankt der Nachfrage und spricht:
«Ich bin zu melden gekommen,
Daß heute Nacht die Sterblichkeit
Bedeutend zugenommen.

«Im Durchschnitt starben täglich zwei,
Doch heute starben sieben,
Vier Männer, drei Frauen – Ich hab den Verlust
Sogleich in die Kladde geschrieben.

«Ich inspizierte die Leichen genau;
Denn diese Schelme stellen
Sich manchmal tot, damit man sie
Hinabwirft in die Wellen.

«Ich nahm den Toten die Eisen ab;
Und wie ich gewöhnlich tue,
Ich ließ die Leichen werfen ins Meer
Des Morgens in der Frühe.

He is as lean as a rake, his nose covered with red warts – 'Well, sea-surgeon,'
asks van Koek, 'how are my black friends?'
    The doctor thanks him for his inquiry and says: 'I have come to report
that there was a significant increase in the mortality-rate last night.
    'On average two died per day, but today seven died, four men, three women
– I entered the loss in the log-book straight away.
    'I examined the corpses carefully; for these rogues sometimes feign death so
as to get tossed down into the waves.
    'I took the irons off the corpses; and as is my wont I had the bodies thrown
into the sea early in the morning.

«Es schossen alsbald hervor aus der Flut
Haifische, ganze Heere,
Sie lieben so sehr das Negerfleisch;
Das sind meine Pensionäre.

«Sie folgten unseres Schiffes Spur,
Seit wir verlassen die Küste;
Die Bestien wittern den Leichengeruch,
Mit schnupperndem Fraßgelüste.

«Es ist possierlich anzusehn,
Wie sie nach den Toten schnappen!
Die faßt den Kopf, die faßt das Bein,
Die andern schlucken die Lappen.

«Ist alles verschlungen, dann tummeln sie sich
Vergnügt um des Schiffes Planken
Und glotzen mich an, als wollten sie
Sich für das Frühstück bedanken.»

Doch seufzend fällt ihm in die Red
Van Koek: Wie kann ich lindern
Das Übel? wie kann ich die Progression
Der Sterblichkeit verhindern?

'Sharks, whole shoals of them, at once shot up out of the waves – they are
very fond of nigger's flesh; they are my pensioners.
'They have followed in our wake ever since we left the coast; the beasts get
the smell of the corpses and sniff with greedy desire.
'It is funny to watch how they snap at the bodies! One seizes the head, an-
other the leg, the others gulp down the flank-meat.
'When everything's been swallowed they play contentedly round the ship's
planks and stare at me, as if they were trying to thank me for their breakfast.'
But van Koek interrupts him with a sigh: 'How can I lessen the evil? How
can I check the spread of the mortality?'

Der Doktor erwidert: «Durch eigne Schuld
Sind viele Schwarze gestorben;
Ihr schlechter Odem hat die Luft
Im Schiffsraum so sehr verdorben.

«Auch starben viele durch Melancholie,
Dieweil sie sich tödlich langweilen;
Durch etwas Luft, Musik und Tanz
Läßt sich die Krankheit heilen.»

Da ruft van Koek: «Ein guter Rat!
Mein teurer Wasserfeldscherer
Ist klug wie Aristoteles,
Des Alexanders Lehrer.

«Der Präsident der Sozietät
Der Tulpenveredlung im Delfte
Ist sehr gescheit, doch hat er nicht
Von Eurem Verstande die Hälfte.

«Musik! Musik! Die Schwarzen solln
Hier auf dem Verdecke tanzen.
Und wer sich beim Hopsen nicht amüsiert,
Den soll die Peitsche kuranzen.»

The doctor replies: 'Many blacks have died through their own fault; their foul breath has ruined the air in the hold.

'And many died from melancholy, for they are bored to death; some air, music and dancing can cure the disease.'

Then van Koek exclaims: 'A good idea! My dear sea-surgeon is as wise as Aristotle, Alexander's tutor.

'The President of the Society of Tulip-growers in Delft is very clever, but he hasn't got half your sense.

'Music! Music! The blacks shall dance here on the deck. And anyone who doesn't enjoy hopping about will be chastised by the whip.'

II

Hoch aus dem blauen Himmelszelt
Viel tausend Sterne schauen,
Sehnsüchtig glänzend, groß und klug,
Wie Augen von schönen Frauen.

Sie blicken hinunter in das Meer,
Das weithin überzogen
Mit phosphorstrahlendem Purpurduft;
Wollüstig girren die Wogen.

Kein Segel flattert am Sklavenschiff,
Es liegt wie abgetakelt;
Doch schimmern Laternen auf dem Verdeck,
Wo Tanzmusik spektakelt.

Die Fiedel streicht der Steuermann,
Der Koch, der spielt die Flöte,
Ein Schiffsjung schlägt die Trommel dazu,
Der Doktor bläst die Trompete.

Wohl hundert Neger, Männer und Fraun,
Sie jauchzen und hopsen und kreisen
Wie toll herum; bei jedem Sprung
Taktmäßig klirren die Eisen.

II

From the high blue firmament many thousand stars look down, gleaming with desire, large and wise, like the eyes of beautiful women.

They gaze down into the sea, which far and wide is covered with a phosphorescently glowing purple haze; the waves murmur voluptuously.

Not a sail flaps on the slave-ship, it lies as if unrigged; but lanterns flicker on the deck, where dance-music blares out.

The helmsman scrapes the fiddle, the cook plays the flute, a ship's boy bangs the drum, the doctor blows the trumpet.

A good hundred niggers, men and women, shout with joy, hop and circle madly round; at each jump the irons rattle in time to the music.

Sie stampfen den Boden mit tobender Lust,
Und manche schwarze Schöne
Umschlingt wollüstig den nackten Genoß –
Dazwischen ächzende Töne.

Der Büttel ist maître des plaisirs,
Und hat mit Peitschenhieben
Die lässigen Tänzer stimuliert,
Zum Frohsinn angetrieben.

Und Dideldumdei und Schnedderedeng!
Der Lärm lockt aus den Tiefen
Die Ungetüme der Wasserwelt,
Die dort blödsinnig schliefen.

Schlaftrunken kommen geschwommen heran
Haifische, viele hundert;
Sie glotzen nach dem Schiff hinauf,
Sie sind verdutzt, verwundert.

Sie merken, daß die Frühstückstund
Noch nicht gekommen, und gähnen,
Aufsperrend den Rachen; die Kiefer sind
Bepflanzt mit Sägezähnen.

They stamp the deck with raging joy, and many a black beauty voluptuously clasps her naked partner – in between come sounds of groaning.

The jailer is the Maître des plaisirs, and with whip-lashes he has stirred up the lazy dancers and urged them on to jollity.

There's a fiddle-de-dee and a rum-ti-ti-tum! The din entices from the depths the monsters of the watery world which were dully sleeping there.

Heavy with sleep many hundreds of sharks come swimming up; they stare up at the ship, they are nonplussed, bewildered.

They note that breakfast-time has not yet come, and yawn, opening wide their throats; their jaws are planted with saw-teeth.

Und Dideldumdei und Schnedderedeng –
Es nehmen kein Ende die Tänze.
Die Haifische beißen vor Ungeduld
Sich selber in die Schwänze.

Ich glaube, sie lieben nicht die Musik,
Wie viele von ihrem Gelichter.
Trau keiner Bestie, die nicht liebt
Musik! sagt Albions großer Dichter.*

Und Schnedderedeng und Dideldumdei –
Die Tänze nehmen kein Ende.
Am Fockmast steht Mynheer van Koek
Und faltet betend die Hände:

«Um Christi willen verschone, o Herr,
Das Leben der schwarzen Sünder!
Erzürnten sie dich, so weißt du ja,
Sie sind so dumm wie die Rinder.

«Verschone ihr Leben um Christi willn,
Der für uns alle gestorben!
Denn bleiben mir nicht dreihundert Stück,
So ist mein Geschäft verdorben.»

There's a fiddle-de-dee and a rum-ti-ti-tum – there's no end to the dancing.
In their impatience the sharks bite their own tails.

I don't think they care for music, like many of their kind. Trust no beast
that does not love music! says Albion's great poet.

There's a rum-ti-ti-tum and a fiddle-de-dee – there's no end to the dancing.
By the foremast stands Mynheer van Koek and he folds his hands in prayer:

'For Christ's sake spare, o Lord, the lives of these black sinners! If they
have angered Thee, Thou knowest that they are as foolish as cattle.

'Spare their lives for Christ's sake, who died for us all! For if 300 of them
don't survive, my business is ruined.'

---

* *The Merchant of Venice*, V, 1.

AFFRONTENBURG*

Die Zeit verfließt, jedoch das Schloß,
Das alte Schloß mit Turm und Zinne
Und seinem blöden Menschenvolk,
Es kommt mir nimmer aus dem Sinne.

Ich sehe stets die Wetterfahn,
Die auf dem Dach sich rasselnd drehte.
Ein jeder blickte scheu hinauf,
Bevor er nur den Mund auftäte.

Wer sprechen wollt, erforschte erst
Den Wind, aus Furcht, es möchte plötzlich
Der alte Brummbär Boreas
Anschnauben ihn nicht sehr ergötzlich.

Die Klügsten freilich schwiegen ganz —
Denn ach, es gab an jenem Orte
Ein Echo, das im Widerklatsch
Boshaft verfälschte alle Worte.

Inmitten im Schloßgarten stand
Ein sphinxgezierter Marmorbronnen,
Der immer trocken war, obgleich
Gar manche Träne dort geronnen.

Castle Contumely *

Time passes, but the castle, the old castle with its tower and battlements and
its foolish human inhabitants — I cannot get it out of my mind.

I constantly see the weather-cock which used to turn creaking on the roof.
Everyone looked timidly up at it before he even opened his mouth.

Whoever wanted to say something would first find out how the wind was
blowing, for fear that the old growler Boreas might suddenly snort at him not
very agreeably.

Those with most sense of course kept quite quiet — for alas, there was an
echo there which maliciously distorted every word as it reported gossip.

In the middle of the castle garden stood a marble fountain adorned with a
sphinx; it was always dry, though many a tear had flowed there.

---

* The country seat at Ottensen, near Hamburg, of Heine's Uncle Salomon.

Vermaledeiter Garten! Ach,
Da gab es nirgends eine Stätte,
Wo nicht mein Herz gekränket ward,
Wo nicht mein Aug geweinet hätte.

Da gabs wahrhaftig keinen Baum,
Worunter nicht Beleidigungen
Mir zugefüget worden sind
Von feinen und von groben Zungen.

Die Kröte, die im Gras gelauscht,
Hat alles mitgeteilt der Ratte,
Die ihrer Muhme Viper gleich
Erzählt, was sie vernommen hatte.

Die hats gesagt dem Schwager Frosch –
Und solcherweis erfahren konnte
Die ganze schmutzge Sippschaft stracks
Die mir erwiesenen Affronte.

Des Gartens Rosen waren schön,
Und lieblich lockten ihre Düfte;
Doch früh hinwelkend starben sie
An einem sonderbaren Gifte.

Accursed garden! Ah, there wasn't a spot in it where my heart had not been wounded, where my eyes had not wept.

There really wasn't a tree there beneath which insults had not been meted out to me by gentle and harsh tongues.

The toad lurking in the grass passed everything on to the rat, and she at once told her cousin, the viper, what she had heard.

She told her brother-in-law the frog – and in this way all that foul tribe could at once learn of the affronts paid me.

The garden's roses were beautiful, and their scent enticed one charmingly; but they soon faded and died from a peculiar poison.

Zu Tod ist auch erkrankt seitdem
Die Nachtigall, der edle Sprosser,
Der jenen Rosen sang sein Lied; –
Ich glaub, vom selben Gift genoß er.

Vermaledeiter Garten! Ja,
Es war, als ob ein Fluch drauf laste;
Manchmal am hellen, lichten Tag
Mich dort Gespensterfurcht erfaßte.

Mich grinste an der grüne Spuk,
Er schien mich grausam zu verhöhnen,
Und aus den Taxubüschen drang
Alsbald ein Ächzen, Röcheln, Stöhnen.

Am Ende der Allee erhob
Sich die Terrasse, wo die Wellen
Der Nordsee, zu der Zeit der Flut,
Tief unten am Gestein zerschellen.

Dort schaut man weit hinaus ins Meer.
Dort stand ich oft in wilden Träumen.
Brandung war auch in meiner Brust –
Das war ein Tosen, Rasen, Schäumen –

The nightingale has also sickened and died since then, the noble songster which sang its song to those roses; – I think it partook of the same poison.

Accursed garden! Yes, it was as if a curse lay heavy upon it; sometimes in full, broad daylight fear of ghosts assailed me.

This green spookiness grinned at me, it seemed to mock me cruelly, and from the yew-bushes there then came a groaning, gasping, moaning.

At the end of the avenue rose the terrace where at high tide the waves of the North Sea are dashed to pieces on the rocks far below.

There you can gaze far out to sea. I often stood there in wild dreams. There was a surging in my breast too – there was a roaring, storming, foaming –

Ein Schäumen, Rasen, Tosen wars,
Ohnmächtig gleichfalls wie die Wogen,
Die kläglich brach der harte Fels,
Wie stolz sie auch herangezogen.

Mit Neid sah ich die Schiffe ziehn
Vorüber nach beglückten Landen –
Doch mich hielt das verdammte Schloß
Gefesselt in verfluchten Banden.

from ZUM LAZARUS

LAß die heilgen Parabolen,
Laß die frommen Hypothesen –
Suche die verdammten Fragen
Ohne Umschweif uns zu lösen.

Warum schleppt sich blutend, elend,
Unter Kreuzlast der Gerechte,
Während glücklich als ein Sieger
Trabt auf hohem Roß der Schlechte?

There was a foaming, storming, roaring as impotent as the waves which were pitifully broken by the hard rock, however proudly they came in.

With envy I watched the ships sail past towards happy lands – but the damned castle held me enchained in its accursed fetters.

from the additional *Lazarus* poems

LEAVE the holy parables, leave the pious hypotheses – try to solve for ourselves these damned questions without beating about the bush.

Why does the just man drag himself along, bleeding and wretched, beneath the weight of the cross, while the bad man trots along on a high horse, happy, as a victor?

Woran liegt die Schuld? Ist etwa
Unser Herr nicht ganz allmächtig?
Oder treibt er selbst den Unfug?
Ach, das wäre niederträchtig.

Also fragen wir beständig,
Bis man uns mit einer Handvoll
Erde endlich stopft die Mäuler –
Aber ist das eine Antwort?

WIE langsam kriechet sie dahin,
Die Zeit, die schauderhafte Schnecke!
Ich aber, ganz bewegungslos
Blieb ich hier auf demselben Flecke.

In meine dunkle Zelle dringt
Kein Sonnenstrahl, kein Hoffnungsschimmer;
Ich weiß, nur mit der Kirchhofsgruft
Vertausch ich dies fatale Zimmer.

Vielleicht bin ich gestorben längst;
Es sind vielleicht nur Spukgestalten
Die Phantasieen, die des Nachts
Im Hirn den bunten Umzug halten.

Where does the fault lie? Is Our Lord perhaps not quite omnipotent? Or is he himself responsible for this disorder? Ah, that would be base.

So we constantly ask until someone eventually stops up our mouths with a handful of earth – but is that an answer?

How slowly she creeps along, time, the loathsome snail! But I, quite incapable of movement, stayed here on the same spot.

Into my dark cell there penetrates no sunbeam, no flicker of hope; I know that I shall exchange this hateful room only for a grave in a churchyard.

Perhaps I died long ago; they are perhaps only ghostly shapes, these chimeras which at night hold their motley processions in my brain.

HEINE

Es mögen wohl Gespenster sein,
Altheidnisch göttlichen Gelichters;
Sie wählen gern zum Tummelplatz
Den Schädel eines toten Dichters. —

Die schaurig süßen Orgia,
Das nächtlich tolle Geistertreiben,
Sucht des Poeten Leichenhand
Manchmal am Morgen aufzuschreiben.

Icʜ sah sie lachen, sah sie lächeln,
Ich sah sie ganz zu Grunde gehn;
Ich hört ihr Weinen und ihr Röcheln,
Und habe ruhig zugesehn.

Leidtragend folgt ich ihren Särgen,
Und bis zum Kirchhof ging ich mit;
Hernach, ich will es nicht verbergen,
Speist ich zu Mittag mit Apptit.

Doch jetzt auf einmal mit Betrübnis
Denk ich der längstverstorbnen Schar;
Wie lodernd plötzliche Verliebnis
Stürmts auf im Herzen wunderbar!

They may well be ghosts of old heathen godlike stamp; they like to choose as their recreation ground the skull of a dead poet. —

In the morning the poet's corpse-hand sometimes tries to record these terrible-sweet orgies, these mad nocturnal ghostly activities.

I sᴀᴡ them laugh, saw them smile, I saw them go to ruin; I heard their weeping and their death-rattle, and watched unmoved.

I followed their coffins as a mourner, and went as far as the cemetery; afterwards, and I won't conceal it, I ate my lunch with a good appetite.

But now, suddenly and with sadness, I think of the long-dead band; there's a strange storm in my heart, like the flame of a sudden infatuation!

Besonders sind es Julchens Tränen,
Die im Gedächtnis rinnen mir;
Die Wehmut wird zu wildem Sehnen,
Und Tag und Nacht ruf ich nach ihr! – –

Oft kommt zu mir die tote Blume
Im Fiebertraum; alsdann zu Mut
Ist mir, als böte sie posthume
Gewährung meiner Liebesglut.

O zärtliches Phantom, umschließe
Mich fest und fester, deinen Mund
Drück ich auf meinen Mund – versüße
Die Bitternis der letzten Stund!

VOM Schöppenstuhle der Vernunft
Bist du vollständig freigesprochen;
Das Urteil sagt: die Kleine hat
Durch Tun und Reden nichts verbrochen.

Ja, stumm und tatlos standest du,
Als mich verzehrten tolle Flammen –
Du schürtest nicht, du sprachst kein Wort,
Und doch muß dich mein Herz verdammen.

It is above all Julia's tears which are running in my memory; melancholy
turns to a wild longing, and I call to her day and night! – –

The dead flower often comes to me in a fevered dream; then it seems as if
she were posthumously permitting my ardours.

O tender phantom, embrace me more and more tightly, I press your mouth
to mine – sweeten the bitterness of my last hour!

You are declared entirely innocent by the jury of Reason; the verdict says:
the girl has committed no offence by word or deed.

Yes, you stood there silent and inactive when mad flames were devouring
me – you didn't poke them, you said not a word, and yet my heart must con-
demn you.

In meinen Träumen jede Nacht
Klagt eine Stimme, die bezichtet
Des bösen Willens dich, und sagt,
Du habest mich zu Grund gerichtet.

Sie bringt Beweis und Zeugnis bei,
Sie schleppt ein Bündel von Urkunden;
Jedoch am Morgen, mit dem Traum,
Ist auch die Klägerin verschwunden.

Sie hat in meines Herzens Grund
Mit ihren Akten sich geflüchtet –
Nur eins bleibt im Gedächtnis mir,
Das ist: ich bin zu Grund gerichtet.

MICH locken nicht die Himmelsauen
Im Paradies, im selgen Land;
Dort find ich keine schönre Frauen
Als ich bereits auf Erden fand.

Kein Engel mit den feinsten Schwingen
Könnt mir ersetzen dort mein Weib;
Auf Wolken sitzend Psalmen singen,
Wär auch nicht just mein Zeitvertreib.

In my dreams each night, a voice complains, accusing you of ill will, and saying: you have brought me to ruin.

It produces proof and testimony, it drags along a bundle of documents; but in the morning the plaintiff has disappeared along with the dream.

She and her documents have taken refuge in the bottom of my heart – only one thing remains clear in my mind, and that is: I have been brought to ruin.

THE heavenly pastures in Paradise, the blessed land, do not attract me; I shan't find any more beautiful women there than I have already found on earth.

No angel with the very best wings could replace my wife there; sitting on clouds and singing psalms wouldn't be my ideal pastime either.

O Herr! ich glaub, es wär das beste,
Du ließest mich in dieser Welt;
Heil nur zuvor mein Leibgebreste,
Und sorge auch für etwas Geld.

Ich weiß, es ist voll Sünd und Laster
Die Welt; jedoch ich bin einmal
Gewöhnt, auf diesem Erdpechpflaster*
Zu schlendern durch das Jammertal.

Genieren wird das Weltgetreibe
Mich nie, denn selten geh ich aus;
In Schlafrock und Pantoffeln bleibe
Ich gern bei meiner Frau zu Haus.

Laß mich bei ihr! Hör ich sie schwätzen,
Trinkt meine Seele die Musik
Der holden Stimme mit Ergötzen.
So treu und ehrlich ist ihr Blick!

Gesundheit nur und Geldzulage
Verlang ich, Herr! O laß mich froh
Hinleben noch viel schöne Tage
Bei meiner Frau im statu quo!

O Lord! I think it would be best if you left me in this world; but heal my bodily infirmities first, and see that there's some money too.

I know this world is full of sin and depravity; but I'm used to walking on these hard pavements* through this vale of tears.

The bustle of the world won't ever vex me, for I seldom go out; I like staying at home with my wife in my dressing-gown and slippers.

Leave me with her! When I hear her chatter, my soul drinks in the music of her lovely voice with delight. Her gaze is so loyal and true!

Just health and more money are all I ask, Lord! Oh, let me live cheerfully on for many a fine day with my wife in the status quo!

* *Pech* also has the meaning of 'bad luck'.

227

DIE WAHLVERLOBTEN

Du weinst und siehst mich an, und meinst,
Daß du ob meinem Elend weinst –
Du weißt nicht, Weib! dir selber gilt
Die Trän, die deinem Aug entquillt.

O, sage mir, ob nicht vielleicht
Zuweilen dein Gemüt beschleicht
Die Ahnung, die dir offenbart,
Daß Schicksalswille uns gepaart?
Vereinigt, war uns Glück hienieden,
Getrennt, nur Untergang beschieden.

Im großen Buche stand geschrieben,
Wir sollten uns einander lieben.
Dein Platz, er sollt an meiner Brust sein,
Hier wär erwacht dein Selbstbewußtsein;
Ich hätt dich aus dem Pflanzentume
Erlöst, emporgeküßt, o Blume,
Empor zu mir, zum höchsten Leben –
Ich hätt dir eine Seel gegeben.

Paired by Destiny

You weep and look at me and think you are weeping at my wretchedness –
you don't know it, woman, but the tear which flows from your eye is for you
yourself.

Oh tell me if a presentiment does not perhaps from time to time come
over you and reveal to you that the will of Destiny has paired us? Together,
happiness was to be our lot here below, and separated, only ruin.

In the great book it was written that we should love one another. Your
place was to be at my breast, your self-assurance would have awakened there;
I would have delivered you from the plant-kingdom, brought you forth to
me, o flower, with a kiss, and to the highest form of life – I would have given
you a soul.

Jetzt, wo gelöst die Rätsel sind,
Der Sand im Stundenglas verrinnt –
O weine nicht, es mußte sein –
Ich scheide, und du welkst allein;
Du welkst, bevor du noch geblüht,
Erlöschest, eh du noch geglüht;
Du stirbst, dich hat der Tod erfaßt,
Bevor du noch gelebet hast.

Ich weiß es jetzt. Bei Gott! du bist es,
Die ich geliebt. Wie bitter ist es,
Wenn im Momente des Erkennens
Die Stunde schlägt des ewgen Trennens!
Der Willkomm ist zu gleicher Zeit
Ein Lebewohl! Wir scheiden heut
Auf immerdar. Kein Wiedersehn
Gibt es für uns in Himmelshöhn.
Die Schönheit ist dem Staub verfallen,
Du wirst zerstieben, wirst verhallen.
Viel anders ist es mit Poeten;
Die kann der Tod nicht gänzlich töten.
Uns trifft nicht weltliche Vernichtung,
Wir leben fort im Land der Dichtung,
In Avalun, dem Feenreiche –
Leb wohl auf ewig, schöne Leiche!

Now, when the riddles are solved and the sand is running out in the hourglass – oh do not weep, it had to be – I depart, and you fade alone; you fade before you have blossomed, you go out before you have shone; you die, Death has seized you before you have lived.

I know now. By God! you are the one I loved. How bitter it is when at the moment of recognition the hour of eternal separation sounds! The welcome is at the same time a farewell! We part today for ever. There is no reunion for us in the heavenly heights. Beauty has fallen to dust, you will be no more, you will fade away. It is quite different with poets; Death cannot entirely kill them. Earthly destruction is not our lot, we live on in the land of poetry, in Avalon, the fairy kingdom – farewell for ever, beautiful corpse!

HEINE

EPILOG

Unser Grab erwärmt der Ruhm.
Torenworte! Narrentum!
Eine beßre Wärme gibt
Eine Kuhmagd, die verliebt
Uns mit dicken Lippen küßt
Und beträchtlich riecht nach Mist.
Gleichfalls eine beßre Wärme
Wärmt dem Menschen die Gedärme,
Wenn er Glühwein trinkt und Punsch
Oder Grog nach Herzenswunsch
In den niedrigsten Spelunken,
Unter Dieben und Halunken,
Die dem Galgen sind entlaufen,
Aber leben, atmen, schnaufen,
Und beneidenswerter sind
Als der Thetis großes Kind –
Der Pelide sprach mit Recht:
Leben wie der ärmste Knecht
In der Oberwelt ist besser
Als am stygischen Gewässer
Schattenführer sein, ein Heros,
Den besungen selbst Homeros.

Epilogue

Fame warms our grave. A fool's words! Madness! An amorous dairy-maid who smells strongly of dung warms us better when she kisses us with thick lips. Again, a better warmth warms a man's entrails when he drinks mulled wine and punch or grog to his heart's content in the lowest taverns, among thieves and rogues who have escaped the gallows, but are alive, breathe, snort, and are more to be envied than Thetis's great child – the son of Peleus said right: to live the life of the poorest serf in the world of men is better than to be Prince of Shadows by the waters of Styx, a hero of whom Homer himself sang.

AUS DER MATRATZENGRUFT

FROM THE MATTRESS-GRAVE

Nachts, erfaßt vom wilden Geiste,
Streck ich die geballten Fäuste
Drohend aus – jedoch erschlafft
Sinkt der Arm, mir fehlt die Kraft.

Leib und Seele sind gebrochen,
Und ich sterbe ungerochen.
Auch kein Blutsfreund, zornentflammt,
Übernimmt das Rächeramt.

Ach! Blutsfreunde sind es eben,
Welche mir den Tod gegeben,
Und die schnöde Meucheltat
Ward verübet durch Verrat.

Siegfried gleich, dem hörnen Recken,
Wußten sie mich hinzustrecken –
Leicht erspäht Familienlist,
Wo der Held verwundbar ist.

At night, seized by a wild spirit, I stretch out my clenched fists threateningly –
but my arm sinks weakly back, I lack the strength.

Body and soul are broken and I die unavenged. And no kinsman, inflamed
by anger, takes over the office of avenger.

Ah! It is precisely my kinsmen who have killed me, and the vile murderous
deed was done by treachery.

They knew how to lay me low as they did Siegfried, the horned hero –
family cunning easily espies where the champion is vulnerable.

Mein Tag war heiter, glücklich meine Nacht.
Mir jauchzte stets mein Volk, wenn ich die Leier
Der Dichtkunst schlug. Mein Lied war Lust und Feuer,
Hat manche schöne Gluten angefacht.
Noch blüht mein Sommer, dennoch eingebracht
Hab ich die Ernte schon in meine Scheuer –
Und jetzt soll ich verlassen, was so teuer,
So lieb und teuer mir die Welt gemacht!
Der Hand entsinkt das Saitenspiel. In Scherben
Zerbricht das Glas, das ich so fröhlich eben
An meine übermütgen Lippen preßte.
O Gott! wie häßlich bitter ist das Sterben!
O Gott! wie süß und traulich läßt sich leben
In diesem traulich süßen Erdenneste!

Mittelalterliche Roheit
Weicht dem Aufschwung schöner Künste:
Instrument moderner Bildung
Ist vorzüglich das Klavier.

My days were serene, my nights happy. My people always cheered me when I struck the lyre of poetry. My song was joy and fire, it fanned many a splendid glow. My summer still blooms, but I have already brought the harvest into my barn – and now I must leave all that made the world so precious, so dear and precious, to me! The stringed instrument sinks from my hand. The glass which I was so joyfully pressing to my arrogant lips, splinters into fragments. O God! how hatefully bitter it is to die! O God! how sweetly and snugly one can live in this snug, sweet earthly nest!

Medieval coarseness gives way to the rise of the fine arts: the instrument of modern culture is primarily the pianoforte.

AUS DER MATRATZENGRUFT

Auch die Eisenbahnen wirken
Heilsam aufs Familienleben,
Sintemal sie uns erleichtern
Die Entfernung von der Sippschaft.

Wie bedaur ich, daß die Darre
Meines Rückgratmarks mich hindert
Lange Zeit noch zu verweilen
In dergleichen Fortschrittswelt!

STUNDEN, Tage, Ewigkeiten
Sind es, die wie Schnecken gleiten;
Diese grauen Riesenschnecken
Ihre Hörner weit ausrecken.

Manchmal in der öden Leere,
Manchmal in dem Nebelmeere
Strahlt ein Licht, das süß und golden,
Wie die Augen meiner Holden.

The railways too have a beneficial effect on family life, since they make it easier for us to get away from our relations.

How I regret that my spinal atrophy will prevent me from staying for a long time yet in this world of progress!

HOURS, days, eternities – they glide by like snails; these huge grey snails stick their horns out far.

Sometimes in the desolate emptiness, sometimes in the sea of mists a light gleams, sweet and golden like the eyes of my dear one.

Doch im selben Nu zerstäubet
Diese Wonne, und mir bleibet
Das Bewußtsein nur, das schwere,
Meiner schrecklichen Misere.

Mir lodert und wogt im Hirn eine Flut
Von Wäldern, Bergen und Fluren;
Aus dem tollen Wust tritt endlich hervor
Ein Bild mit festen Konturen.

Das Städtchen, das mir im Sinne schwebt,
Ist Godesberg, ich denke.
Dort wieder unter dem Lindenbaum
Sitz ich vor der alten Schenke.

Der Hals ist mir trocken, als hätt ich verschluckt
Die untergehende Sonne.
Herr Wirt! Herr Wirt! Eine Flasche Wein
Aus Eurer besten Tonne!

But in the same instant this joy turns to dust, and I am left only with the heavy consciousness of my terrible misery.

A flood of forests, mountains and meadows blazes and surges in my brain; from the mad confusion there eventually emerges a picture with firm contours.

The little town which hovers in my mind's eye is Godesberg, I think. I'm sitting there under the lime-tree once again outside the old tavern.

My throat is as dry as if I had swallowed the setting sun. Landlord! Landlord! A bottle of wine from your finest cask!

Es fließt der holde Rebensaft
Hinunter in meine Seele,
Und löscht bei dieser Gelegenheit
Den Sonnenbrand der Kehle.

Und noch eine Flasche, Herr Wirt! Ich trank
Die erste in schnöder Zerstreuung,
Ganz ohne Andacht! Mein edler Wein,
Ich bitte dich drob um Verzeihung.

Ich sah hinauf nach dem Drachenfels,
Der, hochromantisch beschienen
Vom Abendrot, sich spiegelt im Rhein
Mit seinen Burgruinen.

Ich horchte dem fernen Winzergesang
Und dem kecken Gezwitscher der Finken –
So trank ich zerstreut, und an den Wein
Dacht ich nicht während dem Trinken.

Jetzt aber steck ich die Nase ins Glas,
Und ernsthaft zuvor beguck ich
Den Wein, den ich schlucke; manchmal auch,
Ganz ohne zu gucken, schluck ich.

The friendly juice of the vine flows down into my soul, and in the process it extinguishes the sunburn in my throat.

Another bottle, landlord! I drank the first in a wretchedly distracted state, quite without reverence! O noble wine, I beg your forgiveness.

I gazed up at the Drachenfels which, lit up in a highly romantic way by the evening glow, is with its castle ruins reflected in the Rhine.

I listened to the vine-grower's distant song and the cheeky twittering of the finches – and I drank absent-mindedly, and didn't think of the wine while I was drinking.

But now I put my nose into the glass and I gravely examine the wine before I swallow it; and sometimes, too, I swallow without looking.

Doch sonderbar! Während dem Schlucken wird mir
Zu Sinne, als ob ich verdoppelt,
Ein andrer armer Schlucker sei
Mit mir zusammengekoppelt.

Der sieht so krank und elend aus,
So bleich und abgemergelt.
Gar schmerzlich verhöhnend schaut er mich an,
Wodurch er mich seltsam nergelt.

Der Bursche behauptet, er sei ich selbst,
Wir wären nur Eins, wir beide,
Wir wären ein einziger armer Mensch,
Der jetzt am Fieber leide.

Nicht in der Schenke von Godesberg,
In einer Krankenstube
Des fernen Paris befänden wir uns –
Du lügst, du bleicher Bube!

Du lügst, ich bin so gesund und rot
Wie eine blühende Rose,
Auch bin ich stark, nimm dich in acht,
Daß ich mich nicht erbose!

But how strange! As I swallow it seems to me that I have a double, that another poor wretch is coupled to me.

He looks so sick and wretched, so pale and emaciated. He looks at me with painful scorn and thereby strangely irritates me.

The fellow maintains he is I myself, that the two of us are only one person, that we are one single wretched man now suffering from fever.

He further maintains that we are not in the tavern at Godesberg but in a sick-room in far-off Paris – you lie, pale knave!

You lie, I'm as fit and ruddy as a rose in bloom, and I'm strong too, take care I don't get angry!

Er zuckt die Achseln und seufzt: «O Narr!»
Das hat meinen Zorn entzügelt;
Und mit dem verdammten zweiten Ich
Hab ich mich endlich geprügelt.

Doch sonderbar! jedweden Puff,
Den ich dem Burschen erteile,
Empfinde ich am eignen Leib,
Und ich schlage mir Beule auf Beule.

Bei dieser fatalen Balgerei
Ward wieder der Hals mir trocken,
Und will ich rufen nach Wein den Wirt,
Die Worte im Munde stocken.

Mir schwinden die Sinne, und traumhaft hör
Ich von Kataplasmen reden,
Auch von der Mixtur – einen Eßlöffel voll –
Zwölf Tropfen stündlich in jeden.

GANZ entsetzlich ungesund
Ist die Erde, und zu Grund,
Ja, zu Grund muß alles gehn,
Was hienieden groß und schön.

He shrugs his shoulders and sighs: 'You fool!' That loosed my anger; and
I finally came to blows with my damned second self.

But how strange! every blow I deal out to this fellow I feel on my own body,
and I give myself bruise upon bruise.

During this unfortunate fight my throat grew dry again, and when I try to
order wine from the landlord, the words stick in my mouth.

My senses fail, and in a dream I hear people talking of cataplasms, and also
of The Mixture – a tablespoonful – twelve drops in each every hour.

THIS earth is dreadfully unhealthy, and everything which is great and beauti-
ful here below must fall into decay.

Sind es alten Wahns Phantasmen,
Die dem Boden als Miasmen
Stumm entsteigen und die Lüfte
Schwängern mit dem argen Gifte?

Holde Frauenblumen, welche
Kaum erschlossen ihre Kelche
Den geliebten Sonnenküssen,
Hat der Tod schon fortgerissen.

Helden, trabend hoch zu Roß,
Trifft unsichtbar das Geschoß;
Und die Kröten sich beeifern,
Ihren Lorbeer zu begeifern.

Was noch gestern stolz gelodert,
Das ist heute schon vermodert;
Seine Leier mit Verdruß
Bricht entzwei der Genius.

O wie klug sind doch die Sterne!
Halten sich in sichrer Ferne
Von dem bösen Erdenrund,
Das so tödlich ungesund.

Are they phantasms of former madness which silently emerge from the ground as miasmas and make the air pregnant with their wretched poison?

Pretty female flowers which have scarcely opened their cups to the beloved sun's kisses are already torn away by Death.

Heroes, trotting high on horseback, are hit by an unseen bullet; and toads compete with each other to slobber over their laurels.

What yesterday still glowed proudly has today already rotted away; the guardian angel breaks his lyre in anger.

Oh, how wise the stars are! They keep a safe distance from our evil globe, which is so fatally unhealthy.

AUS DER MATRATZENGRUFT

Kluge Sterne wollen nicht
Leben, Ruhe, Himmelslicht
Hier einbüßen, hier auf Erden,
Und mit uns elendig werden –

Wollen nicht mit uns versinken
In den Twieten, welche stinken,
In dem Mist, wo Würmer kriechen,
Welche auch nicht lieblich riechen –

Wollen immer ferne bleiben
Vom fatalen Erdentreiben,
Von dem Klüngel und Geruddel,
Von dem Erdenkuddelmuddel.

Mitleidsvoll aus ihrer Höhe
Schaun sie oft auf unser Wehe;
Eine goldne Träne fällt
Dann herab auf diese Welt.

DIE Söhne des Glückes beneid ich nicht
Ob ihrem Leben, beneiden
Will ich sie nur ob ihrem Tod,
Dem schmerzlos raschen Verscheiden.

Wise stars don't want to forfeit life, peace, sunlight here on earth, and become wretched like us –
   don't want, like us, to fade away in stinking alley-ways, in the dung creeping with worms – which don't smell very nice either –
   want to keep well away from the wretched bustle of life on earth, from the mob and herd, from the motley crowd on earth.
   Full of compassion they often look down from their heights on our woe; a golden tear then falls down on to this world.

I DON'T envy the sons of Fortune their life, I want only to envy them their death, their painless, rapid passing.

Im Prachtgewand, das Haupt bekränzt,
Und Lachen auf der Lippe,
Sitzen sie froh beim Lebensbankett –
Da trifft sie jählings die Hippe.

Im Festkleid und mit Rosen geschmückt,
Die noch wie lebend blühten,
Gelangen in das Schattenreich
Fortunas Favoriten.

Nie hatte Siechtum sie entstellt,
Sind Tote von guter Miene,
Und huldreich empfängt sie an ihrem Hof
Zarewna Proserpine.

Wie sehr muß ich beneiden ihr Los!
Schon sieben Jahre mit herben,
Qualvollen Gebresten wälz ich mich
Am Boden, und kann nicht sterben!

O Gott, verkürze meine Qual,
Damit man mich bald begrabe;
Du weißt ja, daß ich kein Talent
Zum Martyrtume habe.

In splendid robes and with wreaths in their hair and a laugh on their lips, they sit joyfully at the banquet of life – and the scythe strikes them suddenly.

In festal clothes and adorned with roses which flowered as if they were still alive, Fortune's favourites come to the realm of shadows.

Ill-health had never disfigured them, they are dead men of goodly countenance, and Czarevna Proserpina receives them graciously at her court.

How much I must envy their lot! For seven years now I have been rolling about on the floor with bitter, excruciating infirmities, and cannot die!

O God, shorten my torment so that I may soon be buried; you know I have no talent for martyrdom.

Ob deiner Inkonsequenz, o Herr,
Erlaube, daß ich staune:
Du schufest den fröhlichsten Dichter, und raubst
Ihm jetzt seine gute Laune.

Der Schmerz verdumpft den heitern Sinn
Und macht mich melancholisch;
Nimmt nicht der traurige Spaß ein End,
So werd ich am Ende katholisch.

Ich heule dir dann die Ohren voll,
Wie andre gute Christen –
O Miserere! Verloren geht
Der beste der Humoristen!

MORPHINE

Groß ist die Ähnlichkeit der beiden schönen
Jünglingsgestalten, ob der eine gleich
Viel blässer als der andre, auch viel strenger,
Fast möcht ich sagen viel vornehmer aussieht
Als jener andre, welcher mich vertraulich
In seine Arme schloß – Wie lieblich sanft

Permit me, o Lord, to wonder at your inconsistency: you created the most joyous of poets, and rob him now of his good humour.

Pain dulls my cheerful mind and makes me melancholy; if this sorry joke doesn't soon come to an end, I'll finish up by becoming a Catholic.

I'll then howl your ears full, as other good Christians do – o miserere! That's the end of the best of humorists!

Morphine

GREAT is the similarity between the two fair youthful figures, though one is much paler than the other, and looks much more stern – I might almost say, much more distinguished – than that other one who held me in a cordial em-

War dann sein Lächeln, und sein Blick wie selig!
Dann mocht es wohl geschehn, daß seines Hauptes
Mohnblumenkranz auch meine Stirn berührte
Und seltsam duftend allen Schmerz verscheuchte
Aus meiner Seel – Doch solche Linderung,
Sie dauert kurze Zeit; genesen gänzlich
Kann ich nur dann, wenn seine Fackel senkt
Der andre Bruder, der so ernst und bleich. –
Gut ist der Schlaf, der Tod ist besser – freilich
Das beste wäre, nie geboren sein.

Ich war, o Lamm, als Hirt bestellt,
Zu hüten dich auf dieser Welt.
Hab dich mit meinem Brot geätzt,
Mit Wasser aus dem Born geletzt.
Wenn kalt der Wintersturm gelärmt,
Hab ich dich an der Brust erwärmt.
Hier hielt ich fest dich angeschlossen,
Wenn Regengüsse sich ergossen
Und Wolf und Waldbach um die Wette
Geheult im dunkeln Felsenbette.

brace – how delightfully gentle his smile then was, and how blessed his gaze!
Then it may have happened that the poppy-wreath on his head touched my
brow too and with its strange scent drove all pain from my soul – But such
alleviation does not last long; I can only get completely well again when that
other brother, who is so grave and pale, lowers his torch. – Sleep is good,
Death is better – of course, best of all would be never to have been born.

I was, o lamb, appointed as shepherd, to protect you in this world. I have fed
you with my bread, refreshed you with water from the spring. When winter
storms roared coldly I warmed you at my breast. I held you firmly and close
to me when rain-showers poured down and wolves howled in competition
with forest-streams in the dark rocky ravine. You were not afraid, you did not

AUS DER MATRATZENGRUFT

Du bangtest nicht, hast nicht gezittert.
Selbst wenn den höchsten Tann zersplittert
Der Wetterstrahl – in meinem Schoß
Du schliefest still und sorgenlos.

Mein Arm wird schwach, es schleicht herbei
Der blasse Tod! Die Schäferei,
Das Hirtenspiel, es hat ein Ende.
O Gott, ich leg in deine Hände
Zurück den Stab. – Behüte du
Mein armes Lamm, wenn ich zur Ruh
Bestattet bin – und dulde nicht,
Daß irgendwo ein Dorn sie sticht –
O schütz ihr Vlies vor Dornenhecken
Und auch vor Sümpfen, die beflecken;
Laß überall zu ihren Füßen
Das allerbeste Futter sprießen;
Und laß sie schlafen, sorgenlos,
Wie einst sie schlief in meinem Schoß.

WORTE! Worte! keine Taten!
Niemals Fleisch, geliebte Puppe,
Immer Geist und keinen Braten,
Keine Knödel in der Suppe!

tremble. Even when lightning split the tallest fir-tree – you slept quiet and
free from care in my lap.
My arm grows feeble, pale Death stalks hither! Our shepherd-world and
pastoral games are coming to an end. O God, I place the staff in your hands
again. – You guard my poor lamb when I am laid to rest – and do not allow
any thorns to prick her – oh, protect her fleece from thorny hedges, and also
from swamps which make her dirty; let the very best grazing grow at her feet
wherever she is; and let her sleep, free from care, as once she slept in my lap.

WORDS! words! no deeds! Never flesh, beloved doll, always spirit, and no
roast meat, no dumplings in the soup!

245

Doch vielleicht ist dir zuträglich
Nicht die wilde Lendenkraft,
Welche galoppieret täglich
Auf dem Roß der Leidenschaft.

Ja, ich fürchte fast, es riebe,
Zartes Kind, dich endlich auf
Jene wilde Jagd der Liebe,
Amors Steeple-chase-Wettlauf.

Viel gesünder, glaub ich schier,
Ist für dich ein kranker Mann
Als Liebhaber, der gleich mir
Kaum ein Glied bewegen kann.

Deshalb unsrem Herzensbund,
Liebste, widme deine Triebe;
Solches ist dir sehr gesund,
Eine Art Gesundheitsliebe.

Es träumte mir von einer Sommernacht,
Wo bleich, verwittert, in des Mondes Glanze
Bauwerke lagen, Reste alter Pracht,
Ruinen aus der Zeit der Renaissance.

But perhaps the wild power of the loins which daily gallops on the horse of passion is not good for you.

Yes, I almost fear that it would wear you out, tender child, that wild hunt of love, Amor's steeplechase.

Much better for your health, I almost believe, is a sick man for a lover, one who like me can scarcely move a finger.

Therefore, dearest, devote your energies to the union of our hearts; that will be very good for your health – a kind of health-cure love.

I DREAMED of a summer night when pale, weather-beaten buildings lay in the moon's gleam – remains of old splendour, ruins from the time of the Renaissance.

Nur hie und da, mit dorisch ernstem Knauf,
Hebt aus dem Schutt sich einzeln eine Säule,
Und schaut ins hohe Firmament hinauf,
Als ob sie spotte seiner Donnerkeile.

Gebrochen auf dem Boden liegen rings
Portale, Giebeldächer mit Skulpturen,
Wo Mensch und Tier vermischt, Centaur und Sphinx,
Satyr, Chimäre – Fabelzeitfiguren.

Es steht ein offner Marmorsarkophag
Ganz unverstümmelt unter den Ruinen,
Und gleichfalls unversehrt im Sarge lag
Ein toter Mann mit leidend sanften Mienen.

Karyatiden mit gerecktem Hals,
Sie scheinen mühsam ihn emporzuhalten.
An beiden Seiten sieht man ebenfalls
Viel basrelief gemeißelte Gestalten.

Hier sieht man des Olympos Herrlichkeit
Mit seinen lüderlichen Heidengöttern,
Adam und Eva stehn dabei, sind beid
Versehn mit keuschem Schurz von Feigenblättern.

Only here and there, with grave Doric capital, a column rises solitary from the debris and gazes up into the high firmament, as if it mocked its thunderbolts.

Broken on the ground lie round about portals, gable-roofs with sculptures, in which men and animals are mixed, centaur and sphinx, satyr, chimera – figures from legendary times.

There stands an open marble sarcophagus, quite unmutilated, among the ruins, and likewise undamaged in the coffin there lay a dead man with suffering, gentle features.

Caryatids with craning necks seem to be holding him up with difficulty. On both sides one can also see many figures carved in low relief.

Here one sees the splendour of Olympus with its dissolute heathen gods, Adam and Eve stand alongside, both are provided with a chaste apron of fig-leaves.

Hier sieht man Trojas Untergang und Brand,
Paris und Helena, auch Hektor sah man;
Moses und Aaron gleich daneben stand,
Auch Esther, Judith, Holofern und Haman.

Desgleichen war zu sehn der Gott Amur,
Phöbus Apoll, Vulkanus und Frau Venus,
Pluto und Proserpine und Merkur,
Gott Bacchus und Priapus und Silenus.

Daneben stand der Esel Balaams
– Der Esel war zum Sprechen gut getroffen –
Dort sah man auch die Prüfung Abrahams
Und Lot, der mit den Töchtern sich besoffen.

Hier war zu schaun der Tanz Herodias',
Das Haupt des Täufers trägt man auf der Schüssel,
Die Hölle sah man hier und Satanas,
Und Petrus mit dem großen Himmelsschlüssel.

Abwechselnd wieder sah man hier skulpiert
Des geilen Jovis Brunst und Freveltaten,
Wie er als Schwan die Leda hat verführt,
Die Danaë als Regen von Dukaten.

Here one can see Troy's downfall and burning, Paris and Helen, and one saw Hector too; Moses and Aaron similarly stood by, also Esther, Judith, Holofernes and Haman.

Likewise the god Amor was to be seen, Phoebus Apollo, Vulcan and Madam Venus, Pluto, Proserpina and Mercury, god Bacchus and Priapus and Silenus.

Near by stood Balaam's ass – the ass was a speaking likeness – there too one saw the testing of Abraham, and Lot, who had got drunk with his daughters.

Herodias's dance was to be seen here, someone is holding the Baptist's head on a charger, one saw hell here and Satan, and Peter with the great key of heaven.

In turn one saw sculptured here lascivious Jove's lust and outrages, saw him as the swan seducing Leda, and, as a shower of ducats, Danae.

Hier war zu sehn Dianas wilde Jagd,
Ihr folgen hochgeschürzte Nymphen, Doggen,
Hier sah man Herkules in Frauentracht,
Die Spindel drehend hält sein Arm den Rocken.

Daneben ist der Sinai zu sehn,
Am Berg steht Israel mit seinen Ochsen,
Man schaut den Herrn als Kind im Tempel stehn
Und disputieren mit den Orthodoxen.

Die Gegensätze sind hier grell gepaart,
Des Griechen Lustsinn und der Gottgedanke
Judäas! Und in Arabeskenart
Um beide schlingt der Epheu seine Ranke.

Doch, wunderbar! Derweilen solcherlei
Bildwerke träumend ich betrachtet habe,
Wird plötzlich mir zu Sinn, ich selber sei
Der tote Mann im schönen Marmorgrabe.

Zu Häupten aber meiner Ruhestätt
Stand eine Blume, rätselhaft gestaltet,
Die Blätter schwefelgelb und violett,
Doch wilder Liebreiz in der Blume waltet.

Diana's wild hunt was to be seen here, nymphs follow her, their dresses tied high, and mastiffs; here one saw Hercules in women's clothes, turning the spindle, his arm holding the distaff.

Near by, Sinai is to be seen, on the mount stands Israel with his oxen, one sees the Lord as a child standing in the temple and disputing with the orthodox.

The antitheses are vividly paired here, the Greek's sense of joy and Judaea's concept of God! And the ivy in arabesques entwines its tendrils around both.

But how strange! While I gazed dreaming at such sculptures, it suddenly seems to me that I myself am the dead man in the beautiful marble grave.

But at the head of my resting-place stood a flower, mysteriously shaped, the leaves sulphur-yellow and violet, yet a wild fascination lies in the flower.

Das Volk nennt sie die Blum der Passion
Und sagt, sie sei dem Schädelberg entsprossen,
Als man gekreuzigt hat den Gottessohn,
Und dort sein welterlösend Blut geflossen.

Blutzeugnis, heißt es, gebe diese Blum,
Und alle Marterinstrumente, welche
Dem Henker dienen bei dem Märtyrtum,
Sie trüge sie abkonterfeit im Kelche.

Ja, alle Requisiten der Passion
Sähe man hier, die ganze Folterkammer,
Zum Beispiel: Geißel, Stricke, Dornenkron,
Das Kreuz, den Kelch, die Nägel und den Hammer.

Solch eine Blum an meinem Grabe stand,
Und über meinen Leichnam niederbeugend,
Wie Frauentrauer, küßt sie mir die Hand,
Küßt Stirne mir und Augen, trostlos schweigend.

Doch, Zauberei des Traumes! Seltsamlich,
Die Blum der Passion, die schwefelgelbe,
Verwandelt in ein Frauenbildnis sich,
Und das ist Sie – die Liebste, ja die selbe!

The people call it the passion-flower and say it sprang up on Golgotha when hey crucified the Son of God and his world-redeeming blood flowed there.

This flower, they say, bears witness to the blood, and all the instruments of torture which serve the executioner at a martyrdom are portrayed in its cup.

Yes, one might see here all the requisites of the Passion, the whole torture-chamber, for example: scourge, ropes, crown of thorns, the cross, the cup, the nails and the hammer.

Such a flower stood by my grave, and bending over my corpse, like a woman's grief, it kisses my hand, kisses my brow and eyes, inconsolably silent.

But, magic of dreams! Strangely, the sulphur-yellow passion-flower becomes transformed into the likeness of a woman, and it is she – my dearest one, none other!

Du warst die Blume, du geliebtes Kind,
An deinen Küssen mußt ich dich erkennen.
So zärtlich keine Blumenlippen sind,
So feurig keine Blumentränen brennen!

Geschlossen war mein Aug, doch angeblickt
Hat meine Seel beständig dein Gesichte,
Du sahst mich an, beseligt und verzückt,
Und geisterhaft beglänzt vom Mondenlichte!

Wir sprachen nicht, jedoch mein Herz vernahm,
Was du verschwiegen dachtest im Gemüte –
Das ausgesprochne Wort ist ohne Scham,
Das Schweigen ist der Liebe keusche Blüte.

Lautloses Zwiegespräch! man glaubt es kaum,
Wie bei dem stummen, zärtlichen Geplauder
So schnell die Zeit verstreicht im schönen Traum
Der Sommernacht, gewebt aus Lust und Schauder.

Was wir gesprochen, frag es niemals, ach!
Den Glühwurm frag, was er dem Grase glimmert,
Die Welle frage, was sie rauscht im Bach,
Den Westwind frage, was er weht und wimmert.

You were the flower, beloved child, by your kisses I was bound to recognize you. No flower-lips are so tender, no flower-tears burn with so much fire!

My eye was closed, but my soul constantly gazed at your face, you looked at me, blessed and enraptured, and lit up ghostlike by the moon!

We did not speak, but my heart perceived what you secretly thought in your mind – the spoken word is without shame, silence is love's chaste flower.

Soundless colloquy! One can scarcely believe how swiftly the time passes in silent, tender chat in the beautiful dream of a summer night, woven of joy and dread.

Never ask what we spoke, ah, ask the glow-worm what message it glimmers to the grass, ask the wave what it whispers in the brook, ask the west wind what it breathes and moans.

Frag, was er strahlet, den Karfunkelstein,
Frag, was sie duften, Nachtviol und Rosen –
Doch frage nie, wovon im Mondenschein
Die Marterblume und ihr Toter kosen!

Ich weiß es nicht, wie lange ich genoß
In meiner schlummerkühlen Marmortruhe
Den schönen Freudentraum. Ach, es zerfloß
Die Wonne meiner ungestörten Ruhe!

O Tod! mit deiner Grabesstille, du,
Nur du kannst uns die beste Wollust geben;
Den Krampf der Leidenschaft, Lust ohne Ruh,
Gibt uns für Glück das albern rohe Leben!

Doch wehe mir! es schwand die Seligkeit,
Als draußen plötzlich sich ein Lärm erhoben;
Es war ein scheltend, stampfend wüster Streit,
Ach, meine Blum verscheuchte dieses Toben!

Ja, draußen sich erhob mit wildem Grimm
Ein Zanken, ein Gekeife, ein Gekläffe,
Ich glaubte zu erkennen manche Stimm –
Es waren meines Grabmals Basrelieffe.

Ask what the carbuncle flashes, ask the dame's violet and roses what sweet smell they bring – but never ask what the flower of martyrdom and its dead friend talk of so tenderly in the moonlight!

I do not know how long I enjoyed in my slumber-cool marble chest this beautiful dream of joy. Alas, the bliss of my undisturbed rest melted away!

O Death! with thy stillness of the grave thou alone canst give us the most perfect sensual pleasure; the convulsions of passion, and desire without rest are what foolish, crude life gives us for happiness!

But woe is me! This bliss vanished when outside a noise suddenly arose; it was an arid quarrel, with scoldings and stampings; alas, the din frightened away my flower.

Yes, outside quarrelling, nagging and yelping arose with wild anger; I thought I recognized many a voice – it was the bas-reliefs from my tomb.

Spukt in dem Stein der alte Glaubenswahn?
Und disputieren diese Marmorschemen?
Der Schreckensruf des wilden Waldgotts Pan
Wetteifernd wild mit Mosis Anathemen!

O, dieser Streit wird enden nimmermehr,
Stets wird die Wahrheit hadern mit dem Schönen,
Stets wird geschieden sein der Menschheit Heer
In zwei Partein: Barbaren und Hellenen.

Das fluchte, schimpfte! gar kein Ende nahms
Mit dieser Kontroverse, der langweilgen,
Da war zumal der Esel Balaams,
Der überschrie die Götter und die Heilgen!

Mit diesem I-A, I-A, dem Gewiehr,
Dem schluchzend ekelhaften Mißlaut, brachte
Mich zur Verzweiflung schier das dumme Tier,
Ich selbst zuletzt schrie auf – und ich erwachte.

Does the old religious fanaticism haunt the stone? And are these marble figures in dispute? The cry of terror of the wild wood-god Pan contending wildly with Moses's anathemas!

Oh, this strife will never end, truth will always wrangle with beauty, the hosts of men will always be divided into two parties: barbarians and Hellenes.

What cursing and abuse there was! There was no end to this tedious controversy, and it was above all Balaam's ass that drowned the cries of gods and saints!

With its hee-haw, hee-haw bray, that sobbing, loathsomely ugly sound, the foolish animal brought me to despair, I myself at last cried out – and I awoke.

HEINE

DER SCHEIDENDE

ERSTORBEN ist in meiner Brust
Jedwede weltlich eitle Lust,
Schier ist mir auch erstorben drin
Der Haß des Schlechten, sogar der Sinn
Für eigne wie für fremde Not –
Und in mir lebt nur noch der Tod!

Der Vorhang fällt, das Stück ist aus,
Und gähnend wandelt jetzt nach Haus
Mein liebes deutsches Publikum,
Die guten Leutchen sind nicht dumm;
Das speist jetzt ganz vergnügt zu Nacht,
Und trinkt sein Schöppchen, singt und lacht –
Er hatte recht, der edle Heros,
Der weiland sprach im Buch Homeros':
Der kleinste lebendige Philister
Zu Stukkert am Neckar, viel glücklicher ist er
Als ich, der Pelide, der tote Held,
Der Schattenfürst in der Unterwelt.

The Parting One

EVERY vain worldly joy has died in my breast, and hatred of evil is likewise entirely dead there, even the awareness of my own and others' distress – and only Death is still alive within me!

The curtain falls, the play is over, and my dear German public is now going home yawning, the good folks aren't stupid; they'll now be contentedly eating their supper, drinking their glass of wine, singing and laughing – he was right, the noble hero who once said in Homer's book: The least living philistine in Stuttgart on the Neckar is much more fortunate than I, the son of Peleus, the dead hero, the Prince of Shadows in the Underworld.

INDEX OF TITLES AND FIRST LINES

INDEX OF TITLES AND FIRST LINES

INDEX OF TITLES AND FIRST LINES

261

INDEX OF TITLES AND FIRST LINES

READ MORE IN PENGUIN

In every corner of the world, on every subject under the sun, Penguin represents quality and variety – the very best in publishing today.

For complete information about books available from Penguin – including Puffins, Penguin Classics and Arkana – and how to order them, write to us at the appropriate address below. Please note that for copyright reasons the selection of books varies from country to country.

In the United Kingdom: Please write to *Dept. EP, Penguin Books Ltd, Bath Road, Harmondsworth, West Drayton, Middlesex UB7 ODA*

In the United States: Please write to *Consumer Sales, Penguin USA, P.O. Box 999, Dept. 17109, Bergenfield, New Jersey 07621-0120.* VISA and MasterCard holders call 1-800-253-6476 to order Penguin titles

In Canada: Please write to *Penguin Books Canada Ltd, 10 Alcorn Avenue, Suite 300, Toronto, Ontario M4V 3B2*

In Australia: Please write to *Penguin Books Australia Ltd, P.O. Box 257, Ringwood, Victoria 3134*

In New Zealand: Please write to *Penguin Books (NZ) Ltd, Private Bag 102902, North Shore Mail Centre, Auckland 10*

In India: Please write to *Penguin Books India Pvt Ltd, 706 Eros Apartments, 56 Nehru Place, New Delhi 110 019*

In the Netherlands: Please write to *Penguin Books Netherlands bv, Postbus 3507, NL-1001 AH Amsterdam*

In Germany: Please write to *Penguin Books Deutschland GmbH, Metzlerstrasse 26, 60594 Frankfurt am Main*

In Spain: Please write to *Penguin Books S. A., Bravo Murillo 19, 1° B, 28015 Madrid*

In Italy: Please write to *Penguin Italia s.r.l., Via Felice Casati 20, I–20124 Milano*

In France: Please write to *Penguin France S. A., 17 rue Lejeune, F–31000 Toulouse*

In Japan: Please write to *Penguin Books Japan, Ishikiribashi Building, 2–5–4, Suido, Bunkyo-ku, Tokyo 112*

In Greece: Please write to *Penguin Hellas Ltd, Dimocritou 3, GR–106 71 Athens*

In South Africa: Please write to *Longman Penguin Southern Africa (Pty) Ltd, Private Bag X08, Bertsham 2013*

PENGUIN AUDIOBOOKS

A Quality of Writing that Speaks for Itself

Penguin Books has always led the field in quality publishing. Now you can listen at leisure to your favourite books, read to you by familiar voices from radio, stage and screen. Penguin Audiobooks are ideal as gifts, for when you are travelling or simply to enjoy at home. They are produced to an excellent standard, and abridgements are always faithful to the original texts. From thrillers to classic literature, biography to humour, with a wealth of titles in between, Penguin Audiobooks offer you quality, entertainment and the chance to rediscover the pleasure of listening.

You can order Penguin Audiobooks through Penguin Direct by telephoning (0181) 899 4036. The lines are open 24 hours every day. Ask for Penguin Direct, quoting your credit card details.

Published or forthcoming:

Emma by Jane Austen, read by Fiona Shaw

Persuasion by Jane Austen, read by Joanna David

Pride and Prejudice by Jane Austen, read by Geraldine McEwan

The Tenant of Wildfell Hall by Anne Brontë, read by Juliet Stevenson

Jane Eyre by Charlotte Brontë, read by Juliet Stevenson

Villette by Charlotte Brontë, read by Juliet Stevenson

Wuthering Heights by Emily Brontë, read by Juliet Stevenson

The Woman in White by Wilkie Collins, read by Nigel Anthony and Susan Jameson

Heart of Darkness by Joseph Conrad, read by David Threlfall

Tales from the One Thousand and One Nights, read by Souad Faress and Raad Rawi

Moll Flanders by Daniel Defoe, read by Frances Barber

Great Expectations by Charles Dickens, read by Hugh Laurie

Hard Times by Charles Dickens, read by Michael Pennington

Martin Chuzzlewit by Charles Dickens, read by John Wells

The Old Curiosity Shop by Charles Dickens, read by Alec McCowen

PENGUIN AUDIOBOOKS

Crime and Punishment by Fyodor Dostoyevsky, read by Alex Jennings

Middlemarch by George Eliot, read by Harriet Walter

Silas Marner by George Eliot, read by Tim Pigott-Smith

The Great Gatsby by F. Scott Fitzgerald, read by Marcus D'Amico

Madame Bovary by Gustave Flaubert, read by Claire Bloom

Jude the Obscure by Thomas Hardy, read by Samuel West

The Return of the Native by Thomas Hardy, read by Steven Pacey

Tess of the D'Urbervilles by Thomas Hardy, read by Eleanor Bron

The Iliad by Homer, read by Derek Jacobi

Dubliners by James Joyce, read by Gerard McSorley

The Dead and Other Stories by James Joyce, read by Gerard McSorley

On the Road by Jack Kerouac, read by David Carradine

Sons and Lovers by D. H. Lawrence, read by Paul Copley

The Fall of the House of Usher by Edgar Allan Poe, read by Andrew Sachs

Wide Sargasso Sea by Jean Rhys, read by Jane Lapotaire and Michael Kitchen

The Little Prince by Antoine de Saint-Exupéry, read by Michael Maloney

Frankenstein by Mary Shelley, read by Richard Pasco

Of Mice and Men by John Steinbeck, read by Gary Sinise

Travels with Charley by John Steinbeck, read by Gary Sinise

The Pearl by John Steinbeck, read by Hector Elizondo

Dr Jekyll and Mr Hyde by Robert Louis Stevenson, read by Jonathan Hyde

Kidnapped by Robert Louis Stevenson, read by Robbie Coltrane

The Age of Innocence by Edith Wharton, read by Kerry Shale

The Buccaneers by Edith Wharton, read by Dana Ivey

Mrs Dalloway by Virginia Woolf, read by Eileen Atkins

READ MORE IN PENGUIN

A CHOICE OF CLASSICS

Jacob Burckhardt	**The Civilization of the Renaissance in Italy**
Carl von Clausewitz	**On War**
Meister Eckhart	**Selected Writings**
Friedrich Engels	**The Origins of the Family, Private Property and the State**
Wolfram von Eschenbach	**Parzival**
	Willehalm
Goethe	**Elective Affinities**
	Faust Parts One and Two (in 2 volumes)
	Italian Journey
	The Sorrows of Young Werther
Jacob and Wilhelm Grimm	**Selected Tales**
E. T. A. Hoffmann	**Tales of Hoffmann**
Henrik Ibsen	**A Doll's House and Other Plays**
	Ghosts and Other Plays
	Hedda Gabler and Other Plays
	The Master Builder and Other Plays
	Peer Gynt
Søren Kierkegaard	**Fear and Trembling**
	The Sickness Unto Death
Georg Christoph Lichtenberg	**Aphorisms**
Karl Marx	**Capital** (in three volumes)
Friedrich Nietzsche	**The Birth of Tragedy**
	Beyond Good and Evil
	Ecce Homo
	Human, All Too Human
	A Nietzsche Reader
Friedrich Schiller	**The Robbers/Wallenstein**
Arthur Schopenhauer	**Essays and Aphorisms**
Gottfried von Strassburg	**Tristan**
Adalbert Stifter	**Brigitta and Other Tales**
August Strindberg	**By the Open Sea**